Official Google Cloud Certified
Professional Machine Engineer
Study Guide

Mona Mona

Pratap Ramamurthy

SYBEX®
A Wiley Brand

To my late father, grandparents, mom, and husband (Pratyush Ranjan), mentor (Mark Smith), and friends. Also to anyone trying to study for this exam. Hope this book helps you pass the exam with flying colors!
—*Mona Mona*

To my parents, wonderful wife (Swetha), and two fantastic children: Rishab and Riya.
—*Pratap Ramamurthy*

Acknowledgments

Although this book bears my name as author, many other people contributed to its creation. Without their help, this book wouldn't exist, or at best would exist in a lesser form. Pratap Ramamurthy as my co-author has helped contribute a third of the content of this book. Kim Wimpsett, the development editor, Christine O'Connor, the managing editor, and Saravanan Dakshinamurthy, the production specialist, oversaw the book as it progressed through all its stages. Arielle Guy was the book's proofreader and Judy Flynn was the copyeditor. Last but not the least, thanks to Hitesh Hinduja for being an amazing reviewer throughout the book writing process.

I'd also like to thank Jim Minatel and Melissa Burlock at Wiley, and Dan Sullivan, who helped connect me with Wiley to write this book.

—Mona Mona

This book is the product of hard work by many people, and it was wonderful to see everyone come together as a team, starting with Jim Minatel and Melissa Burlock from Wiley and including Kim Wimpsett, Christine O' Connor, Saravanan Dakshinamurthy, Judy Flynn, Arielle Guy, and the reviewers.

Most importantly, I would like to thank Mona for spearheading this huge effort. Her knowledge from her previous writing experience and leadership from start to finish was crucial to bringing this book to completion.

—Pratap Ramamurthy

About the Authors

Mona Mona is an AI/ML specialist at Google Public Sector. She is the author of the book *Natural Language Processing with AWS AI Services* and a speaker. She was a senior AI/ML specialist Solution Architect at AWS before joining Google. She has 14 certifications and has created courses for AWS AI/ML Certification Specialty Exam readiness. She has authored 17 blogs on AI/ML and also co-authored a research paper on AWS CORD-19 Search: A neural search engine for COVID-19 literature, which won an award at the Association for the Advancement of Artificial Intelligence (AAAI) conference. She can be reached at monasheetal3@gmail.com.

Pratap Ramamurthy loves to solve problems using machine learning. Currently he is an AI/ML specialist at Google Public Sector. Previously he worked at AWS as a partner solution architect where he helped build the partner ecosystem for Amazon SageMaker. Later he was a principal solution architect at H2O.ai, a company that works on machine learning algorithms for structured data and natural language. Prior to that he was a developer and a researcher. To his credit he has several research papers in networking, server profiling technology, genetic algorithms, and optoelectronics. He holds three patents related to cloud technologies. In his spare time, he likes to teach AI using modern board games. He can be reached at pratap.ram@gmail.com.

About the Technical Editors

Hitesh Hinduja is an ardent artificial intelligence (AI) and data platforms enthusiast currently working as a senior manager in Azure Data and AI at Microsoft. He worked as a senior manager in AI at Ola Electric, where he led a team of 30+ people in the areas of machine learning, statistics, computer vision, deep learning, natural language processing, and reinforcement learning. He has filed 14+ patents in India and the United States and has numerous research publications under his name. Hitesh has been associated in research roles at India's top B-schools: Indian School of Business, Hyderabad, and the Indian Institute of Management, Ahmedabad. He is also actively involved in training and mentoring and has been invited as a guest speaker by various corporations and associations across the globe. He is an avid learner and enjoys reading books in his free time.

Kanchana Patlolla is an AI innovation program leader at Google Cloud. Previously she worked as an AI/ML specialist in Google Cloud Platform. She has architected solutions with major public cloud providers in financial services industries on their quest to the cloud, particularly in their Big Data and machine learning journey. In her spare time, she loves to try different cuisines and relax with her kids.

About the Technical Proofreader

Adam Vincent is an experienced educator with a passion for spreading knowledge and helping people expand their skill sets. He is multi-certified in Google Cloud, is a Google Cloud Authorized Trainer, and has created multiple courses about machine learning. Adam also loves playing with data and automating everything. When he is not behind a screen, he enjoys playing tabletop games with friends and family, reading sci-fi and fantasy novels, and hiking.

Google Technical Reviewer

Wiley and the authors wish to thank the Google Technical Reviewer Emma Freeman for her thorough review of the proofs for this book.

Contents at a Glance

Contents

Introduction

When customers have a business problem, say to detect objects in an image, sometimes it can be solved very well using machine learning. Google Cloud Platform (GCP) provides an extensive set of tools to be able to build a model that can accomplish this and deploy it for production usage. This book will cover many different use cases, such as using sales data to forecast for next quarter, identifying objects in images or videos, and even extracting information from text documents. This book helps an engineer build a secure, scalable, resilient machine learning application and automate the whole process using the latest technologies.

The purpose of this book is to help you pass the latest version of the Google Cloud Professional ML Engineer (PMLE) exam. Even after you've taken and passed the PMLE exam, this book should remain a useful reference as it covers the basics of machine learning, BigQuery ML, the Vertex AI platform, and MLOps.

Google Cloud Professional Machine Learning Engineer Certification

A Professional Machine Learning Engineer designs, builds, and productionizes ML models to solve business challenges using Google Cloud technologies and knowledge of proven ML models and techniques. The ML engineer considers responsible AI throughout the ML development process and collaborates closely with other job roles to ensure the long-term success of models. The ML engineer should be proficient in all aspects of model architecture, data pipeline interaction, and metrics interpretation. The ML engineer needs familiarity with foundational concepts of application development, infrastructure management, data engineering, and data governance. Through an understanding of training, retraining, deploying, scheduling, monitoring, and improving models, the ML engineer designs and creates scalable solutions for optimal performance.

Why Become Professional ML Engineer (PMLE) Certified?

There are several good reasons to get your PMLE certification.

Provides proof of professional achievement   Certifications are quickly becoming status symbols in the computer service industry. Organizations, including members of the computer service industry, are recognizing the benefits of certification.

Increases your marketability   According to Forbes (www.forbes.com/sites/louiscolumbus/2020/02/10/15-top-paying-it-certifications-in-2020/?sh=12f63aa8358e), jobs that require GCP certifications are the highest-paying jobs for the second year in a row, paying an average salary of $175,761/year. So, there is a demand from many engineers to get certified. Of the many certifications that GCP offers, the AI/ML certified engineer is a new certification and is still evolving.

Provides an opportunity for advancement   IDC's research (www.idc.com/getdoc .jsp?containerId=IDC_P40729) indicates that while AI/ML adoption is on the rise, the cost, lack of expertise, and lack of life cycle management tools are among the top three inhibitors to realizing AI and ML at scale.

This book is the first in the market to talk about Google Cloud AI/ML tools and the technology covering the latest Professional ML Engineer certification guidelines released on February 22, 2022.

Recognizes Google as a leader in open source and AI   Google is the main contributor to many of the path-breaking open source softwares that dramatically changed the landscape of AI/ML, including TensorFlow, Kubeflow, Word2vec, BERT, and T5. Although these algorithms are in the open source domain, Google has the distinct ability of bringing these open source projects to the market through the Google Cloud Platform (GCP). In this regard, the other cloud providers are frequently seen as trailing Google's offering.

Raises customer confidence   As the IT community, users, small business owners, and the like become more familiar with the PMLE certified professional, more of them will realize that the PMLE professional is more qualified to architect secure, cost-effective, and scalable ML solutions on the Google Cloud environment than a noncertified individual.

How to Become Certified

You do not have to work for a particular company. It's not a secret society. There is no prerequisite to take this exam. However, there is a recommendation to have 3+ years of industry experience, including one or more years designing and managing solutions using Google Cloud.

This exam is 2 hours and has 50–60 multiple-choice questions.

You can register two ways for this exam:

- Take the online-proctored exam from anywhere or sitting at home. You can review the online testing requirements at www.webassessor.com/wa.do?page=certInfo &branding=GOOGLECLOUD&tabs=13.

- Take the on-site, proctored exam at a testing center.

We usually prefer to go with the on-site option as we like the focus time in a proctored environment. We have taken all our certifications in a test center. You can find and locate a test center near you at www.kryterion.com/Locate-Test-Center.

Who Should Buy This Book

This book is intended to help students, developers, data scientists, IT professionals, and ML engineers gain expertise in the ML technology on the Google Cloud Platform and take the Professional Machine Learning Engineer exam. This book intends to take readers through the machine learning process starting from data and moving on through feature engineering, model training, and deployment on the Google Cloud. It also walks readers through best practices for when to pick custom models versus AutoML or pretrained models. Google Cloud AI/ML technologies are presented through real-world scenarios to illustrate how IT professionals can design, build, and operate secure ML cloud environments to modernize and automate applications.

Anybody who wants to pass the Professional ML Engineer exam may benefit from this book. If you're new to Google Cloud, this book covers the updated machine learning exam course material, including the Google Cloud Vertex AI platform, MLOps, and BigQuery ML. This is the only book on the market to cover the complete Vertex AI platform, from bringing your data to training, tuning, and deploying your models.

Since it's a professional-level study guide, this book is written with the assumption that you know the basics of the Google Cloud Platform, such as compute, storage, networking, databases, and identity and access management (IAM) or have taken the Google Cloud Associate-level certification exam. Moreover, this book assumes you understand the basics of machine learning and data science in general. In case you do not understand a term or concept, we have included a glossary for your reference.

How This Book Is Organized

This book consists of 14 chapters plus supplementary information: a glossary, this introduction, and the assessment test after the introduction. The chapters are organized as follows:

Chapter 1: Framing ML Problems   This chapter covers how you can translate business challenges into ML use cases.

Chapter 2: Exploring Data and Building Data Pipelines   This chapter covers visualization, statistical fundamentals at scale, evaluation of data quality and feasibility, establishing data constraints (e.g., TFDV), organizing and optimizing training datasets, data validation, handling missing data, handling outliers, and data leakage.

Chapter 3: Feature Engineering   This chapter covers topics such as encoding structured data types, feature selection, class imbalance, feature crosses, and transformations (TensorFlow Transform).

Chapter 4: Choosing the Right ML Infrastructure   This chapter covers topics such as evaluation of compute and accelerator options (e.g., CPU, GPU, TPU, edge devices) and choosing appropriate Google Cloud hardware components. It also covers choosing the best solution (ML vs. non-ML, custom vs. pre-packaged [e.g., AutoML, Vision API]) based on the business requirements. It talks about how defining the model output should be used to solve the business problem. It also covers deciding how incorrect results should be handled and identifying data sources (available vs. ideal). It talks about AI solutions such as CCAI, DocAI, and Recommendations AI.

Chapter 5: Architecting ML Solutions   This chapter explains how to design reliable, scalable, and highly available ML solutions. Other topics include how you can choose appropriate ML services for a use case (e.g., Cloud Build, Kubeflow), component types (e.g., data collection, data management), automation, orchestration, and serving in machine learning.

Chapter 6: Building Secure ML Pipelines   This chapter describes how to build secure ML systems (e.g., protecting against unintentional exploitation of data/model, hacking). It also covers the privacy implications of data usage and/or collection (e.g., handling sensitive data such as personally identifiable information [PII] and protected health information [PHI]).

Chapter 7: Model Building   This chapter describes the choice of framework and model parallelism. It also covers modeling techniques given interpretability requirements, transfer learning, data augmentation, semi-supervised learning, model generalization, and strategies to handle overfitting and underfitting.

Chapter 8: Model Training and Hyperparameter Tuning   This chapter focuses on the ingestion of various file types into training (e.g., CSV, JSON, IMG, parquet or databases, Hadoop/Spark). It covers training a model as a job in different environments. It also talks about unit tests for model training and serving and hyperparameter tuning. Moreover, it discusses ways to track metrics during training and retraining/redeployment evaluation.

Chapter 9: Model Explainability on Vertex AI   This chapter covers approaches to model explainability on Vertex AI.

Chapter 10: Scaling Models in Production   This chapter covers scaling prediction service (e.g., Vertex AI Prediction, containerized serving), serving (online, batch, caching), Google Cloud serving options, testing for target performance, and configuring trigger and pipeline schedules.

Chapter 11: Designing ML Training Pipelines   This chapter covers identification of components, parameters, triggers, and compute needs (e.g., Cloud Build, Cloud Run). It also talks about orchestration framework (e.g., Kubeflow Pipelines/Vertex AI Pipelines, Cloud Composer/Apache Airflow), hybrid or multicloud strategies, and system design with TFX components/Kubeflow DSL.

Chapter 12: Model Monitoring, Tracking, and Auditing Metadata   This chapter covers the performance and business quality of ML model predictions, logging strategies, organizing and tracking experiments, and pipeline runs. It also talks about dataset versioning and model/dataset lineage.

Chapter 13: Maintaining ML Solutions This chapter covers establishing continuous evaluation metrics (e.g., evaluation of drift or bias), understanding the Google Cloud permission model, and identification of appropriate retraining policies. It also covers common training and serving errors (TensorFlow), ML model failure, and resulting biases. Finally, it talks about how you can tune the performance of ML solutions for training and serving in production.

Chapter 14: BigQuery ML This chapter covers BigQueryML algorithms, when to use BigQueryML versus Vertex AI, and the interoperability with Vertex AI.

Chapter Features

Each chapter begins with a list of the objectives that are covered in the chapter. The book doesn't cover the objectives in order. Thus, you shouldn't be alarmed at some of the odd ordering of the objectives within the book.

At the end of each chapter, you'll find several elements you can use to prepare for the exam.

Exam Essentials This section summarizes important information that was covered in the chapter. You should be able to perform each of the tasks or convey the information requested.

Review Questions Each chapter concludes with 8+ review questions. You should answer these questions and check your answers against the ones provided after the questions. If you can't answer at least 80 percent of these questions correctly, go back and review the chapter, or at least those sections that seem to be giving you difficulty.

WARNING The review questions, assessment test, and other testing elements included in this book are *not* derived from the PMLE exam questions, so don't memorize the answers to these questions and assume that doing so will enable you to pass the exam. You should learn the underlying topic, as described in the text of the book. This will let you answer the questions provided with this book *and* pass the exam. Learning the underlying topic is also the approach that will serve you best in the workplace.

To get the most out of this book, you should read each chapter from start to finish and then check your memory and understanding with the chapter-end elements. Even if you're already familiar with a topic, you should skim the chapter; machine learning is complex enough that there are often multiple ways to accomplish a task, so you may learn something even if you're already competent in an area.

Like all exams, the Google Cloud certification from Google is updated periodically and may eventually be retired or replaced. At some point after Google is no longer offering this exam, the old editions of our books and online tools will be retired. If you have purchased this book after the exam was retired, or are attempting to register in the Sybex online learning environment after the exam was retired, please know that we make no guarantees that this exam's online Sybex tools will be available once the exam is no longer available.

Bonus Digital Contents

This book is accompanied by an online learning environment that provides several additional elements. The following items are available among these companion files:

Practice tests All of the questions in this book appear in our proprietary digital test engine—including the 30-question assessment test at the end of this introduction and the 100+ questions that make up the review question sections at the end of each chapter. In addition, there are two 50-question bonus exams.

Electronic "flash cards" The digital companion files include 50+ questions in flash card format (a question followed by a single correct answer). You can use these to review your knowledge of the exam objectives.

Glossary The key terms from this book, and their definitions, are available as a fully searchable PDF.

Interactive Online Learning Environment and Test Bank

You can access all these resources at www.wiley.com/go/sybextestprep.

Conventions Used in This Book

This book uses certain typographic styles in order to help you quickly identify important information and to avoid confusion over the meaning of words such as on-screen prompts. In particular, look for the following styles:

- *Italicized text* indicates key terms that are described at length for the first time in a chapter. These words probably appear in the searchable online glossary. (Italics are also used for emphasis.)

- A `monospaced font` indicates the contents of configuration files, messages displayed as a text-mode Google Cloud shell prompt, filenames, text-mode command names, and Internet URLs.

In addition to these text conventions, which can apply to individual words or entire paragraphs, a few conventions highlight segments of text:

A note indicates information that's useful or interesting but that's somewhat peripheral to the main text. A note might be relevant to a small number of networks, for instance, or it may refer to an outdated feature.

A tip provides information that can save you time or frustration and that may not be entirely obvious. A tip might describe how to get around a limitation or how to use a feature to perform an unusual task.

Google Cloud Professional ML Engineer Objective Map

Here is where to find the objectives covered in this book.

OBJECTIVE	CHAPTER(S)
Section 1: Architecting low-code ML solutions	
1.1 Developing ML models by using BigQuery ML. Considerations include:	14
▪ Building the appropriate BigQuery ML model (e.g., linear and binary classification, regression, time-series, matrix factorization, boosted trees, autoencoders) based on the business problem	14
▪ Feature engineering or selection by using BigQuery ML	14
▪ Generating predictions by using BigQuery ML	14
1.2 Building AI solutions by using ML APIs. Considerations include:	4
▪ Building applications by using ML APIs (e.g., Cloud Vision API, Natural Language API, Cloud Speech API, Translation)	4
▪ Building applications by using industry-specific APIs (e.g., Document AI API, Retail API)	4
1.3 Training models by using AutoML. Considerations include:	4
▪ Preparing data for AutoML (e.g., feature selection, data labeling, Tabular Workflows on AutoML)	4

OBJECTIVE	CHAPTER(S)
▪ Using available data (e.g., tabular, text, speech, images, videos) to train custom models	4
▪ Using AutoML for tabular data	4
▪ Creating forecasting models using AutoML	4
▪ Configuring and debugging trained models	4

Section 2: Collaborating within and across teams to manage data and models

2.1 Exploring and preprocessing organization-wide data (e.g., Cloud Storage, BigQuery, Cloud Spanner, Cloud SQL, Apache Spark, Apache Hadoop). Considerations include:	3, 5, 6, 8, 13
▪ Organizing different types of data (e.g., tabular, text, speech, images, videos) for efficient training	8
▪ Managing datasets in Vertex AI	8
▪ Data preprocessing (e.g., Dataflow, TensorFlow Extended [TFX], BigQuery)	3, 5
▪ Creating and consolidating features in Vertex AI Feature Store	13
▪ Privacy implications of data usage and/or collection (e.g., handling sensitive data such as personally identifiable information [PII] and protected health information [PHI])	6
2.2 Model prototyping using Jupyter notebooks. Considerations include:	6, 8
▪ Choosing the appropriate Jupyter backend on Google Cloud (e.g., Vertex AI Workbench notebooks, notebooks on Dataproc)	8
▪ Applying security best practices in Vertex AI Workbench	6
▪ Using Spark kernels	8
▪ Integration with code source repositories	8
▪ Developing models in Vertex AI Workbench by using common frameworks (e.g., TensorFlow, PyTorch, sklearn, Spark, JAX)	8
2.3 Tracking and running ML experiments. Considerations include:	5, 12
▪ Choosing the appropriate Google Cloud environment for development and experimentation (e.g., Vertex AI Experiments, Kubeflow Pipelines, Vertex AI TensorBoard with TensorFlow and PyTorch) given the framework	5, 12

OBJECTIVE	CHAPTER(S)
Section 3: Scaling prototypes into ML models	
3.1 Building models. Considerations include:	7
▪ Choosing ML framework and model architecture	7
▪ Modeling techniques given interpretability requirements	7
3.2 Training models. Considerations include:	7, 8
▪ Organizing training data (e.g., tabular, text, speech, images, videos) on Google Cloud (e.g., Cloud Storage, BigQuery)	8
▪ Ingestion of various file types (e.g., CSV, JSON, images, Hadoop, databases) into training	8
▪ Training using different SDKs (e.g., Vertex AI custom training, Kubeflow on Google Kubernetes Engine, AutoML, tabular workflows)	8
▪ Using distributed training to organize reliable pipelines	7, 8
▪ Hyperparameter tuning	8
▪ Troubleshooting ML model training failures	8
3.3 Choosing appropriate hardware for training. Considerations include:	4, 8
▪ Evaluation of compute and accelerator options (e.g., CPU, GPU, TPU, edge devices)	4
▪ Distributed training with TPUs and GPUs (e.g., Reduction Server on Vertex AI, Horovod)	8
Section 4: Serving and scaling models	
4.1 Serving models. Considerations include:	5, 10
▪ Batch and online inference (e.g., Vertex AI, Dataflow, BigQuery ML, Dataproc)	5, 10
▪ Using different frameworks (e.g., PyTorch, XGBoost) to serve models	10
▪ Organizing a model registry	10
▪ A/B testing different versions of a model	10
4.2 Scaling online model serving. Considerations include:	4, 5, 6, 10, 13
▪ Vertex AI Feature Store	13
▪ Vertex AI public and private endpoints	6
▪ Choosing appropriate hardware (e.g., CPU, GPU, TPU, edge)	4

OBJECTIVE	CHAPTER(S)
6.2 Monitoring, testing, and troubleshooting ML solutions. Considerations include:	12, 13
▪ Establishing continuous evaluation metrics (e.g., Vertex AI Model Monitoring, Explainable AI)	12,13
▪ Monitoring for training-serving skew	12
▪ Monitoring for feature attribution drift	12
▪ Monitoring model performance against baselines, simpler models, and across the time dimension	12
▪ Common training and serving errors	13

Exam domains and objectives are subject to change at any time without prior notice and at Google's sole discretion. Please visit its website (https://cloud.google.com/certification/machine-learning-engineer) for the most current information.

How to Contact the Publisher

If you believe you have found a mistake in this book, please bring it to our attention. At John Wiley & Sons, we understand how important it is to provide our customers with accurate content, but even with our best efforts an error may occur.

In order to submit your possible errata, please email it to our Customer Service Team at wileysupport@wiley.com with the subject line "Possible Book Errata Submission."

Assessment Test

1. How would you split the data to predict a user lifetime value (LTV) over the next 30 days in an online recommendation system to avoid data and label leakage? (Choose three.)

    A. Perform data collection for 30 days.

    B. Create a training set for data from day 1 to day 29.

    C. Create a validation set for data for day 30.

    D. Create random data split into training, validation, and test sets.

2. You have a highly imbalanced dataset and you want to focus on the positive class in the classification problem. Which metrics would you choose?

    A. Area under the precision-recall curve (AUC PR)

    B. Area under the curve ROC (AUC ROC)

    C. Recall

    D. Precision

3. A feature cross is created by _____ two or more features.

    A. Swapping

    B. Multiplying

    C. Adding

    D. Dividing

4. You can use Cloud Pub/Sub to stream data in GCP and use Cloud Dataflow to transform the data.

    A. True

    B. False

5. You have training data, and you are writing the model training code. You have a team of data engineers who prefer to code in SQL. Which service would you recommend?

    A. BigQuery ML

    B. Vertex AI custom training

    C. Vertex AI AutoML

    D. Vertex AI pretrained APIs

6. What are the benefits of using a Vertex AI managed dataset? (Choose three.)

    A. Integrated data labeling for unlabeled, unstructured data such as video, text, and images using Vertex data labeling.

    B. Track lineage to models for governance and iterative development.

    C. Automatically splitting data into training, test, and validation sets.

    D. Manual splitting of data into training, test, and validation sets.

7. Masking, encrypting, and bucketing are de-identification techniques to obscure PII data using the Cloud Data Loss Prevention API.

    A. True

    B. False

8. Which strategy would you choose to handle the sensitive data that exists within images, videos, audio, and unstructured free-form data?

    A. Use NLP API, Cloud Speech API, Vision AI, and Video Intelligence AI to identify sensitive data such as email and location out of box, and then redact or remove it.

    B. Use Cloud DLP to address this type of data.

    C. Use Healthcare API to hide sensitive data.

    D. Create a view that doesn't provide access to the columns in question. The data engineers cannot view the data, but at the same time the data is live and doesn't require human intervention to de-identify it for continuous training.

9. You would use _____ when you are trying to reduce features while trying to solve an overfitting problem with large models.

    A. L1 regularization

    B. L2 regularization

    C. Both A and B

    D. Vanishing gradient

10. If the weights in a network are very large, then the gradients for the lower layers involve products of many large terms leading to exploding gradients that get too large to converge. What are some of the ways this can be avoided? (Choose two.)

    A. Batch normalization

    B. Lower learning rate

    C. The ReLU activation function

    D. Sigmoid activation function

11. You have a Spark and Hadoop environment on-premises, and you are planning to move your data to Google Cloud. Your ingestion pipeline is both real time and batch. Your ML customer engineer recommended a scalable way to move your data using Cloud Dataproc to BigQuery. Which of the following Dataproc connectors would you *not* recommend?

    A. Pub/Sub Lite Spark connector

    B. BigQuery Spark connector

    C. BigQuery connector

    D. Cloud Storage connector

12. You have moved your Spark and Hadoop environment and your data is in Google Cloud Storage. Your ingestion pipeline is both real time and batch. Your ML customer engineer recommended a scalable way to run Apache Hadoop or Apache Spark jobs directly on data in Google Cloud Storage. Which of the following Dataproc connector would you recommend?

    A. Pub/Sub Lite Spark connector

    B. BigQuery Spark connector

    C. BigQuery connector

    D. Cloud Storage connector

13. Which of the following is *not* a technique to speed up hyperparameter optimization?

    A. Parallelize the problem across multiple machines by using distributed training with hyperparameter optimization.

    B. Avoid redundant computations by pre-computing or cache the results of computations that can be reused for subsequent model fits.

    C. Use grid search rather than random search.

    D. If you have a large dataset, use a simple validation set instead of cross-validation.

14. Vertex AI Vizier is an independent service for optimizing complex models with many parameters. It can be used only for non-ML use cases.

    A. True

    B. False

15. Which of the following is *not* a tool to track metrics when training a neural network?

    A. Vertex AI interactive shell

    B. What-If Tool

    C. Vertex AI TensorBoard Profiler

    D. Vertex AI hyperparameter tuning

16. You are a data scientist working to select features with structured datasets. Which of the following techniques will help?

    A. Sampled Shapley

    B. Integrated gradient

    C. XRAI (eXplanation with Ranked Area Integrals)

    D. Gradient descent

17. Variable selection and avoiding target leakage are the benefits of feature importance.

    A. True

    B. False

18. A TensorFlow SavedModel is what you get when you call _____. Saved models are stored as a directory on disk. The file within that directory, `saved_model.pb`, is a protocol buffer describing the functional tf.Graph.

   A. `tf.saved_model.save()`

   B. `tf.Variables`

   C. `tf.predict()`

   D. `Tf.keras.models.load_model`

19. What steps would you recommend a data engineer trying to deploy a TensorFlow model trained locally to set up real-time prediction using Vertex AI? (Choose three.)

   A. Import the model to Model Registry.

   B. Deploy the model.

   C. Create an endpoint for deployed model.

   D. Create a model in Model Registry.

20. You are an MLOps engineer and you deployed a Kubeflow pipeline on Vertex AI pipelines. Which Google Cloud feature will help you track lineage with your Vertex AI pipelines?

   A. Vertex AI Model Registry

   B. Vertex AI Artifact Registry

   C. Vertex AI ML metadata

   D. Vertex AI Model Monitoring

21. What is *not* a recommended way to invoke a Kubeflow pipeline?

   A. Using Cloud Scheduler

   B. Responding to an event, using Pub/Sub and Cloud Functions

   C. Cloud Composer and Cloud Build

   D. Directly using BigQuery

22. You are a software engineer working at a start-up that works on organizing personal photos and pet photos. You have been asked to use machine learning to identify and tag which photos have pets and also identify public landmarks in the photos. These features are not available today and you have a week to create a solution for this. What is the best approach?

   A. Find the best cat/dog dataset and train a custom model on Vertex AI using the latest algorithm available. Do the same for identifying landmarks.

   B. Find a pretrained cat/dog dataset (available) and train a custom model on Vertex AI using the latest deep neural network TensorFlow algorithm.

   C. Use the cat/dog dataset to train a Vertex AI AutoML image classification model on Vertex AI. Do the same for identifying landmarks.

   D. Vision AI already identifies pets and landmarks. Use that to see if it meets the requirements. If not, use the Vertex AI AutoML model.

23. You are building a product that will accurately throw a ball into the basketball net. This should work no matter where it is placed on the court. You have created a very large Tensor-Flow model (size more than 90 GB) based on thousands of hours of video. The model uses custom operations, and it has optimized the training loop to not have any I/O operations. What are your hardware options to train this model?

   A. Use a TPU slice because the model is very large and has been optimized to not have any I/O operations.

   B. Use a TPU pod because the model size is larger than 50 GB.

   C. Use a GPU-only instance.

   D. Use a CPU-only instance to build your model.

24. You work in the fishing industry and have been asked to use machine learning to predict the age of lobster based on size and color. You have thousands of images of lobster from Arctic fishing boats, from which you have extracted the size of the lobster that is passed to the model, and you have built a regression model for predicting age. Your model has performed very well in your test and validation data. Users want to use this model from their boats. What are your next steps? (Choose three.)

   A. Deploy the model on Vertex AI, expose a REST endpoint.

   B. Enable monitoring on the endpoint and see if there is any training-serving skew and drift detection. The original dataset was only from Arctic boats.

   C. Also port this model to BigQuery for batch prediction.

   D. Enable Vertex AI logging and analyze the data in BigQuery.

25. You have built a custom model and deployed it in Vertex AI. You are not sure if the predictions are being served fast enough (low latency). You want to measure this by enabling Vertex AI logging. Which type of logging will give you information like time stamp and latency for each request?

   A. Container logging

   B. Time stamp logging

   C. Access logging

   D. Request-response logging

26. You are part of a growing ML team in your company that has started to use machine learning to improve your business. You were initially building models using Vertex AI AutoML and providing the trained models to the deployment teams. How should you scale this?

   A. Create a Python script to train multiple models using Vertex AI.

   B. You are now in level 0, and your organization needs level 1 MLOps maturity. Automate the training using Vertex AI Pipelines.

   C. You are in the growth phase of the organization, so it is important to grow the team to leverage more ML engineers.

   D. Move to Vertex AI custom models to match the MLOps maturity level.

27. What is *not* a reason to use Vertex AI Feature Store?

    A. It is a managed service.

    B. It extracts features from images and videos and stores them.

    C. All data is a time-series, so you can track when the features values change over time.

    D. The features created by the feature engineering teams are available during training time but not during serving time. So this helps in bridging that.

28. You are a data analyst in an organization that has thousands of insurance agents, and you have been asked to predict the revenue by each agent for the next quarter. You have the historical data for the last 10 years. You are familiar with all AI services on Google Cloud. What is the most efficient way to do this?

    A. Build a Vertex AI AutoML forecast, deploy the model, and make predictions using REST API.

    B. Build a Vertex AI AutoML forecast model, import the model into BigQuery, and make predictions using BigQuery ML.

    C. Build a BigQuery ML ARIMA+ model using data in BigQuery, and make predictions in BigQuery.

    D. Build a BigQuery ML forecast model, export the model to Vertex AI, and run a batch prediction in Vertex AI.

29. You are an expert in Vertex AI Pipelines, Vertex AI training, and Vertex AI deployment and monitoring. A data analyst team has built a highly accurate model, and this has been brought to you. Your manager wants you to make predictions using the model and use those predictions. What do you do?

    A. Retrain the model on Vertex AI with the same data and deploy the model on Vertex AI as part of your CD.

    B. Run predictions on BigQuery ML and export the predictions into GCS and then load into your pipeline.

    C. Export the model from BigQuery into the Vertex AI model repository and run predictions in Vertex AI.

    D. Download the BigQuery model, and package into a Vertex AI custom container and deploy it in Vertex AI.

30. Which of the following statements about Vertex AI and BigQuery ML is incorrect?

    A. BigQueryML supports both unsupervised and supervised models.

    B. BigQuery ML is very portable. Vertex AI supports all models trained on BigQuery ML.

    C. Vertex AI model monitoring and logs data is stored in BigQuery tables.

    D. BigQuery ML also has algorithms to predict recommendations for users.

Answers to Assessment Test

1. **A, B, C.** In case of time-series data, the best way to perform a split is to do a time-based split rather than a random split to avoid the data or label leakage. For more information, see Chapter 2.

2. **A.** In the case of an imbalanced class, precision-recall curves (PR curves) are recommended for highly skewed domains. For more information, see Chapter 3.

3. **B.** A feature cross, or synthetic feature, is created by multiplying (crossing) two or more features. It can be multiplying the same feature by itself [A * A] or it can be multiplying values of multiple features such as [A * B * C]. In machine learning, feature crosses are usually performed on one-hot encoded features. For example, binned_latitude × binned_longitude. For more information, see Chapter 3.

4. **A, True.** Cloud Pub/Sub creates a pipeline for streaming the data and Cloud Dataflow is used for data transformation. For more information, see Chapter 5.

5. **A.** If you want to perform ML using SQL, BigQuery ML is the right approach. For more information, see Chapter 5.

6. **A, B, C.** As stated in options A, B, and C, the advantages of using a managed dataset are to have integrated data labeling, data lineage, and automatic labeling features. For more information, see Chapter 5.

7. **A.** Cloud DLP uses all the mentioned techniques to obscure the PII data. For more information, see Chapter 6.

8. **A.** Cloud DLP only applies to data with a defined pattern for masking. If you have image data and a pattern of masking is not defined (for example, you want to redact faces from images), you would use Vision AI to identify the image and then redact the bounding box of the image using Python code. For more information, see Chapter 6.

9. **A.** You will use L1 when you are trying to reduce features and L2 when you are looking for a stable model. Vanishing gradients for the lower layers (closer to the input) can become very small. When the gradients vanish toward 0 for the lower layers, these layers train very slowly or they do not train at all. For more information, see Chapter 7.

10. **A, B.** Batch normalization and lower learning rate can help prevent exploding gradients. The ReLU activation function can help prevent vanishing gradients. For more information, see Chapter 7.

11. **D.** You will not use the Cloud Storage connector as the data is on premises. You would need a connector to move data directly to BigQuery. For more information, see Chapter 8.

12. **D.** The premise of the question is that you've moved the data to Cloud Storage for use. The Cloud Storage connector will allow you to use that data in your Hadoop/Spark jobs without it having to be moved onto the machines in the cluster. For more information, see Chapter 8.

13. C. You can improve performance by using a random search algorithm since it uses fewer trails. Options A, B, and D are all correct ways to improve optimization. For more information, see Chapter 8.

14. B. Vertex AI Vizier is an independent service for optimizing complex models with many parameters. It can be used for both ML and non-ML use cases. For more information, see Chapter 8.

15. D. Vertex AI hyperparameter tuning is not a tool to track metrics when training a neural network; rather, it is used for tuning hyperparameters. For more information, see Chapter 8.

16. A. Sampled Shapley is the only method with Explainable AI, which can help explain tabular or structured datasets. For more information, see Chapter 9.

17. A. Feature importance is a technique that explains the features that make up the training data using a score (importance). It indicates how useful or valuable a feature is relative to other features. For more information, see Chapter 9.

18. A. After TensorFlow model training, you get a SavedModel. A SavedModel contains a complete TensorFlow program, including trained parameters (i.e., `tf.Variables`) and computation. For more information, see Chapter 10.

19. A, B, C. You need to import your models to the Model Registry in Vertex AI and then deploy the model before creating an endpoint. For more information, see Chapter 10.

20. C. Vertex ML Metadata lets you record the metadata and artifacts produced by your ML system and query that metadata to help analyze, debug, and audit the performance of your ML system or the artifacts that it produces. For more information, see Chapter 10.

21. D. You cannot invoke a Kubeflow pipeline using BigQuery as they are used for ETL workloads and not for MLOps. For more information, see Chapter 11.

22. D. The easiest approach is to use Vision AI as it is pretrained and already available. Options A, B, and C are all valid but they are unnecessarily complex given that Vision AI already achieves that. The key point to note is that you only have a week to do this task, so choose the fastest option. For more information, see Chapter 4.

23. C. TPU cannot be used for this case because it has custom TensorFlow operations. So options A and B are not valid. Option C is the best option because it is a large model. Using CPU only is going to be very slow. For more information, see Chapter 4.

24. A, B, D. There is no need to port into BigQuery for batch processing. Based on the question, batch is not a requirement; only online prediction is a requirement. The other options of deploying the model on Vertex AI, creating an endpoint and monitoring and logging, are valid. For more information, see Chapter 12.

25. C. Container logging gives you stderr and stdout from the container. Request-response logs a sample of online predictions. There is no such thing as time stamp logging. Access logging is the correct answer. For more information, see Chapter 12.

26. B. Option B is the correct answer because it recognizes the right level of MLOps maturity and recommends automating the training with pipeline. Option A is wrong because methods like "scripting" methods are considered "ad hoc," not mature enough for this level. Option C is wrong because it does not address the technical nature of the problem. Option D is wrong because moving from AutoML to custom models does not really help in any way here. For more information, see Chapter 13.

27. B. A Vertex AI Feature Store does not extract features from images. It deals only with structured data. For more information, see Chapter 13.

28. C. While all answers are possible, the most efficient is to build a model in BigQueryML and predict in BigQuery. For more information, see Chapter 14.

29. C. Option A is most redundant so not recommended. Option B is a roundabout way of doing this. Option C is the most efficient because it uses an important portability feature between BigQuery and the Vertex AI model registry. Option D is wrong because you don't have to package the model; BigQuery models don't need to be "packaged" into a container. For more information, see Chapter 14.

30. B. Option B is incorrect because you cannot port a model with BigQuery ML TRANSFORM into Vertex AI. All other choices are true. For more information, see Chapter 14.

Chapter

1

Framing ML Problems

Artificial intelligence and machine learning have dramatically changed our lives, and we are still in the early stages of adoption. Google adopted machine learning two decades ago and continues to inspire us all with its innovations. Google's innovations are part of its brand, and millions of customers eagerly look forward to the annual conference Google I/O, which is described as "innovation in the open" for new path-breaking creations. Many innovations, although considered disruptive initially, are adopted rapidly, sometimes by billions of users; they can even achieve common household usage in just a few years.

For example, a universal translator is a device that can translate text or voice from one language to another in near real time; this was a common theme in old sci-fi movies that is now a reality today. Another use case is the ability to search for objects in images by showing an image instead of using a keyword, called "search by image." You might have used the "suggested replies" to emails, which saves you the time and effort to type out an email reply on Android phones. While that use case might save a few minutes of time, other innovations like the AlphaFold AI system saves years, accelerating research by predicting a protein's 3D structure from its amino acid sequence instead of using means based on a physical lab.

Businesses across the globe have started embracing AI and machine learning. These businesses are not "rare innovators" but cut across all domains, in a range of industries including agriculture, healthcare, transportation, retail, and manufacturing. One can safely say that any field can benefit from machine learning by identifying the right use cases.

You see use cases everywhere around you, and the motivations for innovation might be varied. Some industries might be trying to solve critical problems like trying to understand the protein structure of the coronavirus; other industries might be looking for ways to increase efficiency. Sometimes machine learning can solve a problem that was previously impossible to solve, while in other cases it might be providing an incremental improvement to an existing situation. Sometimes these innovations might be competitive, where one business is able to grow rapidly due to innovation that puts pressure on all others, while in other cases all businesses might be trying to come together to solve a single problem. Having a historical understanding of an industry helps you appreciate the previous efforts in solving problems and exploring new approaches.

Innovations all start out as simple use cases that are translated into machine problems, which can then be tackled by machine learning engineers. The ability to identify these use cases and assess the impact of machine learning is the first step in your journey toward certification.

Translating Business Use Cases

The goal of this chapter is to help you to first identify the impact, success criteria, and data available for a use case. Then, match this with a machine learning approach (an algorithm and a metric) as shown in Figure 1.1. We will look at how to fit the ML project into the budget and timeline.

FIGURE 1.1   Business case to ML problem

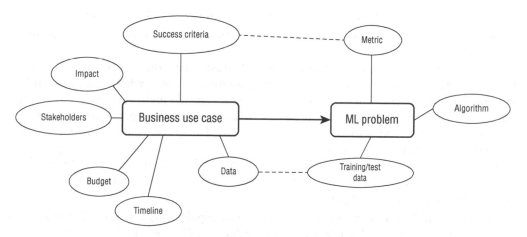

Now, imagine you are being tasked with using ML to solve a problem. You first need to identify the use case and fit it to a machine learning problem.

For example, say you are trying to predict house prices, you can use a regression model. The performance requirements of the model will be determined by the business.

Say, you have had a discussion with the key people and understood the use case; you now need to identify the key *stakeholders*, the people related to the use case. The stakeholders can be executives, the CFO, data engineers, tech support staff who may have to approve the project to proceed. Each of these stakeholders might have very different expectations of this ML project, and your ability to communicate the value could make the difference between approval or rejection. Executives are looking for impact to business, CFOs are typically interested in the budget of the solution, managers might be keen on timelines, and data managers might be interested in data privacy and security. If you are able to understand these five aspects, your pathway to approvals will be smooth.

The stakeholders will help you measure the *impact* of this use case for your company and the end user. The impact could be increasing profit, reducing fraud, improving the quality of life, or even saving lives. The impact is probably the most important element of the use case.

For example, say your company has a learning management system (LMS), a platform where students subscribe to courses. You have data of students' activities and using this you want to improve the experience using machine learning. You could do several things:

- Create a recommendation engine to show new courses for students.

- Churn prediction to see if a student is going to quit the course.

- Churn prediction to see if a teacher is not going to come back.

- Identify what makes a course interesting for students (sample questions, more images, more tables, short videos, etc.).

- Identify what kind of learning a student prefers (auditory, visual, or kinesthetic).

Which of these would be most impactful is a question that can be answered only by the business owner.

Once you have identified the use case with the highest impact on your business, you need to identify the outcome of your machine learning solution. In short, what would happen if you implemented your solution? Sometimes, your model would make accurate predictions, but the environment might react in a counterproductive way to these predictions. This is because the environment is seldom static; the users could adapt or the users could get confused with the behavior of the predictions.

For example, say your company has a video sharing website, and you have millions of videos. You are trying to build an ML model to recommend videos to your users. You could choose from among the following:

- An ML model to recommend unseen videos from popular video creators. The problem is that this is not personalized. What if the user does not like some of the creators?

- An ML model to recommend videos that get a lot of clicks. But what if these are just clickbait, where people click and regret wasting time?

- An ML model to recommend videos that have been watched fully by similar users. This would lead to improving the user experience.

In this example, you need to have a good understanding of the use case, the overall goal, and the end user to be able to find the right fit.

Next, find out if the problem is even solvable using machine learning. Business leaders hear inspiring stories in the media about how a business solves a problem with ML and it sounds magical and the business leaders would love to use it to solve their business problems. They need an expert like you to figure out if it is even feasible to solve their problem using ML. This is not as easy as it sounds; it depends on several things, like existing technology, available data, and budget. For example, natural language processing has advanced leaps and bounds and has made it possible to do things that were impossible just a few years ago, such as using ML to answer a question from a piece of text. Familiarity with the latest advancements in natural language processing would help you identify easier, faster, and better ML methods to solve your business problems.

As the next step, you will need to identify an ML learning approach that fits your use case.

Machine Learning Approaches

Many machine learning problems have been well researched and have elegant solutions, but some algorithms are not perfect and some problems can be solved in multiple ways. Sometimes, a use case will fit perfectly with an ML framework and other times not so well. You need to be aware of the landscape of ML problems. There are several approaches to machine learning methods. Some of these approaches have been studied for decades, and others are fairly new. There are hundreds if not thousands of ways to apply machine learning techniques. To help us get a grasp of the breadth of these methods, we organize them into categories (also called methods, or types or approaches or problems). Each of these approaches solves a specific class of problems, distinguished by the type of data, the type of prediction, and so on.

 On the exam, you will be given the details of a use case and will be expected to understand the nature of the problem and find the appropriate machine learning approach to solve it. To accomplish that, you need to have wide knowledge of the landscape of these machine learning approaches.

We will look at the different ways to classify the approaches in the following sections.

Supervised, Unsupervised, and Semi-supervised Learning

A common method of classifying machine learning approaches is based on the type of learning. When you have a labeled dataset that you can use to train your model, it is called *supervised learning*. For example, supervised learning would be trying to build a model to classify images of dogs or cats and having the ability to use a dataset of images that have been labeled accordingly.

There are some cases where you have only unlabeled data, such as a set of images (without any labels or tags), and you will be asked to classify or group them. This would be an *unsupervised* ML model. Clustering algorithms are a suite of algorithms that belong to this type and are used to group and/or classify data. Autoencoders are also a family of algorithms that belong to this type. Autoencoders are used to reduce the dimensionality of input data, a preprocessing step in many machine learning models.

Another popular unsupervised ML use case is *topic modeling*, a type of document clustering problem. The algorithm takes documents and classifies them into N number of classes based on the commonality of words and sentences in the texts. Comparing this to how a human being would classify books, say, in a library, you may classify them into fiction, nonfiction, science, history, and so on. In other times, you may classify the books based on languages (for example, English, Chinese, Hindi). Similarly, an unsupervised algorithm may or may not classify in the way you expected. The output of unsupervised learning methods cannot be fully controlled, and it is almost never perfect and so requires careful tuning to get required results. Table 1.1 provides the details of some of the popular ML model types that are readily available in Google Cloud.

TABLE 1.1   ML problem types

Name	Data Type	Supervised/Unsupervised
Regression – Tables	Tabular	Supervised
Classification – Tables	Tabular	Supervised
Forecasting	Series	Supervised
Image classification	Image	Supervised
Image segmentation	Image	Supervised
Object detection	Image	Supervised
Video classification	Video	Supervised
Video object tracking	Video	Supervised
Video action recognition	Video	Supervised
Sentiment analysis	Text	Supervised
Entity extraction	Text	Supervised
Translation	Text	Supervised
K-means clustering	Tabular	Unsupervised
Principal component analysis	Tabular	Unsupervised
Topic modeling	Text	Unsupervised
Collaborative filtering/ recommendations	Mixed	Supervised/Unsupervised

Source: Adapted from Google cloud/ https://cloud.google.com/vertex-ai/docs/training-overview last accessed December 16, 2022.

To solve the problem of uncertainty in unsupervised learning, there is a hybrid solution called *semi-supervised learning*, where some data is labeled and other data is not. This is like guiding the algorithm toward the clusters that you want to see. While semi-supervised models are interesting research topics and have some utility, in a majority of use cases, supervised models are used.

There are many other kinds of machine learning models beyond these, including reinforcement learning (where the algorithm is not given data but is given an environment that the agent explores and learns) and active learning algorithm, but they are beyond the scope of the certificate exam.

Another way to classify the machine learning algorithms is based on the type of prediction. The type of data the model will predict determines several aspects of the machine learning algorithm and the method used. We will explore that next.

Classification, Regression, Forecasting, and Clustering

Classification is the process of predicting the "labels" or "classes" or "categories." Given a picture of a pet, classifying dogs versus cats is a classification problem. If there are just two labels, it is called *binary classification*, and if there are more labels, it is called *multiclass classification*. You could have a classification with thousands of labels; for example, the Cloud Vision API can classify millions of different objects in a picture, which is a more difficult problem to solve. You cannot apply the same model for binary classification, multiclass classification, and classification with thousands of classes.

In *regression*, the ML model predicts a number—for example, prediction of house price (given the number of bedrooms, square footage, zip code), prediction of the amount of rainfall (given temperature, humidity, location). Here the predicted value's range depends on the use case. The ML algorithms used for regression are usually different from classification. Typically, you would find structured data (data in rows and columns), as shown in Table 1.2, being used for regression problems.

TABLE 1.2   Structured data

Student ID	Age	Exam Scores (Out of 100)
1	34	75
2	23	59
3	36	92
4	31	67

Forecasting is another type where the input is time-series data and the model predicts the future values. In a time-series dataset (Table 1.3), you get a series of input values that are indexed in time order. For example, you have a series of temperature measurements taken every hour for 10 hours from a sensor. In this case, one temperature reading is related to the previous and next reading because they are from the same sensor, in subsequent hours, and usually only vary to a small extent by the hour, so they are not considered to be "independent" (an important distinction from other types of structured data).

TABLE 1.3   Time-Series Data

	Temperature
Series 1	29, 30, 40, 39, 23, 20
Series 2	10, 11, 13, 23, 43, 34
Series 2	19, 18, 19, 20, 38, 20
Series 4	14, 17, 34, 34, 12, 43

Some forecasting problems can be converted to regression problems by modifying the time-series data into independent and identically distributed (IID) values. This is done either for convenience or availability of data or for preference for a certain type of ML model. In other cases, regression problems can be converted into classification problems by bucketizing the values. We will look into details in the following chapters. There is an art to fitting an ML model to a use case.

Clustering is another type of problem, where the algorithm creates groups in the data based on inherent similarities and differences among the different data points. For example, if we are given the latitude and longitude of every house on Earth, the algorithm might group each of these data points into clusters of cities based on the distances between groups of houses. K-means is a popular algorithm in this type.

ML Success Metrics

A business problem can be solved using many different machine learning algorithms, so which one to choose? An *ML metric* (or a suite of metrics) is used to determine if the trained model is accurate enough. After you train the model (supervised learning), you will predict the values (y) for, say, N data points for which you know the actual value (y). We will use a formula to calculate the metric from these N predictions.

There are several metrics with different properties. If so, what is our metric? What is the formula for calculating the metric? Does the metric align with the business success criteria? To answer these questions, let us look at each class of problems, starting with classification.

Say you are trying to detect a rare fatal disease from an X-ray. This is a binary classification problem with two possible outcomes: positive/negative. You are given a set of a million labeled X-ray images with only 1 percent of the cases with the disease, a positive data point. In this case, a wrong negative (false negative), where we predict that the patient does not have the disease when they actually do have it, might cause the patient to not take timely action and cause harm due to inaction. But a wrong positive prediction (false positive), where we predict that the patient has the disease when in fact they do not, might cause undue concern for the patient. This will result in further medical tests to confirm the prediction. In this case, accuracy (the percentage of correct prediction) is not the correct metric.

Let us now consider an example with prediction numbers for a binary classification for an unbalanced dataset, shown in Table 1.4.

TABLE 1.4   Confusion matrix for a binary classification example

		Predicted	
		Positive Prediction	**Negative Prediction**
Actual	**Positive Class**	5	2
	Negative Class	3	990

There are two possible prediction classes, positive and negative. Usually the smaller class (almost always the more important class) is represented as the positive class. In Table 1.4, we have a total of 1,000 data points and have predictions for each. We have tabulated the predictions against the actual values. Out of 1,000 data points, there are 7 belonging to the positive class and 993 belonging to the negative class. The model has predicted 8 to be in the positive class and 992 in the negative class. The bottom right represents true negatives (990 correctly predicted negatives) and the top left represents true positives (5 correctly predicted positives). The bottom left represents false positives (3 incorrectly predicted as positive) and the top right represents false negatives (2 incorrectly predicted as negative). Now, using the numbers in this confusion matrix, we can calculate various metrics based on our needs.

If this model is to detect cancer, we do not want to miss detecting the disease; in other words, we want a low false negative rate. In this case, *recall* is a good metric.

$$Recall = \frac{True\ Positive}{True\ Positive + False\ Negative}$$

In our case, recall = *5/(5 + 2)* = 0.714. If false positives are higher, the recall metric will be lower because false negative is in the denominator. Recall can range from 0 to 1, and a higher score is better. Intuitively, recall is the measure of what percentage of the positive data points the model was able to predict correctly.

On the other hand, if this is a different use case and you are trying to reduce false positives, then you can use the precision metric.

$$Precision = \frac{True\ Positive}{True\ Positive + False\ Positive}$$

In our case, we have 3 false positives, so our precision score is *5/(5 + 3)* = 0.625. Intuitively, precision quantifies the percentage of positive predictions that were actually correct.

Sometimes, your use case might be interested in reducing both false positives and false negatives simultaneously. In that case, we use a harmonic mean of both precision and recall, and it is called the F1 score. (There is a more general F_β score depending on how you wish to weight precision and recall and F1 is just one case.)

$$F1 = 2 \times \frac{Precision * Recall}{Precision + Recall}$$

In our example, we get 2 x (0.625 x 0.714)/(0.625 + 0.714) = 0.666. Here again, F1 ranges from 0 to 1, and a higher score indicates a higher-quality model. The three metrics are summarized in Table 1.5.

TABLE 1.5   Summary of metrics

	Scenario	Formula
Precision	Lower false positive	$Precision = \dfrac{True\ Positive}{True\ Positive + False\ Positive}$
Recall	Lower false negative	$Recall = \dfrac{True\ Positive}{True\ Positive + False\ Negative}$
F1	Lower false positive and false negative together	$F1 = 2 \times \dfrac{Precision * Recall}{Precision + Recall}$

Area Under the Curve Receiver Operating Characteristic (AUC ROC)

ROC stands for receiver operating characteristic curve (it comes from the field of signal processing) and is a graphical plot that summarizes the performance of a binary classification model (Figure 1.2). The x-axis is the false positive rate, and the y-axis is the true positive rate, and the plot is generated at different classification thresholds. The ideal point for this plot is the top-left corner, which has 100 percent true positive and 0 percent false positive, but in practice you will never see this. You can also calculate the precision, recall, and F1 at each point on the curve. When you visually inspect the curve, a diagonal line is the worst case, and we want the curve to stretch as far from the diagonal as possible.

When you have two models, you get two ROC curves, and the way to compare them is to calculate the area under the curve (AUC).

Once you have chosen the model based on AUC, you can find the threshold point that maximizes your F1 (as indicated in Figure 1.2).

FIGURE 1.2   AUC

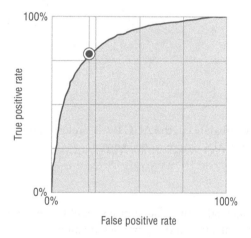

This method has the following advantages:

- **Scale-invariant:** It measures how well the predictions are ranked and not their absolute values.

- **Classification threshold-invariant:** It helps you measure the model irrespective of what threshold is chosen.

 Classification threshold invariance is not always desirable because sometimes there are huge disparities between false positives and false negatives. Therefore, AUC is not usually the best metric for picking a model when there is class imbalance.

The Area Under the Precision-Recall (AUC PR) Curve

The area under the precision-recall curve is a graphical plot that illustrates the relationship between a precision-recall pair (Figure 1.3). The x-axis is the recall and the y-axis is the precision. The best AUC PR curve is a horizontal line across the top. In this curve, the optimal point is the top-right corner, which has 100 percent precision and 100 percent recall, which is never seen in practice but always aimed at.

FIGURE 1.3 AUC PR

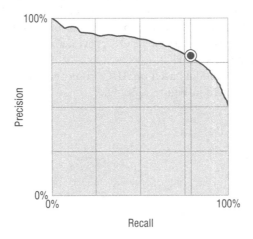

If the dataset is highly imbalanced, the AUC PR is preferred because a high number of true negatives can cause the AUC curve to be skewed.

Regression

Regression predicts a numerical value. The metric should try to show the quantitative difference between the actual value and the predicted value.

MAE   The mean absolute error (MAE) is the average absolute difference between the actual values and the predicted values.

RMSE   The root-mean-squared error (RMSE) is the square root of the average squared difference between the target and predicted values. If you are worried that your model might incorrectly predict a very large value and want to penalize the model, you can use this. Ranges from 0 to infinity.

RMSLE   The root-mean-squared logarithmic error (RMSLE) metric is similar to RMSE, except that it uses the natural logarithm of the predicted and actual values +1. This is an asymmetric metric, which penalizes under prediction (value predicted is lower than actual) rather than over prediction.

MAPE   Mean absolute percentage error (MAPE) is the average absolute percentage difference between the labels and the predicted values. You would choose MAPE when you care about proportional difference between actual and predicted value.

R^2 R-squared (R^2) is the square of the Pearson correlation coefficient (r) between the labels and predicted values. This metric ranges from zero to one; and generally a higher value indicates a better fit for the model.

Responsible AI Practices

AI and machine learning are powerful new tools, and with power comes responsibility. You should consider fairness, interpretability, privacy, and security in your ML solution. You can borrow from best practices in software engineering in tandem with considerations unique to machine learning.

General Best Practices   Always have the end user in mind as well as their user experience. How does your solution change someone's life? Solicit feedback early in the design process. Engage and test with a diverse set of users you would expect to use your solution. This will build a rich variety of perspectives and will allow you to adjust early in the design phase.

Fairness   Fairness is very important because machine learning models can reflect and reinforce unfair biases. Fairness is also difficult in practice because there are several definitions of fairness from different perspectives (academic, legal, cultural, etc.). Also, it is not possible to apply the same "fairness" to all situations as it is very contextual. To start with, you can use statistical methods to measure bias in datasets and to test ML models for bias in the evaluation phase.

Interpretability   Some popular state-of-the-art machine learning models like neural networks are too complex for human beings to comprehend, so they are treated as black boxes. The lack of visibility creates doubt and could have hidden biases. *Interpretability* is the science of gaining insights into models and predictions. Some models are inherently more interpretable (like linear regression, decision trees) and others are less interpretable (deep learning models). One way to improve interpretability is to use *model explanations*. Model explanations quantify the contributions of each input feature toward making a prediction. However, not all algorithms support model explanations. In some domains, model explanations are mandated, so your choice of algorithms is restricted.

Privacy   The only connection between the training data and prediction is the ML model. While the model only provides predictions from input values, there are some cases where it can reveal some details about the training data. This becomes a serious issue if you trained with sensitive data like medical history, for example. Although the science of detecting and preventing data leakage is still an area of active research, fortunately there are now techniques to minimize leakage in a precise and principled fashion.

Security   The threat of cybersecurity is very much applicable to machine learning. In addition to the usual threats to any digital application, there are some unique security challenges to machine learning applications. These threats are ever present, from the data collection phase (poison data), training phase (leakage of training data), and deployment phase (stealing of models). It is important to identify potential threats to the system, keep learning to stay ahead of the curve, and develop approaches to combat these threats.

You can read more at `https://ai.google/responsibilities`.

Summary

In this chapter, you learned how to take a business use case and understand the different dimensions to an ask and to frame a machine learning problem statement as a first step.

Exam Essentials

Translate business challenges to machine learning.   Understand the business use case that wants to solve a problem using machine learning. Understand the type of problem, the data availability, expected outcomes, stakeholders, budget, and timelines.

Understand the problem types.   Understand regression, classification, and forecasting. Be able to tell the difference in data types and popular algorithms for each problem type.

Know how to use ML metrics.   Understand what a metric is, and match the metric with the use case. Know the different metrics for each problem type, like precision, recall, F1, AUC ROC, RMSE, and MAPE.

Understand Google's Responsible AI principles.   Understand the recommended practices for AI in the context of fairness, interpretability, privacy, and security.

Review Questions

1. When analyzing a potential use case, what are the first things you should look for? (Choose three.)

    A. Impact

    B. Success criteria

    C. Algorithm

    D. Budget and time frames

2. When you try to find the best ML problem for a business use case, which of these aspects is not considered?

    A. Model algorithm

    B. Hyperparameters

    C. Metric

    D. Data availability

3. Your company wants to predict the amount of rainfall for the next 7 days using machine learning. What kind of ML problem is this?

    A. Classification

    B. Forecasting

    C. Clustering

    D. Reinforcement learning

4. You work for a large company that gets thousands of support tickets daily. Your manager wants you to create a machine learning model to detect if a support ticket is valid or not. What type of model would you choose?

    A. Linear regression

    B. Binary classification

    C. Topic modeling

    D. Multiclass classification

5. You are building an advanced camera product for sports, and you want to track the ball. What kind of problem is this?

    A. Not possible with current state-of-the-art algorithms

    B. Image detection

    C. Video object tracking

    D. Scene detection

6. Your company has millions of academic papers from several research teams. You want to organize them in some way, but there is no company policy on how to classify the documents. You are looking for any way to cluster the documents and gain any insight into popular trends. What can you do?

    A. Not much. The problem is not well defined.

    B. Use a simple regression problem.

    C. Use binary classification.

    D. Use topic modeling.

7. What metric would you never chose for linear regression?

    A. RMSE

    B. MAPE

    C. Precision

    D. MAE

8. You are building a machine learning model to predict house prices. You want to make sure the prediction does not have extreme errors. What metric would you choose?

    A. RMSE

    B. RMSLE

    C. MAE

    D. MAPE

9. You are building a plant classification model to predict variety1 and variety2, which are found in equal numbers in the field. What metric would you choose?

    A. Accuracy

    B. RMSE

    C. MAPE

    D. R^2

10. You work for a large car manufacturer and are asked to detect hidden cracks in engines using X-ray images. However, missing a crack could mean the engine could fail at some random time while someone is driving the car. Cracks are relatively rare and happen in about 1 in 100 engines. A special camera takes an X-ray image of the engine as it comes through the assembly line. You are going to build a machine learning model to classify if an engine has a crack or not. If a crack is detected, the engine would go through further testing to verify. What metric would you choose for your classification model?

    A. Accuracy

    B. Precision

    C. Recall

    D. RMSE

11. You are asked to build a classification model and are given a training dataset but the data is not labeled. You are asked to identify ways of using machine learning with this data. What type of learning will you use?

    A. Supervised learning

    B. Unsupervised learning

    C. Semi-supervised learning

    D. Reinforcement learning

12. You work at a company that hosts millions of videos and you have thousands of users. The website has a Like button for users to click, and some videos get thousands of "likes." You are asked to create a machine learning model to recommend videos to users based on all the data collected to increase the amount of time users spend on your website. What would be your ML approach?

    A. Supervised learning to predict based on the popularity of videos

    B. Deep learning model based on the amount of time users watch the videos

    C. Collaborative filtering method based on explicit feedback

    D. Semi-supervised learning because you have some data about some videos

13. You work for the web department of a large hardware store chain. You have built a visual search engine for the website. You want to build a model to classify whether an image contains a product. There are new products being introduced on a weekly basis to your product catalog and these new products must be incorporated into the visual search engine. Which of the following options is a bad idea?

    A. Create a pipeline to automate the step: take the dataset, train a model.

    B. Create a golden dataset and do not change the dataset for at least a year because creating a dataset is time-consuming.

    C. Extend the dataset to include new products frequently and retrain the model.

    D. Add evaluation of the model as part of the pipeline.

14. Which of the following options is not a type of machine learning approach?

    A. Supervised learning

    B. Unsupervised learning

    C. Semi-supervised learning

    D. Hyper-supervised learning

15. Your manager is discussing a machine learning approach and is asking you about feeding the output of one model to another model. Select two statements that are true about this kind of approach.

    A. There are many ML pipelines where the output of one model is fed into another.

    B. This is a poor design and never done in practice.

    C. Never feed the output of one model into another model. It may amplify errors.

    D. There are several design patterns where the output of one model (like encoder or transformer) is passed into a second model and so on.

16. You are building a model that is going to predict credit-worthiness and will be used to approve loans. You have created a model and it is performing extremely well and has high impact. What next?

   A. Deploy the model.

   B. Deploy the model and integrate it with the system.

   C. Hand it over to the software integration team.

   D. Test your model and data for biases (gender, race, etc.).

17. You built a model to predict credit-worthiness, and your training data was checked for biases. Your manager still wants to know the reason for each prediction and what the model does. What do you do?

   A. Get more testing data.

   B. The ML model is a black box. You cannot satisfy this requirement.

   C. Use model interpretability/explanations.

   D. Remove all fields that may cause bias (race, gender, etc.).

18. Your company is building an Android app to add funny moustaches on photos. You built a deep learning model to detect the location of a face in a photo, and your model had very high accuracy based on a public photo dataset that you found online. When integrated into an Android phone app, it got negative feedback on accuracy. What could be the reason?

   A. The model was not deployed properly.

   B. Android phones could not handle a deep learning model.

   C. Your dataset was not representative of all users.

   D. The metric was wrong.

19. You built a deep learning model to predict cancer based on thousands of personal records and scans. The data was used in training and testing. The model is secured behind a fire-wall, and all cybersecurity precautions have been taken. Are there any privacy concerns? (Choose two.)

   A. No. There are no privacy concerns. This does not contain photographs, only scans.

   B. Yes. This is sensitive data being used.

   C. No. Although sensitive data is used, it is only for training and testing.

   D. The model could reveal some detail about the training data. There is a risk.

20. You work for an online shoe store and the company wants to increase revenue. You have a large dataset that includes the browsing history of thousands of customers, and also their shopping cart history. You have been asked to create a recommendation model. Which of the following is not a valid next step?

   A. Use your ML model to recommend products at checkout.

   B. Creatively use all the data to get maximum value because there is no privacy concern.

   C. Periodically retrain the model to adjust for performance and also to include new products.

   D. In addition to the user history, you can use the data about product (description, images) in training your model.

Chapter

2

Exploring Data and Building Data Pipelines

GOOGLE CLOUD PROFESSIONAL MACHINE LEARNING ENGINEER EXAM OBJECTIVES COVERED IN THIS CHAPTER:

✓ **5.1 Developing end-to-end ML pipelines. Considerations include:**

- Data and model validation

Data collecting and cleaning is a major step in machine learning as your model is only as good as your data. Most of the time in machine learning is spent cleaning data and feature engineering. In this chapter, we will focus on data cleaning and exploratory data analysis (EDA). We will talk about data visualization and statistical techniques to check for bad data (omitted values, outliers, duplicate values). Then we will cover how to normalize the data and handle bad data (such as having a data schema), how to handle missing data, and how to check for data leakage. We will also cover how you can use TensorFlow Data Validation (TFDV) to validate data for large-scale systems.

Visualization

Data visualization is a data exploratory technique to find trends and outliers in the data. Data visualization helps in the data cleaning process because you can find out whether your data is imbalanced by visualizing the data on a chart. It also helps in the feature engineering process because you can select features and discard features and see how a feature will influence your model by visualizing it.

There are two ways to visualize data:

Univariate Analysis In this analysis, each of the features is analyzed independently, such as the range of the feature and whether outliers exist in the data. The most common visuals used for this are box plots and distribution plots.

Bivariate Analysis In this analysis, we compare the data between two features. This analysis can be helpful in finding correlation between features. Some of the ways you can perform this analysis are by using line plots, bar plots, and scatterplots.

Box Plot

A box plot helps visualize the division of observations into defined intervals known as *quartiles* and how that compares to the entire observation. It represents the data as 25th, 50th, and 75th quartiles. It consists of the body, or interquartile range, where maximum observations are present. Whiskers or straight lines represent the maximum and minimum. Points that lie outside the whiskers will be considered *outliers*.

Figure 2.1 shows a box plot.

FIGURE 2.1 Box plot showing quartiles

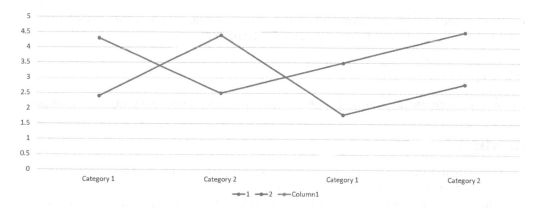

Line Plot

A line plot plots the relationship between two variables and is used to analyze the trends for data changes over time.

Figure 2.2 shows a line plot.

FIGURE 2.2 Line plot

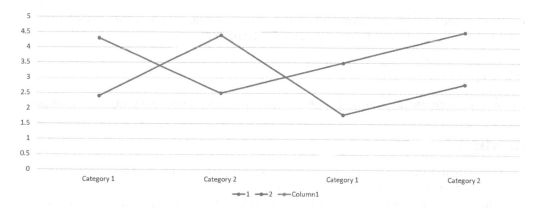

Bar Plot

A bar plot is used for analyzing trends in data and comparing categorical data such as sales figures every week, the number of visitors to a website, or revenue from a product every month.

Figure 2.3 shows a bar plot.

FIGURE 2.3   Bar plot

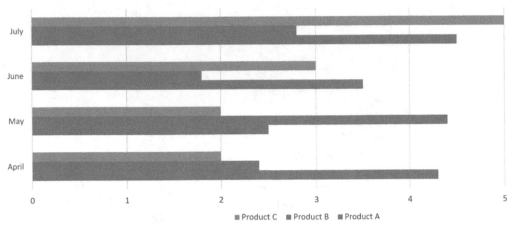

Scatterplot

A scatterplot is the most common plot used in data science and is mostly used to visualize clusters in a dataset and show the relationship between two variables.

Statistics Fundamentals

In statistics, we have three measures of central tendency: mean, median, and mode. They help us describe the data and can be used to clean data statistically.

Mean

Mean is the accurate measure to describe the data when we do not have any outliers present.

Median

Median is used if there is an outlier in the dataset. You can find the median by arranging data values from the lowest to the highest value.

   If there are even numbers, the median is the average of two numbers in the middle, and if there are odd numbers, the median is the middle value. For example, in the dataset 1, 1, 2, 4, 6, 6, 9, the median is 4. For the dataset 1, 1, 4, 6, 6, 9, the median is 5. Take the mean of 4 and 6, or (4+6) / 2 = 5.

Mode

Mode is used if there is an outlier and the majority of the data is the same. Mode is the value or values in the dataset that occur most.

For example, for the dataset 1, 1, 2, 5, 5, 5, 9, the mode is 5.

Outlier Detection

Mean is the measure of central tendency that is affected by the outliers, which in turn impacts standard deviation.

For example, consider the following small dataset:

[15, 18, 7, 13, 16, 11, 21, 5, 15, 10, 9, 210]

By looking at it, one can quickly say 210 is an outlier that is much larger than the other values.

As you can see from Table 2.1, there has been a significant change in mean by adding an outlier compared to median and mode. *Variance* is the average of the squared differences from the mean.

TABLE 2.1 Mean, median, and mode for outlier detection

With Outlier	Without Outlier
Mean: 12.72	Mean: 29.16
Median: 13	Median: 14
Mode: 15	Mode: 15

Standard Deviation

Standard deviation is the square root of the variance. Standard deviation is an excellent way to identify outliers. Data points that lie more than one standard deviation from the mean can be considered unusual.

NOTE   Covariance is a measure of how much two random variables vary from each other.

Correlation

Correlation is simply a normalized form of covariance. The value of the correlation coefficient ranges from −1 to +1. The correlation coefficient is also known as Pearson's correlation coefficient.

Positive Correlation   When we increase the value of one variable, the value of another variable increases respectively; this is called *positive correlation.*

Negative Correlation   When we increase the value of one variable, the value of another variable decreases respectively; this is called *negative correlation.*

Zero Correlation   When the change in the value of one variable does not impact the other substantially, then it is called *zero correlation.*

Correlation is helpful in detecting label leakage. For highly correlated labels, for example, if you are training a cancer prediction model, you are using hospital name as a feature, which is highly correlated with the target variable, whether a person has cancer. This correlation can cause your model to learn on hospital names. Refer to this video for more details: `https://developers.google.com/machine-learning/crash-course/cancer-prediction`.

Data Quality and Reliability

The quality of your model is going to depend on the quality and reliability (or feasibility) of the data. Your model quality will also depend on the size of the training data.

Reliability is the degree to which you can trust your data. If your data is unreliable, that means it has missing values, duplicate values, and bad features; you can consider it as unclean data. If you train a model on unclean data, you are less likely to get useful predictions. To ensure your data is reliable, you can do the following:

- Check for label errors as sometimes humans do labeling and we do make mistakes.
- Check for noise in features, such as, for example, GPS measurements.
- Check for outliers and data skew.

It's important to have a concrete definition of quality while collecting the data. We will discuss several parameters of data quality in the following sections.

Data Skew

Data skew means when the normal distribution curve is not symmetric, the data is skewed. It means that there are outliers in the data or the data distribution is not even.

The skewness for a normal distribution is 0.

The data can be right skewed or left skewed (see Figure 2.4). You can analyze skew by knowing the statistical measure such as mean and median and standard deviation from the dataset.

FIGURE 2.4   Data skew

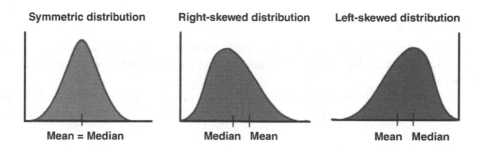

For right-skewed data, a real-world example can be income data because most people will have an average income and only 0.01 percent will have income higher than rest of the population (billionaires such as Jeff Bezos), leading to outliers, or right skew.

Skewed data does not work well with models because having extreme outliers affects the model's capability to predict well. With several transformations such as log transformation and normalization, you can transform skewed distribution to normal distribution by removing outliers. If the skewness is in the target variable, you can use the Synthetic Minority Oversampling Technique (SMOTE), undersampling, or oversampling.

Data Cleaning

The goal of normalization is to transform features to be on a similar scale. This improves the performance and training stability of the model. (See `https://developers.google.com/machine-learning/data-prep/transform/normalization`.)

Scaling

Scaling means converting floating-point feature values from their natural range into a standard range—for example, from 1,000–5,000 to 0 to 1 or –1 to +1. Scaling is useful when a feature set consists of multiple features. It has the following benefits:

- In deep neural network training, scaled features help gradient descent converge better than non-scaled features.

- Scaling removes the possibility of "NaN traps" as every number value is scaled to a range of numbers.
- Without scaling, the model will give too much importance to features having a wider range.

 You would use scaling when your data is uniformly distributed or has no skew with few or no outliers; for example, age can be scaled because every range will have a uniform number of people representing age.

Log Scaling

Log scaling is used when some of the data samples are in the power of law, or very large. For example, you would use log scaling when some of the sample is 10,000 while some is in the range 0–100.

So, taking a log will bring them to same range. For example, log of (100,000) = 100 and log of (100) = 10. Therefore, your data will be scaled to the 0 to 100 range with log scaling.

Z-score

This is another scaling method where the value is calculated as standard deviations away from the mean. You would calculate the z-score as follows when you have a few outliers:

Scaled value = (value – mean) / stddev

For example, given

Mean = 100

Standard deviation = 20

Original value = 130

the scaled value is 1.5. The z-score lies between –3 to +3, so anything outside of that range will be an outlier.

Clipping

In the case of extreme outliers, you can cap all feature values above or below to a certain fixed value. You can perform feature clipping before or after other normalization techniques.

Handling Outliers

An outlier is a value that is the odd one out or an observation that lies far from the rest of the data points because it is too large or too small. They may exist in data due to human error or skew.

You need to use the following visualization techniques and statistical techniques (some of which were discussed in previous sections) to detect outliers:

- Box plots
- Z-score
- Clipping
- Interquartile range (IQR)

Once an outlier is detected, you can either remove it from the dataset so that it does not affect model training or impute or replace outlier data to either mean, median, mode, or boundary values.

Establishing Data Constraints

The data analysis and exploration process leads to key insights and outcomes such as data quality issues (missing values, outliers, and type conversions).

To have a consistent and reproducible check, you need to set up the data constraint by defining a schema for your ML pipeline.

A schema with defined metadata describes the property of your data, such as data type (numerical vs. categorical), allowed range, format, and distribution of values of the data. A schema is an output of the data analysis process.

The following are the advantages of having a schema:

- For feature engineering and data transformation, your categorical data and numerical data needs to be transformed. Having a schema enables metadata-driven preprocessing.
- You can validate new data using the data schema and catch anomalies such as skews and outliers during training and prediction.

Exploration and Validation at Big-Data Scale

The volume of data is growing at a fast pace. To train deep neural networks, a large amount of data is needed. The challenge to validate these large datasets is that the data needs to be validated in memory. You will need multiple machines to scale data validation for large datasets.

TensorFlow Data Validation (TFDV) can be used to understand, validate, and monitor ML data at scale (see Figure 2.5).

TFDV is used for detecting data anomalies and schema anomalies in the data. It is a part of the *TensorFlow Extended (TFX)* platform and provides libraries for data validation and schema validation for large datasets in an ML pipeline. The key TFX libraries are Tensor-Flow Data Validation, TensorFlow Transform, used for data preprocessing and feature engineering, TensorFlow Model Analysis for ML model evaluation and analysis, and TensorFlow Serving for serving ML models.

FIGURE 2.5   TensorFlow Data Validation

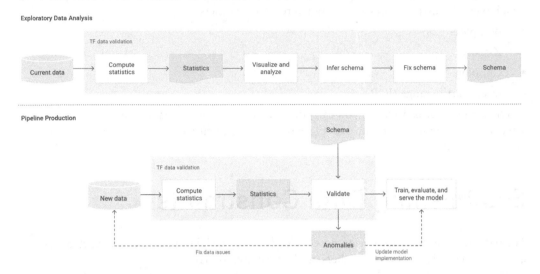

You can use TFDV in these ways:

Exploratory Data Analysis Phase   You can use TFDV to produce a data schema to understand the data for your ML pipeline. This schema can act as a defined contract between your ML pipeline and data. Whenever your schema is violated, you need to fix either your data or the pipeline.

Production Pipeline Phase   After your model is deployed, this schema can be used to define a baseline to detect any new data causing skew or drift in the model during training and serving.

Running TFDV on Google Cloud Platform

TFDV core application programming interfaces (APIs) are built on the Apache Beam open source software development kit (SDK) for building batch and streaming pipelines. Dataflow is a managed service that runs Apache Beam data processing pipelines at scale.

Dataflow integrates natively with the data warehousing serverless service BigQuery and data lakes (Google Cloud Storage) as well as Vertex AI Pipelines machine learning.

Organizing and Optimizing Training Datasets

You learned in the previous section how to check for data quality. In this section, we will talk about data sampling, imbalanced data, and how to split your dataset. We generally divide the data into training, test, and validation dataset (see Figure 2.6).

FIGURE 2.6   Dataset representation

Training Dataset   This is the actual dataset that we use to train the model, and our model learns from this data.

Validation Dataset   This is a subset of data that is used for the evaluation of the model. This data is used for hyperparameter tuning. The model does not use this data to learn from it, unlike training data. It is used for improving the model behavior after training.

Test Dataset   This is the sample of data used to test or evaluate the performance of your model. The test set is different from the training and validation sets as it's used after model training and model validation. The test set should not contain the data samples in the validation or training set because it might cause data leakage. Also, you should never train your data using the test set.

Imbalanced Data

When two classes in a dataset are not equal, the result is imbalanced data. In the example shown in Figure 2.7, there is less chance of credit card fraud in the dataset compared to No fraud.

In the case of credit card transactions, suppose, out of all transactions, 1,000 are not fraud examples and only five are fraud transactions. This is a classic representation of imbalanced data. In this scenario, we do not have enough transactions to train the model to classify whether a credit card transaction is fraud. The training model will spend more time on no-fraud scenarios.

In a random sampling, you can perform either *oversampling*, which means duplicating samples from the minority class, or *undersampling*, which means deleting samples from the majority class. Both of these approaches include bias because they introduce either more samples or fewer samples to remove imbalance.

FIGURE 2.7 Credit card data representation

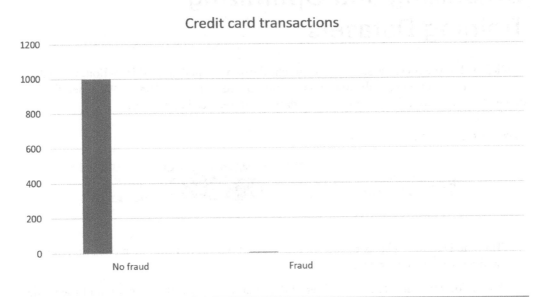

Credit card transactions

 An effective way to handle imbalanced data is to downsample and upweight the majority class.

Let's now consider the previous example and downsample the majority class, which is no-fraud examples. Downsampling by 10 will improve the balance (see Figure 2.8).

FIGURE 2.8 Downsampling credit card data

Credit card transactions

Now let's upweight the downsampled class. Since we downsampled by a factor of 10, the example weight should be 10. *Example weight* means counting an individual example as more important during training. An example weight of 10 means the model treats the example as 10 times as important (when computing loss) as it would for an example of weight 1. Refer to `https://developers.google.com/machine-learning/data-prep/construct/sampling-splitting/imbalanced-data` to learn more.

One of the advantages of downsampling and upweighting the downsampled class is faster model convergence because we have more of the minority class examples compared to the data before downsampling and upweighting.

Data Splitting

Mostly with general data cleaning, you would start with random splitting of the data. For example, consider datasets having naturally clustered examples.

Say you want your model to classify the topics in the text of a book. The topics can be horror, love story, and drama. A random split would be a problem in that case.

Why would having a random split cause a skew? It can cause a skew because stories with the same type of topic are written on the same timeline. If the data is split randomly, the test set and training set might contain the same stories.

To fix this, try splitting the data based on the time the story was published. For example, you can put stories written in June in the training set and stories published in July in the test set.

Another simple approach to fixing this problem would be to split the data based on when the story was published. For example, you could train on stories for the month of April and then use the second week of May as the test set to prevent overlap.

Data Splitting Strategy for Online Systems

For online systems, it's recommended to split the data by time as the training data is older than the serving data. By splitting data by time, you ensure your validation set mirrors the lag of time between training and prediction.

Here are the steps:

1. Perform data collection for 30 days.

2. Create a training set for data from day 1 to day 29.

3. Create a validation set for data for day 30.

Generally, time-based splits work best with very large datasets, such as, for example, data with millions of examples.

When it is clustered data—for example, a book or an online system—you have to make sure that you split the data in a way that your model will not get trained using information not available at prediction time. That's why you should use a time-based approach rather than a random split. For data splitting, you should always use domain knowledge to understand when a random split will work versus when to do a time-based split.

Handling Missing Data

Why do we have missing data? In real-world scenarios, you would have missing data as a result of failure to record data, or it could be due to data corruption. Some examples of missing data in structured data can be NaN values or a null value for a given feature. So, to train your model effectively, you would need to think of ways to handle missing data.

The following list includes some of the ways to handle missing data:

- Delete the rows or columns with missing values such as null or NaN. If a column has more than half of the rows as null, then the entire column can be dropped. The rows that have one or more column values as null can also be dropped. The disadvantage of this approach is that information is lost and the model will perform poorly if a large percentage of data is missing in a complete dataset.

- Replace missing values for numeric continuous columns or features such as age or interest rate in your dataset having missing values. You can replace missing values with the mean, median, or mode of remaining values in the column. This method can prevent the loss of data compared to removing or deleting the columns or rows. This method works well with small datasets. Also, this method does not factor in the covariance between features and can cause data leakage, which we will discuss in the next section.

- For missing values in categorical columns (string or numerical), the missing values can be replaced with the most frequent category. This method is called the imputation method. If the number of missing values is very large, then missing values can be replaced with a new category. The disadvantage of this method is encoding the extra added features while one-hot encoding.

- You can use the last valid observation to fill in the missing value. This is known as the *last observation carried forward (LOCF)* method. This method can reduce bias.

- For the time-series dataset, you can use the interpolation of the variable before and after a time stamp for a missing value.

- ML algorithms that can ignore missing values in data can also be used. For example, the k-nearest neighbors (k-NN) algorithm can ignore a column from a distance measure when a value is missing. Naive Bayes can also support missing values when making a prediction.

    Also, the Random Forest algorithm works well on nonlinear and categorical data. It adapts to the data structure, taking into consideration the high variance or the bias, producing better results on large datasets.

- Use machine learning to predict missing values. The correlation between the variable containing the missing value and other variables can be used to predict missing values. The regression or classification model can be used for the prediction of missing values based on non-missing variables.

Data Leakage

Data leakage happens when you expose your machine learning model to the test data during training. As a result, your model performs great during training and testing, but when you expose the model to unseen data, it underperforms. Data leakage leads to overfitting in the model as the model has already learned from the test and training data.

The following are some of the reasons for data leakage:

- The target variable is the output that your model is trying to predict, and features are the data that is fed into the model to make a prediction or predict the target variable. The cause of data leakage is that by mistake you have added your target variable as your feature.

- While splitting the test data and the training data for model training, you have included the test data with the training data.

- The presence of features that expose the information about the target variable will not be available after the model is deployed. This is also called label leakage and can be detected by checking the correlation between the target variable and the feature.

- Applying preprocessing techniques (normalizing features, removing outliers, etc.) to the entire dataset will cause the model to learn not only the training set but also the test set, which leads to data leakage.

A classic example of data leakage is time-series data. For example, when dealing with time-series data, if we use data from the future when doing computations for current features or predictions, we would highly likely end up with a leaked model. It generally happens when the data is randomly split into train and test subsets.

These are the situations where you might have data leakage:

- If the model's predicted output is as good as actual output, it might be because of a data leakage. This means the model might be somehow memorizing the data or might have been exposed to the actual data.

- While doing the exploratory data analysis, having features that are very highly correlated with the target variable might be a data leakage.

Data leakage happens primarily because of the *way* we split our data and *when* we split our data. Now, let's understand how to prevent data leakage:

- Select features that are not correlated with a given target variable or that don't contain information about the target variable.

- Split the data into test, train, and validation sets. The purpose of the validation set is to mimic the real-life scenario and it will help identify any possible case of overfitting.

- Preprocess the training and test data separately. You would perform normalization on training data rather than on the complete dataset to avoid any leakage.

- In case of time-series data, have a cutoff value on time as it prevents you from getting any information after the time of prediction.

- Cross-validation is another approach to avoid data leakage when you have limited data. However, if data leakage still happens, then scale or normalize the data and compute the parameters on each fold of cross-validation separately.

Furthermore, the difference in production data versus training data must be reflected in the difference between the validation data split and the training data split and between the testing data split and the validation data split.

For example, if you are planning on making predictions about user lifetime value (LTV) over the next 30 days, then make sure that the data in your validation data split is from 30 days after the data in your training data split and that the data in your testing data split is from 30 days before your validation data split.

Summary

In this chapter, we discussed why we need to visualize data and the various ways to visualize data, such as using box plots, line plots, and scatterplots. Then we covered statistical fundamentals such as mean, median, mode, and standard deviation and why they are relevant when finding outliers in data. Also, you learned how to check data correlation using a line plot.

You learned about various data cleaning and normalizing techniques such as log scaling, scaling, clipping, and using a z-score to improve the quality of data.

We also discussed establishing data constraints and why it's important to define a data schema in an ML pipeline and the need to validate data. We covered using TFDV for validating data at scale and why you need TFDV to validate data schema for large-scale deep learning systems. Then we discussed the strategy used for splitting the data and spoke about the data splitting strategy for an imbalanced dataset. We covered splitting based on time for online systems and clustered data.

Last, we covered strategies for how to deal with missing data and data leakage.

Exam Essentials

Be able to visualize data.   Understand why we need to visualize data and various ways to do so, such as using box plots, line plots, and scatterplots.

Understand the fundamentals of statistical terms.   Be able to describe mean, median, mode, and standard deviation and how they are relevant in finding outliers in data. Also know how to check data correlation using a line plot.

Determine data quality and reliability or feasibility.   Understand why you want data without outliers and what data skew is, and learn about various data cleaning and normalizing techniques such as log scaling, scaling, clipping, and z-score.

Establish data constraints.   Understand why it's important to define a data schema in an ML pipeline and the need to validate data. Also, you need to understand TFDV for validating data at scale.

Organize and optimize training data.   You need to understand how to split your dataset into training data, test data, and validation data and how to apply the data splitting technique when you have clustered and online data. Also understand the sampling strategy when you have imbalanced data.

Handle missing data.   Know the various ways to handle missing data, such as removing missing values; replacing missing values with mean, median, or mode; or using ML to create missing values.

Avoid data leaks.   Know the various ways data leakage and label leakage can happen in the data and how to avoid it.

Review Questions

1. You are the data scientist for your company. You have a dataset that includes credit card transactions, and 1 percent of those credit card transactions are fraudulent. Which data transformation strategy would likely improve the performance of your classification model?

   A. Write your data in TFRecords.

   B. Z-normalize all the numeric features.

   C. Use one-hot encoding on all categorical features.

   D. Oversample the fraudulent transactions.

2. You are a research scientist building a cancer prediction model from medical records. Features of the model are patient name, hospital name, age, vitals, and test results. This model performed really well on held-out test data but performed poorly on new patient data. What is the reason for this?

   A. Strong correlation between feature hospital name and predicted result.

   B. Random splitting of data between all the features available.

   C. Missing values in the feature hospital name and age.

   D. Negative correlation between the feature hospital name and age.

3. Your team trained and tested a deep neural network model with 99 percent accuracy. Six months after model deployment, the model is performing poorly due to change in input data distribution. How should you address input data distribution?

   A. Create alerts to monitor for skew and retrain your model.

   B. Perform feature selection and retrain the model.

   C. Retrain the model after hyperparameter tuning.

   D. Retrain your model monthly to detect data skew.

4. You are an ML engineer who builds and manages a production system to predict sales. Model accuracy is important as the production model has to keep up with market changes. After a month in production, the model did not change but the model accuracy was reduced. What is the most likely cause of the reduction in model accuracy?

   A. Accuracy dropped due to poor quality data.

   B. Lack of model retraining.

   C. Incorrect data split ratio in validation, test, and training data.

   D. Missing data for training.

5. You are a data scientist in a manufacturing firm. You have been asked to investigate failure of a production line based on sensor readings. You realize that 1 percent of the data samples are positive examples of a faulty sensor reading. How will you resolve the class imbalance problem?

   A. Generate 10 percent positive examples using class distribution.

   B. Downsample the majority data with upweighting to create 10 percent samples.

   C. Delete negative examples until positive and negative examples are equal.

   D. Use a convolutional neural network with the softmax activation function.

6. You are the data scientist of a meteorological department asked to build a model to predict daily temperatures. You split the data randomly and then transform the training and test datasets. Temperature data for model training is uploaded hourly. During testing, your model performed with 99 percent accuracy; however, in production, accuracy dropped to 70 percent. How can you improve the accuracy of your model in production?

   A. Split the training and test data based on time rather than a random split to avoid leakage.

   B. Normalize the data for the training and test datasets as two separate steps.

   C. Add more data to your dataset so that you have fair distribution.

   D. Transform data before splitting, and cross-validate to make sure the transformations are applied to both the training and test sets.

7. You are working on a neural-network-based project. The dataset provided to you has columns with different ranges and a lot of missing values. While preparing the data for model training, you discover that gradient optimization is having difficulty moving weights. What should you do?

   A. Use feature construction to combine the strongest features.

   B. Use the normalization technique to transform data.

   C. Improve the data cleaning step by removing features with missing values.

   D. Change the hyperparameter tuning steps to reduce the dimension of the test set and have a larger training set.

8. You are an ML engineer working to set a model in production. Your model performs well with training data. However, the model performance degrades in production environment and your model is overfitting. What can be the reason for this? (Choose three.)

   A. Applying normalizing features such as removing outliers to the entire dataset

   B. High correlation between the target variable and the feature

   C. Removing features with missing values

   D. Adding your target variable as your feature

Chapter

3

Feature Engineering

GOOGLE CLOUD PROFESSIONAL MACHINE LEARNING ENGINEER EXAM OBJECTIVES COVERED IN THIS CHAPTER:

✓ **2.1 Exploring and preprocessing organization-wide data (e.g., Cloud Storage, BigQuery, Cloud Spanner, Cloud SQL, Apache Spark, Apache Hadoop). Considerations include:**

- Data preprocessing (e.g., Dataflow, TensorFlow Extended [TFX], BigQuery)

✓ **5.1 Developing end-to-end ML pipelines. Considerations include:**

- Data and model validation

- Ensuring consistent data pre-processing between training and serving

Feature Engineering

In the previous chapter, we discussed why it's important to have quality data. We covered some of the ways to get quality data such as removing missing values, removing outliers, and using data normalization. In this chapter, we will cover feature-engineering techniques. We will also cover encoded structured data type, class imbalance, feature cross, and TensorFlow Transform to perform feature engineering.

Feature engineering is the process of transforming raw data coming from various sources such as log files and weather readings to useful features for model training. The features can be numerical or categorical. Let's understand the primary reasons for data transformation.

Transforming for Data Compatibility　Data consists of both numeric features and non-numeric features. Your model cannot perform mathematical computation on string type data. That is why it's important to transform such features into a vector or numerical representation understood by the model.

You also need to resize your input data to match to the input node in your model; for example, linear models and feed-forward neural networks have a fixed number of input nodes. So your input data must always be the same size.

Transforming for Data Quality　This type of transformation helps the model perform better. For example, converting your text features into lowercase can lead to better performance as can tokenizing, or normalizing numeric features before model training.

Now that you understand why feature engineering is important, let's discuss when to apply feature transformation during model training or the model prediction phase in the next section.

Consistent Data Preprocessing

Consistent data preprocessing is needed as you can apply transformations while generating the data either on disk or within the model. Let's discuss the approaches:

Pretraining Data Transformation　This means data transformation is performed before model training on a complete dataset. Your transformation code lives separate from your machine learning model. Advantages of this approach is that computation is performed only once and it can look at the entire dataset to determine the transform.

Some of the disadvantages of this approach are that the same transformation needs to be reproduced at prediction time, and if data changes at prediction, it can lead to skew, especially in the case of online serving or prediction. Another challenge is updating the transformation. If you want to update the data transformation, you would have to rerun the transform on the entire dataset, leading to slow iterations and more compute time.

Inside Model Data Transformation   In this, the transformation is part of the model code as the model takes in untransformed or raw data as input and transforms it within the model before training. One of the advantages of this approach is that it is easy to decouple your data and transformation. Even if your transformation technique changes, you can still use the same data. You are also using the same transformation during training and serving since it's part of the model. A disadvantage of this method is that if the transform is large or computation heavy, it can increase model latency. Transformations are done by data batches, which can be a problem if you are trying to normalize the data by setting mean values with batches of data and not entire datasets.

This can be solved by *tf.Transform*, which we will cover in the section "TensorFlow Transform" later in this chapter.

Encoding Structured Data Types

A good feature should be related to business objectives, be known at prediction time, be numeric with magnitude, and have enough examples. Let's look at various types of data in feature engineering that we are going to use throughout this chapter.

Categorical Data   This data type defines the category, and the data takes only a number of values—for example, yes/no type of data in your data column, male/female as values in the gender category, and so on.

Numeric Data   This represents data in the form of scalar value or continuous data such as observations, recordings, and measurements.

Why Transform Categorical Data?

Some algorithms can work with categorical data directly, such as, for example, decision trees. However, most ML algorithms cannot operate on label data directly. They require all input variables and output variables to be numeric, which is why categorical data must be converted to numeric data. If the categorical variable is an output variable, you would have to convert the numeric output back to categorical data during predictions.

Mapping Numeric Values

Integer and floating-point data don't need special encoding because they can be multiplied by a numeric weight. You may need to apply two kinds of transformations to numeric data: normalizing and bucketing.

Normalizing

We covered normalization techniques such as scaling, log scaling, z score, and clipping in the Data Cleaning section of Chapter 2, "Exploring Data and Building Data Pipelines." You would perform normalization in two cases with numeric data:

- **Numeric features that have distinctly different ranges (for example, age and income):** In this case, the model gradient descent can slow down convergence due to various data ranges. That is why AdaGrad and Adam optimization techniques can help, because they create a separate learning rate for each feature.

- **Numeric features that cover a wide range such as a city:** This type of dataset model will generate a NaN data error if it is not normalized. In this situation, even optimizers such as Adam and AdaGrad can't prevent NaN errors when there is a wide range of values in a single feature.

Bucketing

Bucketing is transforming numeric data to categorical data. For example, latitude can be a floating-point value, and it's difficult to represent it while predicting house price with respect to location. Two ways to do bucketing are as follows:

- **Creating buckets with equal-spaced boundaries:** You create a range of buckets and some buckets might have more data points compared to others. For example, to represent rainfall, you can bucket by range (0–50 cm, 50–100 cm); you might have more data points in the rainfall range 0–50 cm in an area with less intense rainfall.

- **Buckets with quantile boundaries:** Each bucket has the same number of points. The boundaries are not fixed and could encompass a narrow or wide span of values.

 Bucketing with equally spaced boundaries is an easy method that works for a lot of data distributions. For skewed data, however, try bucketing with quantile bucketing.

Mapping Categorical Values

There are ways to convert or transform your categorical data into numerical data so that your model can understand it.

Label Encoding or Integer Encoding

In label encoding, you would use indexing using a vocabulary. If the number of categories of a data field is small, such as breeds of dog or days of the week, you can make a unique feature for each category and assign an integer value. For example, ratings can be assigned such as "satisfactory" is 1, "good" is 2, and "best" is 3. You can apply integer ratings only if the categories represent limited ranges or ordinal values.

One-Hot Encoding

One-hot encoding is the process of creating dummy variables. This technique is used for categorical variables where order does not matter. The one-hot encoding technique is used when the features are nominal (do not have any order). Let's discuss what is an ordinal relationship in categorical data first; for example, ordinal variables can be socioeconomic status (low income, middle income, high income), education level (high school, BS, MS, PhD), income level (less than 50K, 50K–100K, over 100K), satisfaction rating (extremely dislike, dislike, neutral, like, extremely like). For categorical variables where no such ordinal relationship exists, such integer encoding is not enough.

In one-hot encoding, for every categorical feature, a new variable is created. It is a process by which categorical variables are converted into binary representation for the integer encoding or integer values. Let's look at the example of two colors, as shown in Table 3.1. Each can be represented by binary values.

TABLE 3.1 One-hot encoding example

Categorical Value	Integer Encoding or Creating a Vocabulary Mapping	One-Hot Encoding
Red	0	00
Blue	1	01

Sometimes you have large binary spaces to represent, which might lead to sparse representation with lots of 0s.

Out of Vocab (OOV)

For situations where categorical data contains outliers, you can create a single category called *out of vocabulary* for all the outliers rather than giving them unique representation because they occur very rarely in a dataset. When you use this approach, the ML system won't waste time training on each of those rare outliers.

Feature Hashing

Hashing works by applying a hash function to the categorical features and using their hash values as indices directly rather than looking into vocabulary. Hashing often causes collisions, and that is why for important terms, hashing can be worse than selecting a vocabulary. The advantage of hashing is that it doesn't require you to assemble a vocabulary in case the feature distribution changes heavily over time.

Hybrid of Hashing and Vocabulary

In this approach you can use a vocabulary for the most important categories in your data and replace the out-of-bucket vocabulary categories with categories by hashing. The advantage of this approach is that each out-of-box category is represented with hashing and the model still learns the categories outside your vocabulary.

Embedding

Embedding is a categorical feature represented as a continuous-valued feature. Deep learning models frequently convert the indices from an index to an embedding. Mostly, embeddings are used for text classification or document classification where you have a bag of words or a document of words.

Feature Selection

Feature selection means selecting a subset of features or reducing the number of input variables that are most useful to a model in order to predict the target variable.

Dimensionality reduction is one of the most popular techniques for reducing the number of features. The advantage of this is that it reduces the noise from data and overfitting problems. A lower number of dimensions in data means less training time and computational resources and increases the overall performance of machine learning algorithms. There are two ways this can be accomplished:

- Keep the most important features only: some of the techniques used are backward selection and Random Forest.

- Find a combination of new features: some of the techniques used are principal component analysis (PCA) and t-distributed stochastic neighbor embedding (t-SNE).

Class Imbalance

We covered data class imbalance in Chapter 2 and in this section, we will talk about class imbalance specific to classification models.

Classification models rely on some key outcomes we covered in Chapter 1, "Framing ML":

- A **true positive** is an outcome when the model correctly predicts the positive class; for example, the patients who took tests were actually sick with the virus.

- **True negative** is an outcome when the model correctly predicts the negative class, which means the patient who took the test has negative results and they actually are not sick.

- A **false positive** is an outcome where the model incorrectly predicts the positive class, meaning the patients were actually not sick but the test predicted them as sick.

- **False negative** is an outcome where the model incorrectly predicts the negative class, meaning the patients were sick but the test determined them as not sick.

In this scenario, false negatives are a problem because you do not want sick patients identified as not sick. So you would work on minimizing the false negatives outcome in your classification model.

Classification Threshold with Precision and Recall

In order to map a logistic regression value to a binary category, you define a **classification threshold** (also called the **decision threshold**). It is a value that a human chooses, not a value chosen by model training and usually for most cases this threshold is assumed to be 0.5. A logistic regression model outputs a value between 0 and 1. Suppose the classification threshold is 0.6 set by the human and the value predicted by the model is 0.7, then the model predicts the positive class. This choice of classification threshold strongly influences the number of false positives and false negatives. Mostly, classification thresholds are problem-specific and must be fine-tuned. Precision Recall curve indicates how well a model predicts the positive class. Precision refers to the number of true positives divided by the total number of positive prediction while recall also known as the true positive rate (TPR). Recall is is the percentage of data samples that a machine learning model correctly identifies as belonging to a class of interest which is the "positive class" out of the total samples for that class.

Both precision and recall are important to evaluate a model. However, if you improve precision, it will reduce recall and vice versa.

If you want to minimize false positives, then raise the classification threshold. For these problems, precision is really important to you. For example, if you would rather have your model classify a spam email as not spam than the other way around. When you care more about positives than negatives, precision should be used.

 If you raise the classification threshold, it will reduce false positives, thus raising precision.

If you want to minimize false negatives, then lower the classification threshold. For these problems, recall is really important to you. In other words, you prefer that your model classify a non-sick patient as sick but it will be a problem if a sick patient is identified as non-sick. In such scenarios, if you care more about your negatives than positives, recall should be used.

Recall answers the question, out of all possible positives, how many did the model correctly identify?

If you decrease or lower the classification threshold, it will reduce false negatives, thus raising recall.

Area under the Curve (AUC)

In this section, we will cover two types of areas under the curve with classification problems.

AUC ROC   This is used for a balanced dataset in classification problems that have an equal number of examples for both the classes we are trying to predict.

AUC PR   This is used when a dataset in classification problems is imbalanced, such as, for example, credit card transactions to identify fraud or not fraud. Suppose you have 10,000 credit card transactions, the data for a fraud would be 1 in 1,000 such transactions.

AUC ROC

An ROC curve (receiver operating characteristic curve) is a graph showing the performance of a classification model at all classification thresholds. This curve plots two parameters: true positive rate and false positive rate. You can refer to this link to see what the graph looks like:

```
https://developers.google.com/machine-learning/crash-course/
classification/roc-and-auc
```

AUC ROC (area under the ROC curve) measures the two-dimensional area underneath the entire ROC curve. It refers to a number between 0.0 and 1.0 representing a binary classification model's ability to separate positive classes from negative classes.

The closer the AUC is to 1.0, the better the model's ability to separate classes from each other. AUC ROC curves are used when the class is balanced or when you want to give equal weight to both classes (negative and positive class) prediction ability.

AUC PR

A PR curve is a graph with Precision values on the y-axis and Recall values on the x-axis. The focus of the PR curve on the minority class makes it an effective diagnostic for imbalanced binary classification models.

The area under the precision-recall (AUC PR) curve measures the two-dimensional area underneath the precision-recall (PR) curve. In case of an imbalanced class, precision-recall curves (PR curves) are recommended for highly skewed domains. AUC PR gives more attention to the minority class. It can be used in conjunction with downsampling or upsampling, which we covered in Chapter 2.

Feature Crosses

A *feature cross*, or synthetic feature, is created by multiplying (crossing) two or more features. It can be multiplying the same feature by itself [A * A] or it can be multiplying values of multiple features, such as [A * B * C]. In machine learning, feature crosses are usually performed on one-hot encoded features—for example, binned_latitude × binned_longitude. (For more information, see `https://developers.google.com/machine-learning/crash-course/feature-crosses/video-lecture`.)

There are two ways to use feature cross:

- A feature cross is used when a single feature on its own has less predictive ability compared to combined features. For example, we have a model that needs to predict how crowded the street-based location of people is at a certain time of the day. If we build a feature cross from both these features, [location (market, curbside) × time of the day], then we'll end up with vastly more predictive ability than either feature on its own. For example, if there is a farmers market on Tuesday evening, it will be more crowded. If there is no farmers market on Tuesday evening, it will be less crowded.

- In linear problems with highly complex models, a feature cross is used to represent nonlinearity in a linear model by multiplying (crossing) two or more features. Linear learners scale well to massive data. Using feature crosses on massive datasets is one efficient strategy for learning highly complex models. Let's look at an example. As shown in Figure 3.1, a dot represents sick people, and a rectangle represents healthy people. It is difficult to separate by line or by a linear method.

FIGURE 3.1   Difficult to separate by line or a linear method

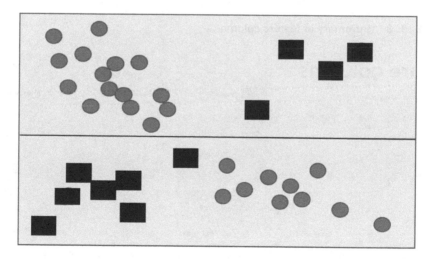

This is a linear problem, but seeing the data distribution of these variables, it's hard to separate the dots from the rectangles by using a straight line, or it's hard to classify these by using a linear method, as shown in Figure 3.2. It's difficult to separate classes by line.

That is why we will cross these features, dot versus rectangle, to create a feature cross—for example, AB = A * B. Please refer to this link to understand the concept of encoding nonlinearity: `https://developers.google.com/machine-learning/crash-course/feature-crosses/encoding-nonlinearity`.

FIGURE 3.2   Difficult to separate classes by line

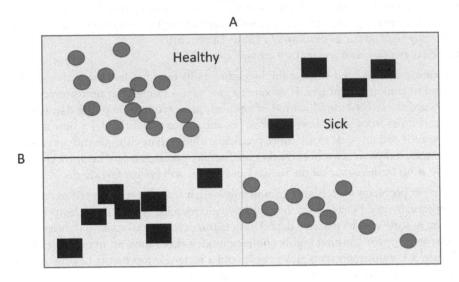

Figure 3.3 summarizes all the feature engineering techniques for converting numerical and categorical data we covered so far.

FIGURE 3.3   Summary of feature columns

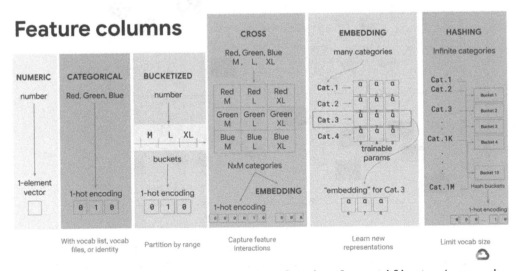

TensorFlow Transform

Increasing the performance of a TensorFlow model requires an efficient input pipeline. First we will discuss the TF Data API and then we'll talk about TensorFlow Transform.

TensorFlow Data API *(tf.data)*

An efficient data input pipeline can drastically improve the speed of your model execution by reducing device idle time. Consider incorporating the following best practices as detailed here to make your data input pipeline more efficient:

- Prefetch transformation to overlap preprocessing and model execution of a training step. This transformation decouples the time when data is produced to the time when data is consumed. The *tf.data* API provides the *tf.data.Dataset.prefetch* transformation.

- The *tf.data.Dataset.interleave* transformation parallelizes the data reading. By using the interleave transformation, you can mitigate the impact of the various data extraction overhead.

- Use the cache transformation to cache data in memory during the first epoch. The *tf.data.Dataset.cache* transformation can cache a dataset, either in memory or on local storage. This will save some operations (like file opening and data reading) from being executed during each epoch.

- Vectorize user-defined functions on a batch of datasets. The dataset is passed in to the map transformation.

- Reduce memory usage when applying the interleave, prefetch, and shuffle transformations.

TensorFlow Transform

The TensorFlow Transform library is part of TensorFlow Extended (TFX) and allows you to perform transformations prior to training the model and to emit a TensorFlow graph that reproduces these transformations during training. Using tf.Transform avoids the training-serving skew. In Google Cloud, you can create transform pipelines using Cloud Dataflow. Some of the steps that TF Transform takes for transformations during training and serving are analyzing training data, transforming training data, transforming evaluation data, producing metadata, feeding the model, and serving data, as shown in Figure 3.4.

You can run the previous pipeline using Cloud Dataflow and BigQuery:

1. Read training data from BigQuery.
2. Analyze and transform training data using tf.Transform Cloud Dataflow.
3. Write transformed training data to Cloud Storage as TFRecords.
4. Read evaluation data from BigQuery.

5. Transform evaluation data using the transform_fn produced by step 2 in Cloud Dataflow.

6. Write transformed training data to Cloud Storage as TFRecords.

7. Write transformation artifacts to Cloud Storage for creating and exporting the model.

FIGURE 3.4   TensorFlow Transform

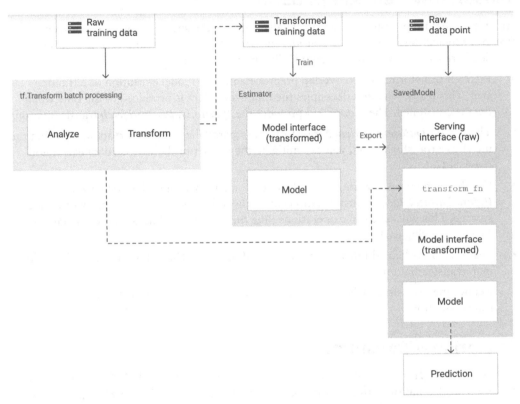

Source: Adapted from Google Cloud

Table 3.2 shows how you can run a TFX pipeline using Google Cloud Platform (GCP) services.

TABLE 3.2   Run a TFX pipeline on GCP

Step	TFX library	GCP service
Data extraction & validation	TensorFlow Data Validation	Cloud Dataflow
Data transformation	TensorFlow Transform	Cloud Dataflow

Step	TFX library	GCP service
Model training & tuning	TensorFlow (tf.Estimators and tf.Keras)	Vertex AI Training
Model evaluation & validation	TensorFlow Model Analysis	Cloud Dataflow
Model serving for prediction	TensorFlow Serving	Vertex AI Prediction

GCP Data and ETL Tools

We will cover the complete data analytics ecosystem in detail, from collecting to storing data, in Chapter 8, "Model Training and Hyperparameter Tuning." Here are two tools that will help with data transformation and ETL in Google Cloud:

- **Cloud Data Fusion** is a code-free web UI–based managed service that helps build and manage extract, transform, load (ETL) or extract, load, transform (ELT) pipelines from various data sources. The web UI helps you to clean and prepare data with no infrastructure management. It also supports Cloud Dataproc, which is another service to run and manage Hadoop and Spark workloads on Google Cloud. Using Dataproc as an execution environment, Cloud Data Fusion allows you to run MapReduce and Spark streaming pipelines. Refer to this link to learn more: `https://cloud.google.com/data-fusion#section-9`.

- **Dataprep by Trifacta** (`https://cloud.google.com/dataprep`) is a serverless intelligent tool for visually exploring, cleaning, and preparing structured and unstructured data for analysis, reporting, and machine learning at any scale. There is no infrastructure to deploy or manage. Also, there is no infrastructure to manage as it is serverless and no need to write code as it is UI–based. It suggests your next data transformation and predicts with each UI input.

Summary

In this chapter, we discussed feature engineering and why it's important to transform numerical and categorical features for model training and serving.

Then we discussed various techniques to transform numerical features, such as bucketing and normalization. We also discussed the technique to transform categorical features such as linear encoding, one-hot encoding, out of vocabulary, hashing, and embedding.

You learned why it's important to select features and some of the techniques for dimensionality reduction such as PCA. Then we covered class imbalance and how precision and recall impacts the classification. For imbalanced classes, AUC PR is more effective than AUC ROC.

We also discussed why feature crosses are important and the benefits of feature crossing.

We covered how to represent data for TensorFlow using tf.data and then we covered tf.Transform and how to process pipelines using tf.Transform on Google Cloud. You learned about some of the Google Cloud data processing and ETL tools such as Cloud Data Fusion and Cloud Dataprep.

Exam Essentials

Use consistent data processing.   Understand when to transform data, either before training or during model training. Also know the benefits and limitations of transforming data before training.

Know how to encode structured data types.   Understand techniques to transform both numeric and categorical data such as bucketing, normalization, hashing, and one-hot encoding.

Understand feature selection.   Understand why feature selection is needed and some of the techniques of feature selection, such as dimensionality reduction.

Understand class imbalance.   Understand true positive, false positive, accuracy, AUC, precision, and recall in classification problems and how to effectively measure accuracy with class imbalance.

Know where and how to use feature cross.   You need to understand why feature cross is important and the scenarios in which you would need it.

Understand TensorFlow Transform.   You need to understand TensorFlow Data and TensorFlow Transform and how to architect tf.Transform pipelines on Google Cloud using BigQuery and Cloud Data Fusion.

Use GCP data and ETL tools.   Know how and when to use tools such as Cloud Data Fusion and Cloud Dataprep. For example, in case you are looking for a no-code solution to clean data, you would use Dataprep for data processing and, in case you are looking for a no-code and UI–based solution for ETL (extract, transform, load), you would use Cloud Data Fusion.

Review Questions

1. You are the data scientist for your company. You have a dataset that which has all categorical features. You trained a model using some algorithms. With some algorithms this data is giving good result but when you change the algorithm the performance is getting reduced. Which data transformation strategy would likely improve the performance of your model?

   A. Write your data in TFRecords.

   B. Create a feature cross with categorical feature.

   C. Use one-hot encoding on all categorical features.

   D. Oversample the features.

2. You are working on a neural network–based project. The dataset provided to you has columns with different ranges. While preparing the data for model training, you discover that gradient optimization is having difficulty moving weights to an optimized solution. What should you do?

   A. Use feature construction to combine the strongest features.

   B. Use the normalization technique.

   C. Improve the data cleaning step by removing features with missing values.

   D. Change the partitioning step to reduce the dimension of the test set and have a larger training set.

3. You work for a credit card company and have been asked to create a custom fraud detection model based on historical data using AutoML Tables. You need to prioritize detection of fraudulent transactions while minimizing false positives. Which optimization objective should you use when training the model?

   A. An optimization objective that minimizes log loss.

   B. An optimization objective that maximizes the precision at a recall value of 0.50.

   C. An optimization objective that maximizes the area under the precision-recall curve (AUC PR) value.

   D. An optimization objective that maximizes the area under the curve receiver operating characteristic (AUC ROC) curve value.

4. You are a data scientist working on a classification problem with time-series data and achieved an area under the receiver operating characteristic curve (AUC ROC) value of 99 percent for training data with just a few experiments. You haven't explored using any sophisticated algorithms or spent any time on hyperparameter tuning. What should your next step be to identify and fix the problem?

   A. Address the model overfitting by using a less complex algorithm.

   B. Address data leakage by applying nested cross-validation during model training.

   C. Address data leakage by removing features highly correlated with the target value.

   D. Address the model overfitting by tuning the hyperparameters to reduce the AUC ROC value.

5. You are training a ResNet model on Vertex AI using TPUs to visually categorize types of defects in automobile engines. You capture the training profile using the Cloud TPU profiler plug-in and observe that it is highly input bound. You want to reduce the bottleneck and speed up your model training process. Which modifications should you make to the `tf.data` dataset? (Choose two.)

   A. Use the interleave option to read data.

   B. Set the prefetch option equal to the training batch size.

   C. Reduce the repeat parameters.

   D. Decrease the batch size argument in your transformation.

   E. Increase the buffer size for shuffle.

6. You have been asked to develop an input pipeline for an ML training model that processes images from disparate sources at a low latency. You discover that your input data does not fit in memory. How should you create a dataset following Google-recommended best practices?

   A. Create a tf.data.Dataset.prefetch transformation.

   B. Convert the images into TFRecords, store the images in Cloud Storage, and then use the tf.data API to read the images for training.

   C. Convert the images to tf.Tensor objects, and then run Dataset.from_tensor_slices().

   D. Convert data into TFRecords.

7. Different cities in California have markedly different housing prices. Suppose you must create a model to predict housing prices. Which of the following sets of features or feature crosses could learn city-specific relationships between roomsPerPerson and housing price?

   A. Two feature crosses: [binned latitude x binned roomsPerPerson] and [binned longitude x binned roomsPerPerson]

   B. Three separate binned features: [binned latitude], [binned longitude], [binned roomsPerPerson]

   C. One feature cross: [binned latitude x binned longitude x binned roomsPerPerson]

   D. One feature cross: [latitude x longitude x roomsPerPerson]

8. You are a data engineer for a finance company. You are responsible for building a unified analytics environment across a variety of on-premises data marts. Your company is experiencing data quality and security challenges when integrating data across the servers, caused by the use of a wide range of disconnected tools and temporary solutions. You need a fully managed, cloud-native data integration service that will lower the total cost of work and reduce repetitive work. Some members on your team prefer a codeless interface for building an extract, transform, load (ETL) process. Which service should you use?

   A. Cloud Data Fusion

   B. Dataprep

   C. Cloud Dataflow

   D. Apache Flink

9. You work for a global footwear retailer and need to predict when an item will be out of stock based on historical inventory data. Customer behavior is highly dynamic since footwear demand is influenced by many different factors. You want to serve models that are trained on all available data but track your performance on specific subsets of data before pushing to production. What is the most streamlined, scalable, and reliable way to perform this validation?

   A. Use the tf.Transform to specify performance metrics for production readiness of the data.

   B. Use the entire dataset and treat the area under the receiver operating characteristic curve (AUC ROC) as the main metric.

   C. Use the last relevant week of data as a validation set to ensure that your model is performing accurately on current data.

   D. Use k-fold cross-validation as a validation strategy to ensure that your model is ready for production.

10. You are transforming a complete dataset before model training. Your model accuracy is 99 percent in training, but in production its accuracy is 66 percent. What is a possible way to improve the model in production?

   A. Apply transformation during model training.

   B. Perform data normalization.

   C. Remove missing values.

   D. Use tf.Transform for creating production pipelines for both training and serving.

Chapter

4

Choosing the Right ML Infrastructure

GOOGLE CLOUD PROFESSIONAL MACHINE LEARNING ENGINEER EXAM OBJECTIVES COVERED IN THIS CHAPTER:

✓ **3.3 Choosing appropriate hardware for training. Considerations include:**

- Evaluation of compute and accelerator options (e.g., CPU, GPU, TPU, edge devices)

✓ **4.2 Scaling online model serving. Considerations include:**

- Choosing appropriate hardware (e.g., CPU, GPU, TPU, edge)

In this chapter, we will discuss the hardware requirements for training on different types of data and for the various different scenarios of deployment. The hardware requirements depend on the type of machine learning (ML) algorithm you choose, the training method (custom, AutoML, or pretrained), and the data type as well.

Generally, ML models for video and images require a large number of computations for each loop of training, including matrix multiplications, additions, subtractions, and differentials. These operations are performed on very large matrices, which sometimes could be several megabytes for each data point. When you have millions of data points, it becomes a problem for traditional general-purpose CPUs. So, GPUs (which were originally used in rendering videos or in gaming consoles) were repurposed to train ML models. Later Google created custom ASICs called Tensor Processing Units (TPUs), which perform even better. These techniques were originally applied to video and images and then were applied to natural language processing tasks. They greatly improved the performance of translations, text classifications, and in-general text-to-text problems (where both the input and output of a model is text).

Let's explore the available hardware options for training and deploying models.

Pretrained vs. AutoML vs. Custom Models

When you have an ML problem to solve, say image classification, you have three ways to deal with approaching it:

- Pretrained
- AutoML
- Custom

Figure 4.1 shows the differences between the models, and we'll elaborate on each in this chapter.

The first method is to use any pretrained models that might be available and ready to use. These are models that have already been trained on large datasets by Google. These pretrained models are already deployed and can be readily used via APIs. Google manages the deployment of these models; therefore, as a user, you only think about the number of times you call the APIs.

FIGURE 4.1   Pretrained, AutoML, and custom models

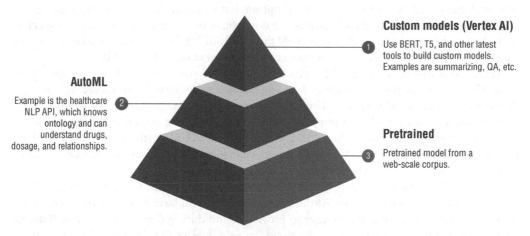

Custom models (Vertex AI)

Use BERT, T5, and other latest tools to build custom models. Examples are summarizing, QA, etc.

AutoML

Example is the healthcare NLP API, which knows ontology and can understand drugs, dosage, and relationships.

Pretrained

Pretrained model from a web-scale corpus.

The biggest advantage of using pretrained models is the ease of use and the speed with which you can incorporate ML into your application. In this case, you do not have to think about the algorithm, the training method, the training hardware, the deployment hardware, scalability, and so on.

A pretrained model should be tried first. Only if the pretrained model does not meet your requirements should you consider AutoML or custom models.

A pretrained model should be your first choice. Carefully consider a pretrained model and evaluate if it fits your use case. You can start by using a pretrained model in your application, and then if you think you need a better model, you can move to an AutoML or custom model.

Pretrained models are used by thousands of users, and with millions of requests coming in, they are maintained by a team of engineers. Of all the users looking to use ML in their application, a majority will choose pretrained models. Figure 4.1 shows these models as a pyramid. You will notice that the bottom layer, which is wide, represents the number of users who use pretrained models.

You do not even have to be an ML engineer to use pretrained models. Any developer can make use of pretrained models using APIs. They can be used with ease using the Python, Java, and Node.js SDKs. We provide a detailed list of pretrained models that are available later in this chapter.

When using the pretrained models, you are not provisioning any cloud resources, and you are consuming only through an API. This is called a *serverless* method, and you will be charged based on the number of times you make a request to the API. Some of the APIs have a free tier. This is one of the reasons the pretrained models using APIs are so popular.

Now, while the pretrained models work well for a majority of users, sometimes they may not work for you. It is the most convenient option, but it is also the least customizable. Say you used the Vision API to classify plants but now you want to identify the exact subspecies of a plant. While the Vision API can provide thousands of labels, it might not have names for subspecies of plants. In this case, you may consider the next option: AutoML.

Vertex AI AutoML is a method by which you can build your own model using your own data. There are some popular machine learning problems that have been researched for decades and understood very well. These problems—such as image classification and text translation, for example—have been used many times in the past and all the nuances and variations have been identified. AutoML chooses the best ML algorithm, and the only thing that it needs is the data. Like a "just add water" cake mix, AutoML can be considered "just add data." You then have to format the data and work on quality control.

Unlike with pretrained models, you have to provision cloud resources for training and deploying the model on instances. At the time of training, you have to decide on the number of hours of instance time that you have to provision, and during deployment, you will decide on whether the model is deployed in the cloud, on field devices like Android phones, or in other IoT devices. We will look at the hardware provisioning options later in this chapter.

AutoML is the second level in the pyramid shown in Figure 4.1, where users who want to train models with their own data usually go. AutoML provides you with the ability to build your own models and at the same time does not require a team of ML experts to build them.

 TIP AutoML should be your choice if a pretrained model does not work for you and you do not have a team of ML engineers.

Say you find that your use case is unique and there is no AutoML available for it. In that case, you can use custom models in Vertex AI. This is the top tier in the pyramid in Figure 4.1, and it offers you a lot of flexibility for the choice of algorithm, hardware provisioning, and data types. The reason this is in the top of the pyramid is because of the flexibility, but at the same time, it also has the smallest base because the number of customers who have the expertise to use custom models is small. We will look at the hardware provisioning options for this training method later in this chapter.

Pretrained Models

When you are trying to solve a problem with machine learning, the first step is to see if there is a pretrained model. Pretrained models are machine learning models that have been trained on extremely large datasets and perform very well in benchmark tests. These models are supported by very large engineering and research teams and are retrained frequently.

As a customer, you can start using these models in just a few minutes through the web console (or the CLI, Python, Java, or Node.js SDK).

Any developer who is trying to solve a problem using machine learning should first check if there is a pretrained model available on the Google Cloud platform, and if so, use it.

Google Cloud has several pretrained models available:

- Vision AI
- Video AI
- Natural Language AI
- Translation AI
- Speech-to-Text and Text-to-Speech

In addition to pretrained models, Google Cloud has platforms that offer solutions to certain kinds of problems and include pretrained models as well as the ability to uptrain the existing models:

- Document AI
- Contact Center AI

Vision AI

Vision AI provides you with convenient access to ML algorithms for processing images and photos without having to create a complete machine learning infrastructure. Using this service, you can perform image classification, detect objects and faces, and read handwriting (through optical character recognition).

You can also try the service quickly from the convenience of your browser at `https://cloud.google.com/vision`. In production, typically you upload an image to the service or point to an image URL to analyze.

When you try service using your browser, you get four types of predictions, as shown in Figure 4.2. First you see objects detected in the photo.

FIGURE 4.2 Analyzing a photo using Vision AI

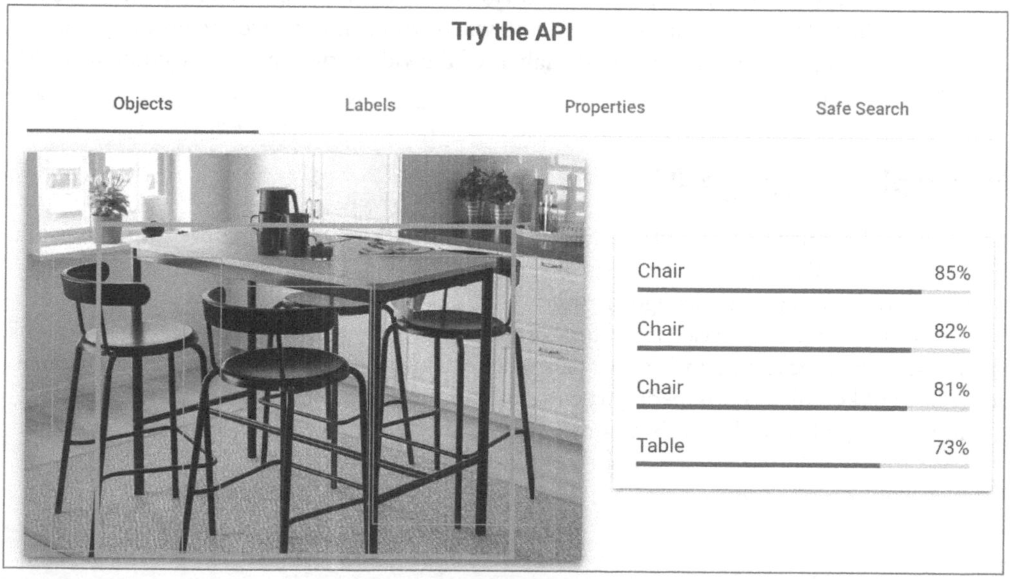

Second, you get a set of labels for your image; in our example, the labels we get are Table, Furniture, Plant, Houseplant, Cabinetry, Wood, and so on. Third, you get the dominant colors for these images, which can be used to organize your images based on a palette. Last, you get the "Safe Search" classification, which is whether the image falls in one of these categories: Adult, Spoof, Medical, Violence, and Racy. These classifications can be used to label images for use cases where you want to restrict sharing certain kinds of images, such as to avoid showing adult content to young audiences.

Video AI

This API has pretrained machine learning models that recognize objects, places, and actions in videos. It can be applied to stored video or to streaming video where the results are returned in real time.

You can use this service to recognize more than 20,000 different objects, places, and actions in videos. You can use the results as metadata in your video that can be used to search videos from your video catalog. For example, you can use the service to tag sports videos, and more specifically the type of sport. You can also process livestreams; for example, if you have a street camera looking at traffic, you can count the number of cars that cross an intersection.

Here are several examples of use cases for Video AI:

- **Use Case 1:** This API can be used to build a video recommendation system, using the labels generated by the API and a user's viewing history. This provides you with an ability to recommend based on details from within the video and not just external metadata and can greatly increase user experience.

- **Use Case 2:** Another use case is to create an index of your video archives using the metadata from the API. This is perfect for mass media companies that have petabytes of data that are not indexed.

- **Use Case 3:** Advertisements inserted into videos sometimes could be completely irrelevant to the videos. This is another use case where you can improve the user experience by comparing the time-frame-specific labels of the video content and the content of the advertisements.

Natural Language AI

The Natural Language AI provides insights from unstructured text using pretrained machine learning models. The main services it provides are entity extraction, sentiment analysis, syntax analysis, and general categorization.

The entity extraction service identifies entities such as the names of people, organizations, products, events, locations, and so on. This service also enriches the entities with additional information like links to Wikipedia articles if it finds any. Although entity extraction may sound like a simple problem, it is a nontrivial task. For example, in the sentence "Mr. Wood is a good actor," it takes a good amount of understanding that "Mr. Wood" is a person and not a type of wood.

Sentiment analysis provides you a positive, negative, or neutral score with magnitude for each sentence, for each entity, and the whole text. The syntax analysis can be used to identify the part of speech, dependency between words, lemma, and the morphology of text. Finally, it also classifies documents into one of more than 700 predefined categories. For more details, see `https://cloud.google.com/natural-language`.

Here are some use cases for Natural Language AI:

- **Use Case 1:** Measure the customer sentiment toward a particular product. Use entity analysis to find important details from documents like emails, chat, and social media and the sentiment analysis for each of these entities to understand customer opinion on specific products.

- **Use Case 2:** Use Healthcare Natural Language API to understand details specific to healthcare text like clinical notes or healthcare research documents. You can use this to extract medical insights like drugs, dosage, and conditions and build powerful healthcare apps. Note: Healthcare Natural Language API is a separate service from Google's Natural Language AI.

Translation AI

Use Translation AI to detect more than 100 languages, from Afrikaans to Zulu, and translate between any pairs of languages in that list. It uses Google Neural Machine Translation (GNMT) technology that was pioneered by Google and is now considered industry standard. For more information, refer to `https://ai.googleblog.com/2016/09/a-neural-network-for-machine.html`.

This service has two levels, Basic and Advanced. There are many differences, but the main difference is the Advanced version can use a *glossary* (a dictionary of terms mapped from source language to target language) and also can translate entire documents (PDFs, DOCs, etc.). There is also price difference.

You can translate text in ASCII or in UTF-8 format. In addition, you can also translate audio in real time using the Media Translation API, typically used for streaming services.

The Media Translation API (separate from the Translation API) directly translates audio in source language into audio in target languages. This helps with low-latency streaming applications and scales quickly.

Speech-to-Text

You can use the Speech-to-Text service to convert recorded audio or streaming audio into text. This is a popular service for creating subtitles for video recordings and streaming video as well. This is also commonly combined with a translate service to generate subtitles for multiple languages. For more details, see `https://cloud.google.com/speech-to-text#section-10`.

Text-to-Speech

Customers use the Text-to-Speech service to provide realistic speech with humanlike intonation. This is based on the state-of-the-art speech synthesis expertise from DeepMind (an AI subsidiary of Google). It currently supports 220+ voices across 40+ languages and variants. You can create a unique voice to represent your brand at all your touchpoints. See here for the list of languages supported: `https://cloud.google.com/text-to-speech/docs/voices`.

AutoML

AutoML, or automated ML, is the process of automating the time-consuming tasks of model training. AutoML is available for popular, well understood, and practically feasible ML problems like image classification, text classification, translation, and so on. You as a user only bring in the data and configure a few settings and the rest of the training is automated. You either leverage the easy-to-use web console or use a Python, Java, or Node.js SDK to initiate the AutoML training job.

There is AutoML training available for many data types and use cases. We can broadly categorize them into four categories:

- Structured data
- Images/video
- Natural language
- Recommendations AI/Retail AI

AutoML for Tables or Structured Data

Structured data is data that adheres to a well-defined schema and is usually in the form of a rectangular table. With tables there are two methods of training models:

- **BigQuery ML:** This is a SQL-based approach to training models. You can use this if you are a data analyst and are comfortable writing SQL queries. You can both train and make predictions using BigQuery and automatically add the predictions to tables. This is a serverless approach for ML training and prediction. We cover this in detail in Chapter 14, "BigQuery ML."
- **Vertex AI Tables:** This is the second method to train ML models that can be triggered using Python, Java, or Node.js, or using REST API. Vertex AI tables provide you with the ability to deploy the model on an endpoint and serve predictions through a REST API.

We will cover the available AutoML Tables algorithms in Table 4.1.

TABLE 4.1   Vertex AI AutoML Tables algorithms

Data Type	ML Problem	Metrics
Table (IID)	Classification	AUC ROC, AUC ROC, Logloss, Precision at Recall, Recall at Precision
Table (IID)	Regression	RMSE, RMSLE, MAE
Time-series data	Forecasting	RMSE, RMSLE, MAPE, Quantile loss

While configuring the AutoML job, there are a few things that are relevant from the hardware perspective. The "budget" is the last step in the web console, where you specify the maximum number of hours that you allow the job to run (see Figure 4.3). If the training job is not completed within the budget, AutoML will use the best model that was trained within the budget. There is another setting called Enable early stopping in figure below, which will end the training job if it identifies that the model training has completed, in which case you will be charged for only the number of node hours that were used.

FIGURE 4.3   Vertex AI AutoML, providing a "budget"

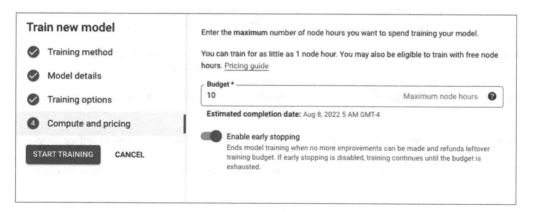

There are minimum values to the budget you can provide for the AutoML job. For example, for Object Detection AutoML, the minimum is 20 hours. Another important aspect to remember is that although all AutoML jobs require you to provide node hours for the budget, not all node hours are the same. The price of each node hour is different for the different types of AutoML jobs because the hardware used for different AutoML jobs is different.

From the model type perspective, forecasting is a special case. Vertex AI offers three model training methods for forecasting:

AutoML   This is the built-in model that is good for a wide variety of forecasting use cases.

Seq2seq+   This type of model takes in a sequence and produces another sequence. This model is effective when the dataset size is less than 1 GB.

Temporal Fusion Transformer   This is a deep neural network model that also uses the attention mechanism. It is designed to produce high accuracy and interpretability for a wide range of use cases.

AutoML for Images and Video

Machine learning problems on image and video data used to be cumbersome and time-consuming for machine learning experts until recently. Vertex AI AutoML makes it extremely easy to build models for these kinds of problems. Table 4.2 neatly summarizes all the available AutoML algorithms for these data types.

TABLE 4.2   AutoML algorithms

Data Type	ML Problem	AutoML Details
Image	Image classification (single)	Predict one correct label from a list of labels provided by user during training.
Image	Multiclass classification	Predict all the correct labels that you want assigned to an image.
Image	Object detection	Predict all the locations of objects that you're interested in.
Image	Image segmentation	Predict per-pixel areas of an image with a label.
Video	Classification	Get label predictions for entire videos, shots, and frames.
Video	Action recognition	Identify the action moments in video.
Video	Object tracking	Get labels, tracks, and time stamps for objects you want to track in a video.

One more consideration in AutoML related to hardware is the AutoML Edge model. These models are to be deployed to the edge devices, so the models are trained and configured to use less memory and low latency. The edge devices currently supported are iPhones, Android phones (Google Pixel, Samsung Galaxy, etc.), and Edge TPU devices, and this set will continue to increase as Google supports more.

When you choose an AutoML Edge model, there are options to help you find the right trade-off between accuracy and latency. For Edge TPU, we see the options shown in Figure 4.4.

FIGURE 4.4   Choosing the size of model in Vertex AI

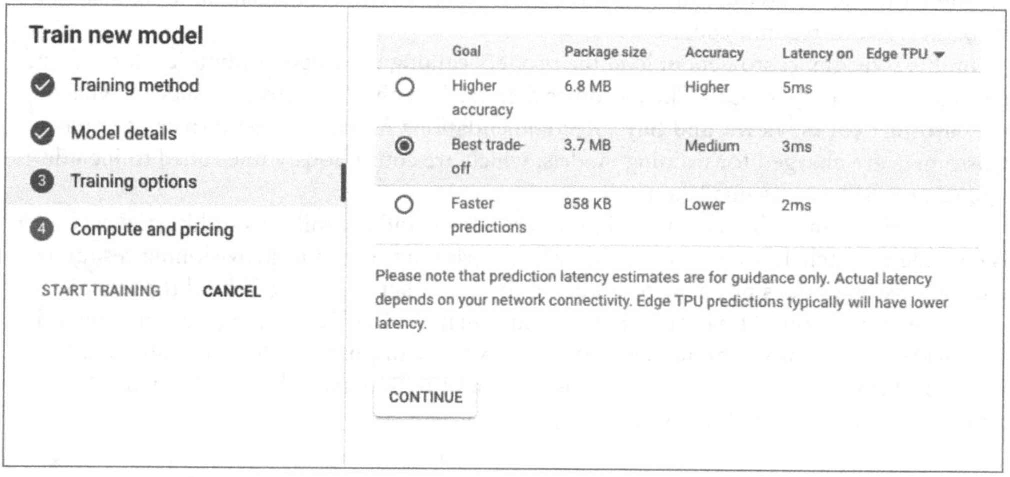

AutoML for Text

Machine learning models for text are also very well understood now, and you can build your own models easily using Vertex AI AutoML text. There are four popular problems that are solved using AutoML, including classification and sentiment analysis. Table 4.3 shows the full list.

TABLE 4.3   Problems solved using AutoML

Data Type	ML Problem	AutoML Details
Text	Text classification	Predict the one correct label that you want assigned to a document.
Text	Multi-label classification	Predict all the correct labels that you want assigned to a document.
Text	Entity extraction	Identify entities within your text items.
Text to text	Translation	Convert text from source language to target language.

Recommendations AI/Retail AI

GCP has an AutoML solution for the retail domain. Retail Search offers retailers a Google-quality search that can be customized and built upon Google's understanding of user intent and context.

The Vision API Product Search (a service under Vision AI) can be trained on reference images of products in your catalog, which can then be searched using an image.

The third part of the solution is Recommendations AI, which can understand nuances behind customer behavior, context, and SKUs in order to drive engagement across channels through relevant recommendations.

In this solution, customers upload the product catalog with details about each product, photos, and other metadata. The customer then feeds in the "user events" such as what the customer clicks, views, and buys. Recommendations AI uses this data to create models. Customers are charged for training models, which are continuously fine-tuned to include updates to the "user events" data.

In addition, when the recommendations are served and get millions of hits, the customer is charged for each 1,000 requests. This is a serverless approach to provisioning resources and the customer does not have to bother about the exact hardware behind the scenes.

Recommendations AI has an easy-to-use automated machine learning training method. It provides several different models that serve a variety of purposes for an online retail presence. From the exam perspective, it is important to understand Table 4.4, which describes the different recommendation types.

TABLE 4.4   Summary of the recommendation types available in Retail AI

Recommendation Type	What Does It Predict?	Usage	Data Used	Optimization Objective
Others you may like	The next product the user is likely to buy	Product page	Customer behavior and product relevance	Click-through rate
Frequently bought together (shopping cart expansion)	Items frequently bought together for a specific product within the same shopping session	Checkout page	User behavior in shopping cart	Revenue per order
Recommended for you	The next product the user likely will buy	Home page	User viewing history and context	Click-through rate
Similar items	Other products with similar attributes	Product page	Product catalog	Click-through rate

Source: Adapted from Google cloud/ https://cloud.google.com/retail/docs/models#model-types last accessed December 16, 2022.

Document AI

When you want to extract details from documents, like digitized scanned images of old printed documents, books, or forms, you can use Document AI. These are pages that can contain text in paragraph format and also tables and pictures. Some of this text could be printed and sometimes it could be handwritten. This is also a common type of document seen in government offices like the DMV where people fill out forms.

Forms contain a mix of printed text, with blank spaces where people fill out their details. This could be written with different types of ink (blue or black pen, etc.), and sometimes people make mistakes while writing. So, the ML model needs to understand the structure of the document (where to expect "name" and "address") and have a tolerance for hand-written text.

Another example is government documents like passports, driver's licenses, and tax filings. These are documents that have better structure but still have some variability.

If we can extract important details (like "firstname," "lastname," "address," etc.) from forms, we have structured data, which can now be stored in a database and can be analyzed. This is the extraction phase.

Document AI is a platform that understands documents and helps you to do the following:

- Detect document quality.
- Deskew.
- Extract text and layout information.
- Identify and extract key/value pairs.
- Extract and normalize entities.
- Split and classify documents.
- Review documents (human in the loop).
- Store, search, and organize documents (Document AI Warehouse)

Document AI has two important concepts: *processors* and a *Document AI Warehouse*.

A Document AI processor is an interface between the document and a machine learning model that performs the actions. There are general processors, specialized processors (procurement, identity, lending, and contract documents), and custom processors. You can train the custom processor by providing a training dataset (labeled set of documents) for your custom needs. For the full list of processor types, visit `https://cloud.google.com/document-ai/docs/processors-list`.

A Document AI Warehouse is a platform to store, search, organize, govern, and analyze documents along with their structured metadata.

Dialogflow and Contact Center AI

Dialogflow is a conversational AI offering from Google Cloud that provides chatbots and voicebots. This is integrated into a telephony service and other services to provide you with a Contact Center AI (CCAI) solution. Let us look at the services provided by this solution.

Virtual Agent (Dialogflow)

You can rapidly develop advanced virtual agents for enterprises that can handle topic switching and supplemental questions and provide multichannel support 24/7. It should be designed in such a way that the virtual agent is able to handle a majority of the cases. The complex calls will be forwarded to a human agent.

 The idea is to have the virtual agent handle a majority of common cases and the human agents handle the more complex calls. This is designed using the data collected from historical calls to the data center.

Agent Assist

When the human agent is handling a call, the Agent Assist can provide support by identifying intent and providing ready-to-send responses and answers from a centralized knowledge base as well as transcript calls in real time.

Insights

This service uses natural language processing to call drivers and measure sentiment to help leadership understand the call center operations so they can improve outcomes.

CCAI

The Contact Center AI platform is a complete cloud native platform to support multichannel communications between customers and agents.

Although Dialogflow and CCAI use advanced machine learning techniques, especially in natural language, they are mostly hidden from the machine learning engineer. An in-depth understanding of CCAI is beyond the scope of this exam.

Custom Training

When you have chosen custom training, you have full flexibility to choose a wide range of hardware options to train your model on.

Graphics processing units (GPUs) can accelerate the training process of deep learning models. Models used for natural language, images, and videos need compute-intensive operations like matrix multiplications that can benefit by running on massively parallel architectures like GPUs.

If you train a deep learning model on a single CPU, it could take days, weeks, or sometimes months to complete. However, if you can offload the heavy computation to a GPU, it can reduce the time by an order of magnitude. What used to take days might take hours to complete.

To understand the advantages of specialized hardware, let us first see how a CPU works.

How a CPU Works

A CPU is a processor that can run a general workload, including software applications, data applications, and so on. The CPU is designed to be very flexible and supports a large number of operations.

A CPU loads data from memory, performs some operation on the value, and stores the result back into memory for every single operation. This architecture works very well for general-purpose software applications. However, a CPU performs computation serially, which is very inefficient when trillions of calculations are required, very typical when training ML models on large datasets.

GPU

GPUs bring in additional firepower. A graphics processing unit (GPU) is a specialized chip designed to rapidly process data in memory to create images; it was originally intended to process movies and render images in video games. A GPU does not work alone and is a sub-processor that helps the CPU in some tasks.

GPUs contain thousands of arithmetic logic units (ALUs) in a single processor. So instead of accessing the memory for each operation, a GPU loads a block of memory and applies some operation using the thousands of ALUs in parallel, thereby making it faster. Using the GPUs for large matrix multiplications and differential operations could improve the speed by an order of magnitude in time.

To use GPUs, you must use an A2 or N1 machine series. GPU currently has the following GPUs available:

- NVIDIA_TESLA_T4
- NVIDIA_TESLA_K80
- NVIDIA_TESLA_P4
- NVIDIA_TESLA_P100
- NVIDIA_TESLA_V100
- NVIDIA_TESLA_A100

In your `WorkerPoolSpec`, specify the type of GPU that you want to use in the `machineSpec.acceleratorType` field and the number of GPUs that you want each VM in the worker pool to use in the `machineSpec.acceleratorCount` field.

When you are trying to configure GPUs with instance types, there are several restrictions based on instance types, instance memory, and so on. Some restrictions are as follows:

- The type of GPU that you choose must be available in the location where you are performing custom training. Not all types of GPUs are available in all regions.

  Here is a page that lists the available locations: `cloud.google.com/vertex-ai/docs/general/locations`.

- There are restrictions on the number of GPUs per instance. For example, you can use two or four NVIDIA TESLA_T4 GPUs on a VM but not three. There is a full table provided by Google for reference, which is subject to change as more instance types and GPUs are introduced; see the link in the tip below.

▪ The GPU configuration must have sufficient virtual CPUs and memory compared to the machine type that goes with it. For example, if you use the n1-standard-16 machine type in your worker pool, then each VM has 16 virtual CPUs and 60 GB of memory. Since each NVIDIA_TESLA_V100 GPU can provide up to 12 virtual CPUs and 76 GB of memory, you must use at least 2 GPUs for each n1-standard-16 VM to support its requirements. (One GPU provides insufficient resources, and you cannot specify 3 GPUs.)

Google provides a compatibility table that specifies the number of GPUs for each instance type for quick reference. For the exam, you do not have to remember anything but the constraints listed earlier.

```
https://cloud.google.com/vertex-ai/docs/training/
configure-compute#gpu-compatibility-table
```

TPU

As ML engineers used GPUs to train very large neural networks, they started to notice the next bottleneck. The GPU is still a semi-general-purpose processor that has to support many different applications, including video processing software. Therefore, in this way GPUs have the same problem as CPUs. For every calculation in the thousands of ALUs, a GPU must access registers or shared memory to read operands and store the intermediate calculation results. To take performance to the next level, Google designed TPUs.

Tensor Processing Units (TPUs) are specialized hardware accelerators designed by Google specifically for machine learning workloads. See Figure 4.5 for the system architecture of a TPU-v4.

FIGURE 4.5   TPU system architecture

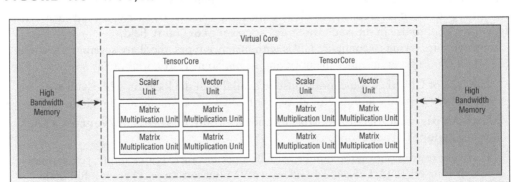

Instead of having an ALU that performs one operation at a time in a CPU, each TPU has multiple matrix multiply units (MXUs).

Each MXU has 128 × 128 multiply/accumulators. Each MXU is capable of performing 16,000 multiply-accumulate operations in each cycle using the bfloat16 number format.

The primary task for TPUs is matrix processing, which is a combination of multiply and accumulate operations. TPUs contain thousands of multiply-accumulators that are directly connected to each other to form a large physical matrix.

TPUs can perform huge operations on huge matrices, which are the core of the training loop in neural networks.

How to Use TPUs

TPUs can be connected in groups called Pods that scale up your workloads with little to no code changes.

Cloud TPU provides the following TPU configurations:

- A single TPU device

- A TPU Pod (a group of TPU devices connected by high-speed interconnects)

- A TPU slice (a subdivision of a TPU Pod)

- A TPU VM

 The general recommendation is to start your machine learning project with a single TPU and scale out to a TPU Pod for production.

Advantages of TPUs

TPUs accelerate the computational speed beyond GPUs. Models that take months to train on CPUs might take a few days to train on GPUs but might run in a matter of hours on TPUs. Simply put, TPUs could provide an order of magnitude improvement over GPUs.

When to Use CPUs, GPUs, and TPUs

TPUs are great for specific workloads, but in some situations, it might be better to use GPUs or even CPUs. Here are the guidelines to choose the right hardware for your use case:

- CPUs
  - Rapid prototyping that needs flexibility
  - Models that train fast
  - Small models that work with small batch size
  - Custom TensorFlow operations written in C++
  - Limited by available I/O or the networking bandwidth of the host

- GPUs
  - Models for which source code does not exist or is too tedious to change
  - Models with a significant number of custom TensorFlow operations so they need to run at least partially on a CPU
  - Models with TensorFlow ops that are not available on TPUs
  - Medium-to-large models with medium-sized batch
- TPUs
  - Models that have a majority of matrix computations
  - Models that have no custom TensorFlow operations
  - Models that train for weeks or months
  - Large and very large models with very large effective batch sizes

Cloud TPUs are *not* suited to the following workloads:

- Programs that require frequent branching (if/else or conditional) or are dominated element-wise by algebra. TPUs are not designed to perform conditionals but they are designed for large-scale matrix multiplications.
- Sparse data (data that has lot of zeros and only a small fraction of nonzero values), which leads to sparse memory access, is not suitable.
- High precision is not well suited for TPUs. Do not expect double precision operations.
- Deep neural networks that contain custom TensorFlow operations written in C++, especially if the custom operations in the main training loop are not suitable for TPUs.

To effectively gain from the TPUs, you should run multiple iterations of the training loop on the TPU. This is not a theoretical requirement but a practical requirement to remove dramatic inefficiency caused otherwise. You can find these guidelines and more information about TPUs in the documentation at `https://cloud.google.com/tpu/docs/tpus`.

Cloud TPU Programming Model

The main bottleneck when using TPUs is the data transfer between the Cloud TPU and host memory. This data transfer happens through the PCIe bus that is much slower than the TPU interconnect and the on-chip high bandwidth memory (HBM). If you do use a partial compilation of a model, where part of execution happens on TPU and the rest happens on host, the TPU will be idle, waiting for data. The right programming model is to execute much of the training loop on the TPU, ideally all of it.

Provisioning for Predictions

In the previous section we looked at the hardware provisioning aspects during the training phase. Now, in this section we will look at the predictions phase.

The prediction workload is very different from the training workload. During training, we will provision resources that will be utilized for a particular duration, which will be deprovisioned on completion.

Prediction can happen in two methods: online and batch. Online prediction is where the model is deployed on a server, and can be queried using a convenient interface like REST. Here the response time is expected to be near real-time. Batch prediction is where a large volume of input data is already available and stored and prediction is initiated as a "batch job." Here, the user expects the job to be completed in near reasonable time (not real-time) but the focus is on the cost of prediction.

In comparison to the training workload, prediction (especially online prediction) is a continuous workload, which also needs to be continuously scaled up or down based on demand. The batch prediction workload differs significantly from both as well.

In this context, the two most important considerations when provisioning for predictions are scaling behavior and finding the ideal machine type. Let us look at these two considerations in detail.

Scaling Behavior

If you use an autoscaling configuration, Vertex AI automatically scales to use more prediction nodes when the CPU usage of your existing nodes gets high. If you are using GPU nodes, make sure to configure the appropriate trigger because there are three resources (CPU, memory, and GPU) that have to be monitored for usage.

Finding the Ideal Machine Type

To determine the ideal machine type for a custom prediction container from a cost perspective, deploy that container as a docker container to a Compute Engine instance directly, then benchmark the instance by calling prediction calls until the instance hits 90+ percent CPU utilization. Determine the *queries per second (QPS) cost per hour* of different machine types. As an example, if a custom container contains a Python web server process that can only effectively use 1 core and that process is calling a multithreaded ML model (such as most implementations of XGBoost), as QPS increases, the web server will start to "block" XGBoost because every XGBoost prediction will wait on the web server process. If this deployed to a 2- or 4-core machine shape, the container will hit the QPS limits and the CPU utilization will be high, so the container is deployed to Vertex AI, and it will autoscale effectively.

Be aware of single-threaded web server limitations in your custom container; it may not scale even when deployed in a 32-core machine shape.

So, you need to include the model type, serving wrapper code in case of custom models, effective utilization of resources (CPU, memory, GPU), latency and throughput requirements, and price to determine the instance type to use.

You have the option of using GPUs to accelerate predictions, but there are some restrictions. The restrictions are:

- GPUs can only be used for a TensorFlow SavedModel or when you use a custom container that has been designed to take advantage of GPUs. You cannot use GPUs for scikit-learn or XGBoost models.

- GPUs are not available in some regions.

- You can use only one type of GPU DeployedModel resource or BatchPredictionJob, and there are limitations on the number of GPUs you can add depending on which machine type you are using.

The above considerations were about predictions in the cloud. There are many use cases where the trained model needs to be deployed at the edge devices. Let us explore these use cases below.

Edge TPU

An important part of the Internet of Things (IoT) are the edge devices. These devices collect real-time data, make decisions, take action, and communicate with other devices or with the cloud. Since such devices have limited bandwidth and sometimes may operate completely offline, there is increasing demand for running inference on the device itself, called *edge inference*.

The Google-designed Edge TPU coprocessor accelerates ML inference on these edge devices. A single Edge TPU can perform 4 trillion operations per second (4 TOPS), on just 2 watts of power.

The Edge TPU is available for your own prototyping and production devices in several form factors, including a single-board computer, a system-on-module, the Edge TPU, and all available products. This is sold under the brand name of Coral.ai.

TPUs are popularly used for training but usually are not used for serving in the cloud. However, Edge TPUs are used for deploying models at the edge.

Deploy to Android or iOS Device

ML Kit (`https://developers.google.com/ml-kit`) brings Google's machine learning expertise to mobile developers in a powerful and easy-to-use package. You can make your iOS and Android apps more engaging, personalized, and helpful with solutions that are optimized to run on device.

You can train your ML model on Google Cloud, use AutoML or a custom model, and deploy the model into your Android or iOS app. The prediction happens in the device for low response times to save on bandwidth and to enable prediction in offline mode as well.

Summary

In this chapter, you learned about different pretrained models that are available on Google Cloud. You also learned about AutoML models and the applicability to different scenarios. In the main part of the chapter, you learned about the different hardware options available for training your models, the difference in the training workload and prediction workload. Google Cloud provides you with a wide variety of hardware accelerators in the form of GPUs and TPUs. Finally, going beyond the cloud, you were introduced to the ideas of deploying to the edge devices.

Exam Essentials

Choose the right ML approach.   Understand the requirements to choose between pretrained models, AutoML, or custom models. Understand the readiness of the solution, the flexibility, and approach.

Provision the right hardware for training.   Understand the various hardware options available for machine learning. Also understand the requirements of GPU and TPU hardware and the instance types that support the specialized hardware. Also learn about hardware differences in training and deployment.

Provision the right hardware for predictions.   Learn the difference between provisioning during training time and during predictions. The requirements for predictions are usually scalability and the CPU and memory constraints, so CPUs and GPUs are used in the cloud. However, TPUs are used in the edge devices.

Understand the available ML solutions.   Instead of provisioning hardware, take a serverless approach by using pretrained models and solutions that are built to solve a problem in a domain.

Review Questions

1. Your company deals with real estate, and as part of a software development team, you have been asked to add a machine learning model to identify objects in photos uploaded to your website. How do you go about this?

   A. Use a custom model to get best results.

   B. Use AutoML to create object detection.

   C. Start with Vision AI, and if that does not work, use AutoML.

   D. Combine AutoML and a custom model to get better results.

2. Your company is working with legal documentation (thousands of pages) that needs to be translated to Spanish and French. You notice that the pretrained model in Google's Translation AI is good, but there are a few hundred domain-specific terms that are not translated in the way you want. You don't have any labeled data and you have only a few professional translators in your company. What do you do?

   A. Use Google's translate service and then have a human in the loop (HITL) to fix each translation.

   B. Use Google AutoML Translation to create a new translation model for your case.

   C. Use Google's Translation AI with a "glossary" of the terms you need.

   D. Not possible to translate because you don't seem to have data.

3. You are working with a thousand hours of video recordings in Spanish and need to create subtitles in English and French. You already have a small dataset with hundreds of hours of video for which subtitles have been created manually. What is your first approach?

   A. There is no "translated subtitle" service so use AutoML to create a "subtitle" job using the existing dataset and then use that model to create translated subtitles.

   B. There is no "translated subtitle" service, and there is no AutoML for this so you have to create a custom model using the data and run it on GPUs.

   C. There is no "translated subtitle" service, and there is no AutoML for this so you have to create a custom model using the data and run it on TPUs.

   D. Use the pretrained Speech-to-Text (STT) service and then use the pretrained Google Translate service to translate the text and insert the subtitles.

4. You want to build a mobile app to classify the different kinds of insects. You have enough labeled data to train but you want to go to market quickly. How would you design this?

   A. Use AutoML to train a classification model, with AutoML Edge as the method. Create an Android app using ML Kit and deploy the model to the edge device.

   B. Use AutoML to train a classification model, with AutoML Edge as the method. Use a Coral.ai device that has edge TPU and deploy the model on that device.

   C. Use AutoML to train an object detection model with AutoML Edge as the method. Use a Coral.ai device that has edge TPU and deploy the model on that device.

   D. Use AutoML to train an image segmentation model, with AutoML Edge as the method. Create an Android app using ML Kit and deploy the model to the edge device.

5. You are training a deep learning model for object detection. It is taking too long to converge, so you are trying to speed up the training. While you are trying to launch an instance (with GPU) with Deep Learning VM Image, you get an error that the "NVIDIA_TESLA_V100 was not found." What could be the problem?

    A. GPU was not available in the selected region.

    B. GPU quota was not sufficient.

    C. Preemptible GPU quota was not sufficient.

    D. GPU did not have enough memory.

6. Your team is building a convolutional neural network for an image segmentation problem on-prem on a CPU-only machine. It takes a long time to train, so you want to speed up the process by moving to the cloud. You experiment with VMs on Google Cloud to use better hardware. You do not have any code for manual placements and have not used any custom transforms. What hardware should you use?

    A. A deep learning VM with n1-standard-2 machine with 1 GPU

    B. A deep learning VM with more powerful e2-highCPU-16 machines

    C. A VM with 8 GPUs

    D. A VM with 1 TPU

7. You work for a hardware retail store and have a website where you get thousands of users on a daily basis. You want to display recommendations on the home page for your users, using Recommendations AI. What model would you choose?

    A. "Others you may like"

    B. "Frequently bought together"

    C. "Similar items"

    D. "Recommended for you"

8. You work for a hardware retail store and have a website where you get thousands of users on a daily basis. You want to increase your revenue by showing recommendations while customers check out. What type of model in Recommendations AI would you choose?

    A. "Others you may like"

    B. "Frequently bought together"

    C. "Similar items"

    D. "Recommended for you"

9. You work for a hardware retail store and have a website where you get thousands of users on a daily basis. You have a customer's browsing history and want to engage the customer more. What model in Recommendations AI would you choose?

    A. "Others you may like"

    B. "Frequently bought together"

    C. "Similar items"

    D. "Recommended for you"

10. You work for a hardware retail store and have a website where you get thousands of users on a daily basis. You do not have browsing events data. What type of model in Recommendations AI would you choose?

A. "Others you may like"

B. "Frequently bought together"

C. "Similar items"

D. "Recommended for you"

11. You work for a hardware retail store and have a website where you get thousands of users on a daily basis. You want to show details to increase cart size. You are going to use Recommendations AI for this. What model and optimization do you choose?

A. "Others you may like" with "click-through rate" as the objective

B. "Frequently bought together" with "revenue per order" as the objective

C. "Similar items" with "revenue per order" as the objective

D. "Recommended for you" with "revenue per order" as the objective

12. You are building a custom deep learning neural network model in Keras that will summarize a large document into a 50-word summary. You want to try different architectures and compare the metrics and performance. What should you do?

A. Create multiple AutoML jobs and compare performance.

B. Use Cloud Composer to automate multiple jobs.

C. Use the pretrained Natural Language API first.

D. Run multiple jobs on the AI platform and compare results.

13. You are building a sentiment analysis tool that collates the sentiment of all customer calls to the call center. The management is looking for something to measure the sentiment; it does not have to be super accurate, but it needs to be quick. What do you think is the best approach for this?

A. Use the pretrained Natural Language API to predict sentiment.

B. Use Speech-to-Text (STT) and then pass through the pretrained Natural Language API to predict sentiment.

C. Build a custom model to predict the sentiment directly from voice calls, which captures the intonation.

D. Convert Speech-to-Text and extract sentiment using BERT algorithm.

14. You have built a very large deep learning model using some custom TensorFlow operations written in C++ for object tracking in videos. Your model has been tested on CPU and now you want to speed up training. What would you do?

A. Use TPU-v4 in default setting because it involves using very large matrix operations.

B. Customize the TPU-v4 size to match with the video and recompile the custom TensorFlow operations for TPU.

C. Use GPU instances because TPUs do not support custom operations.

D. You cannot use GPU or TPU because neither supports custom operations.

15. You want to use GPUs for training your models that need about 50 GB of memory. What hardware options do you have?

A. n1-standard-64 with 8 NVIDIA_TESLA_P100

B. e2-standard-32 with 4 NVIDIA_TESLA_P100

C. n1-standard-32 with 3 NVIDIA_TESLA_P100

D. n2d-standard-32 with 4 NVIDIA_TESLA_P100

16. You have built a deep neural network model to translate voice in real-time cloud TPUs and now you want to push it to your end device. What is the best option?

A. Push the model to the end device running Edge TPU.

B. Models built on TPUs cannot be pushed to the edge. The model has to be recompiled before deployment to the edge.

C. Push the model to any Android device.

D. Use ML Kit to reduce the size of the model to push the model to any Android device.

17. You want to use cloud TPUs and are looking at all options. Which of the below are valid options? (Choose two.)

A. A single TPU VM

B. An HPC cluster of instances with TPU

C. A TPU Pod or slice

D. An instance with both TPU and GPU to give additional boost

18. You want to train a very large deep learning TensorFlow model (more than 100 GB) on a dataset that has a matrix in which most values are zero. You do not have any custom TensorFlow operations and have optimized the training loop to not have an I/O operation. What are your options?

A. Use a TPU because you do not have any custom TensorFlow operations.

B. Use a TPU Pod because the size of the model is very large.

C. Use a GPU.

D. Use an appropriately sized TPUv4 slice.

19. You have been tasked to use machine learning to precisely predict the amount of liquid (down to the milliliter) in a large tank based on pictures of the tank. You have decided to use a large deep learning TensorFlow model. The model is more than 100 GB and trained on a dataset that is very large. You do not have any custom TensorFlow operations and have optimized the training loop to not have I/O operations. What are your options?

A. Use a TPU because you do not have any custom TensorFlow operations.

B. Use a TPU Pod because the size of the model is very large.

C. Use a GPU.

D. Use TPU-v4 of appropriate size and shape for the use case.

20. You are a data scientist trying to build a model to estimate the energy usage of houses based on photos, year built, and so on. You have built a custom model and deployed this custom container in Vertex AI. Your application is a big hit with home buyers who are using it to predict energy costs for houses before buying. You are now getting complaints that the latency is too high. To fix the latency problem, you deploy the model on a bigger instance (32-core) but the latency is still high. What is your next step? (Choose two.)

A. Increase the size of the instance.

B. Use a GPU instance for prediction.

C. Deploy the model on a computer engine instance and test the memory and CPU usage.

D. Check the code to see if this is single-threaded and other software configurations for any bugs.

Chapter

5

Architecting ML Solutions

GOOGLE CLOUD PROFESSIONAL MACHINE LEARNING ENGINEER EXAM OBJECTIVES COVERED IN THIS CHAPTER:

✓ **2.1 Exploring and preprocessing organization-wide data (e.g., Cloud Storage, BigQuery, Cloud Spanner, Cloud SQL, Apache Spark, Apache Hadoop). Considerations include:**

- Data preprocessing (e.g., Dataflow, TensorFlow Extended [TFX], BigQuery)

✓ **2.3 Tracking and running ML experiments. Considerations include:**

- Choosing the appropriate Google Cloud environment for development and experimentation (e.g., Vertex AI Experiments, Kubeflow Pipelines, Vertex AI TensorBoard with TensorFlow and PyTorch) given the framework

✓ **4.1 Serving models. Considerations include:**

- Batch and online inference (e.g., Vertex AI, Dataflow, BigQuery ML, Dataproc)

In the previous chapter, we discussed various options to run your workloads in Google Cloud. In this chapter, we will talk about the best practices to design a reliable, scalable, and highly available ML solution on the Google Cloud Platform (GCP) using our artificial intelligence/machine learning (AI/ML) stack of services. We will introduce the Google AI/ML stack and talk about choosing appropriate services for ML use cases from the stack based on your ease of use and your skill level with AI/ML. Then we will talk about various services to collect and manage data while doing ML on GCP. After that, we will talk about how you can automate the various steps such as data prep, data transform, training, tuning, and deployment using GCP AI/ML pipelines. Last, you will learn about some best practices for hosting or deploying your ML models in production for serving requests.

Designing Reliable, Scalable, and Highly Available ML Solutions

To design highly reliable, scalable, and available ML solutions, you need to think through how to automate and orchestrate the various steps of an AI/ML pipeline.

Your ML pipeline has the following steps:

1. Data collection
2. Data transform
3. Model training
4. Model tuning
5. Model deploying
6. Model monitoring

Moreover, this process is an iterative process because you might need to retrain the model based on your metrics of evaluation (accuracy, confidence score, etc.).

You need a scalable storage solution to manage and store your data—for example, Google Cloud Storage. Then you need a scalable infrastructure to run transform jobs, such as, for example, running PySpark transform jobs on Google Cloud Dataflow. Once you have transformed your data, you need scalable compute to train your model. To create large models that cannot fit into your laptops, you need distributed training.

For custom model training (TensorFlow, Scikit, PyTorch, or other frameworks), you can use Google Vertex AI training because you do not have to worry about spinning up infrastructure for training and managing that infrastructure to stop when the training is over. You also have the choice to use Vertex AI AutoML and Vertex AI APIs in case you are not doing custom training using TensorFlow, Scikit, or PyTorch. Once the training is over, you might want to tune your model with various hyperparameters by running 100 of such training jobs having combinations of the various hyperparameters from your search space. This is where you can use Vertex AI hyperparameter tuning to automate running multiple training jobs in a scalable manner. You would also want to track these variables and your multiple training results in a managed, scalable, and reliable manner. This is where Vertex AI Experiments can help track the parameters of your training runs as well as the results. Since you are able to track your experiments, this helps you with faster model selection.

Finally, once you pick the best training job with the best accuracy, you have to think of deploying this model in production. You also need to worry about scaling your production model; Vertex AI Prediction can help scale your prediction endpoints in production in a fully managed way.

Once your model is deployed in production, you need to think about monitoring the hosted model to check for any kind of model drift. This is where Vertex AI Model Monitoring will help. You also need to think about reproducing this complete pipeline from data collection to model deployment because ML is an iterative process. Vertex AI Pipelines can help here.

Table 5.1 summarizes the services we have mentioned for architecting a highly available scalable managed solution.

TABLE 5.1 ML workflow to GCP services mapping

ML Workflow	Google Cloud Service
Data collection	Google Cloud storage, Pub/Sub (streaming data), BigQuery
Data transformation	Dataflow
Model training	Custom models (Vertex AI Training and Vertex AutoML)
Tuning and experiment tracking	Vertex AI hyperparameter tuning and Vertex AI Experiments
Deployment and monitoring	Vertex AI Prediction and Vertex AI Model Monitoring
Orchestration and CI/CD	Vertex AI Pipelines
Explanations and responsible AI	Vertex Explainable AI, model cards

Choosing an Appropriate ML Service

Google Cloud ML services and solutions are divided into three layers based on ease of use and implementation, as shown in Figure 5.1.

FIGURE 5.1   Google AI/ML stack

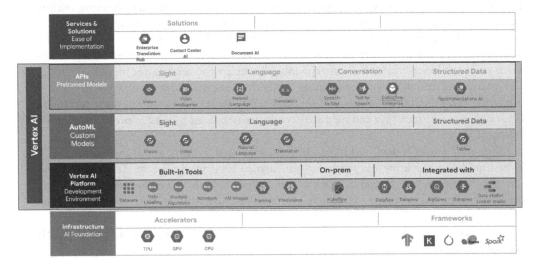

The top layer are AI solutions such as Document AI, Contact Center AI, and Enterprise Translation Hub. These are managed Software as a Service (SaaS) offerings, which are easier to implement and manage with no code. The AI solutions are built on top of the middle layer of Vertex AI services.

The middle layer consists of Vertex AI, which includes the following:

- Vertex AI pretrained APIs for most common use cases in sight, language, conversation, and structured data. The APIs are serverless and scalable.

- Vertex AI AutoML for enriching the vertex AI API use cases with your own data to create models specific to your business use case. For example, you can train an AutoML Vision model by providing some examples of your company logo to detect images of trucks with your company logo on the road.

- Vertex AI Workbench, which is a development environment for the entire data science workflow. This can range from data labeling, training, tuning, deploying, and monitoring your own custom model, which does not fit any use case of using AI services and AutoML. An example is building a text summarization model.

The bottom layer consists of infrastructure such as a compute instance and containers (Google Kubernetes Engine) with a choice of TPUs, GPUs, and storage. You would need to manage the infrastructure yourself for scalability and reliability.

Google Cloud provides BigQuery ML and Vertex AI AutoML to help automate creation of custom models for some common problem domains. The rest of the tools provided by Vertex AI help you build fully custom models for any problem domain. We are going to cover BigQuery ML in detail in Chapter 14 , "BigQuery ML.". Table 5.2 discusses when to use AutoML versus BigQuery ML versus a Vertex AI custom model.

TABLE 5.2   When to use BigQuery ML vs. AutoML vs. a custom model

GCP Service	When to Use
BigQuery ML	You have structured data stored in a BigQuery data warehouse because BigQuery ML requires a tabular dataset. You are comfortable with SQL and the models available in BigQuery ML match the problem you are trying to solve. We are going to cover all the models in Chapter 14.
AutoML (in the context of Vertex AI)	Your problem fits into one of the types that AutoML supports, such as classification, object detection, sentiment analysis, and translation.
	Your data (text, video, images, and tabular) matches the format and fits within the limits set by each type of AutoML model.
Vertex AI custom-trained models	Your problem does not match the criteria listed in this table for BigQuery ML or AutoML.
	You are already running training on-premises or on another cloud platform, and you need consistency across the platforms.

You can train AutoML tabular models from the BigQuery ML because BigQuery supports a tabular data environment. You can also get a custom-trained TensorFlow model and use it in BigQuery ML on tabular data stored in BigQuery tables.

Data Collection and Data Management

Google Cloud provides several data stores to handle your combination of latency, load, throughput, and size requirements for features:

- Google Cloud Storage

- BigQuery
- Vertex AI's datasets to manage training and annotation sets
- Vertex AI Feature Store
- NoSQL data store

Google Cloud Storage (GCS)

Google Cloud Storage is a service for storing your objects in Google Cloud. You can use GCS for storing image, video, audio, and unstructured data. You can combine these individual data types into large files of size at least 100 MB (`https://cloud.google` `.com/architecture/ml-on-gcp-best-practices#store-image-video-audio-` `and-unstructured-data-on-cloud-storage`) and in between 100 to 10,000 shards to improve read and write throughput. This applies to sharded TFRecord files if you're using TensorFlow or Avro files if you're using any other framework.

BigQuery

The best practice is to store tabular data in BigQuery. For training data it's better to store the data as tables instead of views for better speed. BigQuery functionality is available by using the following:

- The Google Cloud console, search for BigQuery
- The bq command-line tool
- The BigQuery REST API
- Vertex AI Jupyter Notebooks using BigQuery Magic or BigQuery Python client.

  We are going to cover BigQuery ML in Chapter 14.
  Table 5.3 lists Google Cloud tools that make it easier to use the API.

TABLE 5.3   Google Cloud tools to read BigQuery data

Framework	Google Cloud tool to read data from BigQuery
TensorFlow or Keras	tf.data.dataset reader for BigQuery and tfio.BigQuery. BigQueryClient() (`www.tensorflow.org/io/api_docs/python/tfio/` `BigQuery/BigQueryClient`)
TFX	BigQuery client
Dataflow	BigQuery I/O connector
Any other framework	BigQuery Python Client library

Vertex AI Managed Datasets

Google Cloud recommends using Vertex AI managed datasets to train custom models instead of writing your training application to ingest training data directly from storage such as Google Cloud Storage or from local storage. Primarily four data formats are supported: image, video, tabular (CSV, BigQuery tables), and text.

The advantages of using managed storage are as follows:

- Manage datasets in a central location.

- Integrated data labeling for unlabeled unstructured data such as video, text, and images using Vertex AI data labeling.

- Easy to track lineage to models for governance and iterative development.

- Compare model performance by training AutoML and custom models using the same datasets.

- Generate data statistics and visualizations.

- Automatically split data into training, test, and validation sets.

Managed datasets are not required if you want more control over splitting your data in your training code or if lineage between your data and model isn't critical to your application.

When you have unlabeled and unstructured data, you can use the Vertex AI data labeling service to label the data in Google Cloud Storage or Vertex AI–managed datasets. This is a service just to label the data and it does not store data. You can use third-party crowd-sourced human labelers or your own labelers to label the data.

Vertex AI Feature Store

Vertex AI Feature Store is a fully managed centralized repository for organizing, storing, and serving ML features. You can use Vertex AI Feature Store independently or as part of Vertex AI workflows. For example, you can fetch data from Vertex AI Feature Store to train custom or AutoML models in Vertex AI. When you're training a model with structured data, users can define features and then ingest (import) feature values from various data sources. Any permitted user can search and retrieve values from the Feature Store. For example, you can find features and then do a batch export to get training data for ML model creation or you can create a new feature if the feature does not exist. You can also retrieve feature values in real time to perform fast online predictions.

The benefit of using Feature Store is that you do not have to compute feature values and save them in various locations such as in tables in BigQuery and as files in Google Cloud Storage. Moreover, Feature Store can help detect drifts and mitigate data skew because features are created in a centralized manner.

NoSQL Data Store

For static feature lookup during prediction, analytical data stores such as BigQuery are not engineered for low-latency singleton read operations such as where the result is a single row with many columns. An example of a query like this is "Select 100 columns from several tables for a specific customer ID." Therefore, static reference features are collected, prepared, and stored in a NoSQL database that is optimized for singleton lookup operations.

Table 5.4 shows the NoSQL data store options for managed data stores in Google Cloud. As ML specialists, we have worked with Memorystore for use cases needing submillisecond latency. We have worked with data stores in use cases to store user login details in data stores where latency can be in milliseconds and Bigtable for millisecond latency with dynamic changing data.

TABLE 5.4   NoSQL data store options

	Memorystore	Datastore	Bigtable
Description	Memorystore is a managed in-memory database. When you use its Redis offering, you can store intermediate data for submillisecond read access. Keys are binary-safe strings, and values can be of different data structures.	Datastore is a fully managed, scalable NoSQL document database built for automatic scaling, high performance, and ease of application development. Data objects in Datastore are known as entities. An entity has one or more named properties in which you store the feature values required by your model or models.	Bigtable is a massively scalable NoSQL database service engineered for high throughput and for low-latency workloads. It can handle petabytes of data, with millions of reads and writes per second at a latency that's on the order of milliseconds. The data is structured as a sorted key-value map. Bigtable scales linearly with the number of nodes.
Retrieval	Submillisecond retrieval latency on a limited amount of quickly changing data, retrieved by a few thousand clients.	Millisecond retrieval latency on slowly changing data where storage scales automatically.	Millisecond retrieval latency on dynamically changing data, using a store that can scale linearly with heavy reads and writes.

	Memorystore	Datastore	Bigtable
Use cases	User-feature lookup in real-time bidding that requires submillisecond retrieval time. Media and gaming applications that use precomputed predictions. Storing intermediate data for a real-time data pipeline for creating input features.	Product recommendation system on an e-commerce site that's based on information about logged-in users.	Fraud detection that leverages dynamically aggregated values. Applications in Fintech and Adtech are usually subject to heavy reads and writes. Ad prediction that leverages dynamically aggregated values over all ad requests and historical data. Booking recommendation based on the overall customer base's recent bookings.

You should avoid storing data in block storage such as a Network File System (NFS) or a virtual machine (VM) hard disk as it's harder to manage them and tune performance than in Google Cloud Storage or Big-Query. Also avoid reading data directly from databases such as Cloud SQL; instead, store data in BigQuery, Google Cloud Storage, or a NoSQL data store for performance.

Automation and Orchestration

Machine learning workflows define which phases are implemented during a machine learning project. The typical phases include data collection, data preprocessing, building datasets, model training and refinement, evaluation, and deployment to production. To integrate an ML system in a production environment, you need to orchestrate the steps in your ML pipeline. In addition, you need to automate the execution of the pipeline for the continuous training of your models.

ML pipelines are there to connect the various steps of your ML solution. Kubeflow is a machine learning toolkit that provides a pipeline solution called Kubeflow Pipelines, built atop Kubernetes. Google introduced Vertex AI Pipelines because maintaining Kubernetes can be challenging and time-intensive. It's a serverless product to run pipelines, so your machine learning team can focus on what they're there to do: ML.

Use Vertex AI Pipelines to Orchestrate the ML Workflow

Vertex AI Pipelines is a managed service that helps you to automate, monitor, and govern your ML systems by orchestrating your ML workflow in a serverless manner and storing your workflow's artifacts using Vertex ML Metadata. By storing the artifacts of your ML workflow in Vertex ML Metadata, you can analyze the lineage of your workflow's artifacts such as training data, hyperparameters, and code that were used to create the model. Vertex AI Pipelines can run pipelines built using the Kubeflow Pipelines SDK v1.8.9 or higher or TensorFlow Extended v0.30.0 or higher.

For TensorFlow, use TensorFlow Extended to define your pipeline and the operations for each step, then execute it on Vertex AI's serverless pipelines system.

For all other frameworks, use Kubeflow Pipelines with Vertex AI Pipelines. Use Vertex AI to launch and interact with the platform.

 Managed pipeline steps can be calls to a Google Cloud service. Vertex AI Pipelines supports experiments, which is GA now in Google Cloud Platform. Kubeflow Pipelines already supports Kubeflow experiments. So you might get questions on the exam on experiment tracking; Kubeflow will be the correct answer because exam questions were written keeping in mind GA services.

This has two outcomes:

- You can use pipelines regardless of the ML environment you choose.
- You need a small number of nodes with modest CPU and RAM since most work will happen within a managed service.

Use Kubeflow Pipelines for Flexible Pipeline Construction

Kubeflow is an open source Kubernetes framework for developing and running portable ML workloads. Kubeflow Pipelines is a Kubeflow service that lets you compose, orchestrate, and automate ML systems. You can choose to deploy your Kubernetes workloads locally, on-premises, or to a cloud environment such as Google Cloud or other cloud platforms. Kubeflow Pipelines SDK is recommended for most users who want to author managed pipelines. Kubeflow Pipelines is flexible, letting you use simple code to construct pipelines, and it provides Google Cloud Pipeline Components, which lets you include Vertex AI functionality like AutoML in your pipeline.

Kubeflow Pipelines lets you orchestrate and automate a production ML pipeline by executing the required Google Cloud services. In Figure 5.2, Cloud SQL serves as the ML metadata store for Kubeflow Pipelines.

FIGURE 5.2 Kubeflow Pipelines and Google Cloud managed services

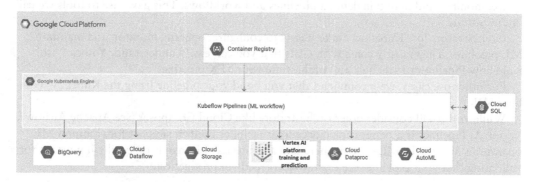

Kubeflow Pipelines components aren't limited to executing TensorFlow Extended (TFX)–related services on Google Cloud. These components can execute Dataproc for Spark ML jobs, AutoML, and other compute workloads.

Use TensorFlow Extended SDK to Leverage Pre-built Components for Common Steps

TensorFlow provides prebuilt components for common steps in the Vertex AI workflow like data ingestion, data validation, and training. TFX provides a bunch of frameworks, libraries, and components for defining, launching, and monitoring machine learning models in production. TensorFlow Extended SDK is recommended if any of the following is true:

- You already use TensorFlow.
- You use structured and textual data.
- You work with a lot of data.

We covered Google Cloud implementation of a TFX pipeline in Chapter 3, "Feature Engineering." See also this page:

```
https://neptune.ai/blog/deep-dive-into-ml-models-in-production-
using-tfx-and-kubeflow
```

When to Use Which Pipeline

Vertex AI Pipelines can run pipelines built using the Kubeflow Pipelines SDK v1.8.9 or higher or TensorFlow Extended v0.30.0 or higher.

If you use TensorFlow in an ML workflow that processes terabytes of structured data or text data, we recommend that you build your pipeline using TFX. By default, TFX creates a directed acyclic graph (DAG) of your ML pipeline. It uses Apache Beam under the hood for managing and implementing pipelines, and this can be easily executed on distributed processing backends like Apache Spark, Google Cloud Dataflow, and Apache Flink.

While TFX running Apache Beam using Cloud Dataflow is cool, it is difficult to configure, monitor, and maintain defined pipelines and workflows. This gave rise to tools we call *orchestrators*.

Orchestrators like Kubeflow make it easy to configure, operate, monitor, and maintain ML pipelines. They mostly come with GUIs that you can easily understand. You can use Kubeflow Pipelines to schedule and orchestrate your TFX pipeline.

For other use cases, we recommend that you build your pipeline using the Kubeflow Pipelines SDK.

While you could consider other orchestrators like Cloud Composer (see Apache Airflow), Vertex AI Pipelines is a better choice because it includes built-in support for common ML operations and tracks ML–specific metadata and lineage. Lineage is especially important for validating that your pipelines are operating correctly in production.

Serving

After you train, evaluate, and tune a machine learning (ML) model, the model is deployed to production for predictions. An ML model can provide predictions in two ways: offline prediction and online prediction.

Offline or Batch Prediction

You perform offline or batch prediction when you are getting your data in batches and you run a batch job pointing to the trained model to predict offline. Some of the use cases for offline or batch processing can be recommendations, demand forecasting, segment analysis, and classifying large batches of text to determine the topic to which they belong. You can use Vertex AI batch prediction to run a batch prediction job for your data stored in BigQuery or Google Cloud Storage.

Figure 5.3 shows a typical high-level architecture on Google Cloud for performing offline batch prediction.

FIGURE 5.3 Google Cloud architecture for performing offline batch prediction

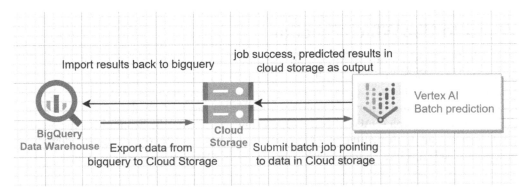

Online Prediction

This prediction happens in near real time when you send a request to your deployed model endpoint and you get the predicted response back. This can be a model deployed to an HTTPS endpoint, and you can use microservice architecture to call this endpoint from your web applications or mobile applications. Use cases where you need response in near real time while making ML predictions are real-time bidding and real-time sentiment analysis of Twitter feeds.

There are two ways you can have online predictions, described here:

Synchronous In this the caller waits until it receives the prediction from the ML service before performing the subsequent steps. You can use Vertex AI online predictions to deploy your model as a real-time HTTPS endpoint. You can also use App Engine or GKE (Google Kubernetes Engine) as an ML gateway to perform some feature preprocessing before sending your request from client applications, as shown in Figure 5.4.

FIGURE 5.4 Google Cloud architecture for online prediction

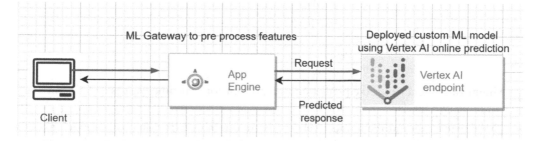

Asynchronous In this the end user may not query a model endpoint directly. The end user may get notified or may poll a Feature Store or data store for prediction in real time. There are two methods by which this can happen.

> **Push** The model generates predictions and pushes them to the end user as a notification. For example, in fraud detection, you would use this method when you want to notify other systems to take action when a potentially fraudulent transaction is identified. See Figure 5.5 for reference.
>
> **Poll** The model generates predictions and stores them in a low latency read database such as a NoSQL data store. The end user periodically polls the database for available predictions. An example is targeted marketing, where the system checks the propensity scores predicted in real time for active customers in order to decide whether to send an email with a promotion or a retention offer.

FIGURE 5.5   Push notification architecture for online prediction

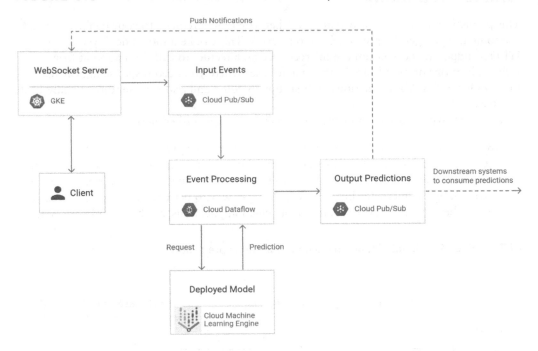

Minimizing latency to serve prediction is important for real-time use cases. This can happen at these two levels:

- **Minimize latency at the model level:** You need to minimize the time your model takes to make a prediction when invoked with a request. You can minimize latency by building a smaller model because it will have less neural network layers and will need less compute to process the prediction.

  You can use accelerators such as Cloud GPU and TPU to serve your model endpoint. Typically, you use TPUs only when you have large deep-learning models and large batch sizes.

- **Minimize latency at the serving level:** This is where you minimize the time your system takes to serve the prediction when it receives the request. This includes storing your input features in a low latency read lookup data store, precomputing predictions in an offline batch-scoring job, and caching the predictions.

For training TensorFlow models, you can optimize the SavedModel using the Graph Transformation Tools. Refer to the blog "Optimizing Tensor-Flow Models for Serving" at https://medium.com/google-cloud/optimizing-tensorflow-models-for-serving-959080e9ddbf.

Summary

In this chapter, we discussed best practices for designing a reliable, scalable, and highly available ML solution on Google Cloud Platform (GCP). Then we discussed when to use which service from the three layers of the GCP AI/ML stack. We covered data collection and data management strategy for managing data in the integrated Vertex AI platform with BigQuery. We also covered data storage options for submillisecond and millisecond latency such as NoSQL data store. Then we covered automation and orchestration techniques for ML pipelines such as Vertex AI Pipelines, Kubeflow Pipelines, and TFX pipelines.

We discussed how you can serve the model using both batch mode and real time to serve the predictions. We covered a few architecture patterns to create batch predictions as well as online predictions using Vertex AI Prediction. Last, we discussed some ways to improve model latency while using real-time serving.

Exam Essentials

Design reliable, scalable, and highly available ML solutions.   Understand why you need to design a scalable solution and how Google Cloud AI/ML services can help architect a scalable and highly available solution.

Choose an appropriate ML service.   Understand the AI/ML stack of GCP and when to use each layer of the stack based on your use case and expertise with ML.

Understand data collection and management.   Understand various types of data stores for storing your data for various ML use cases.

Know how to implement automation and orchestration.   Know when to use Vertex AI Pipelines vs. Kubeflow vs. TFX pipelines. We will cover the details in Chapter 11, "Designing ML Training Pipelines."

Understand how to best serve data.   You need to understand the best practices when deploying models. Know when to use batch prediction versus real-time prediction and how to manage latency with online real-time prediction.

Review Questions

1. You work for an online travel agency that also sells advertising placements on its website to other companies. You have been asked to predict the most relevant web banner that a user should see next. Security is important to your company. The model latency requirements are 300ms@p99, the inventory is thousands of web banners, and your exploratory analysis has shown that navigation context is a good predictor.

   You want to implement the simplest solution. How should you configure the prediction pipeline?

   A. Embed the client on the website, and then deploy the model on the Vertex AI platform prediction.

   B. Embed the client on the website, deploy the gateway on App Engine, and then deploy the model on the Vertex AI platform prediction.

   C. Embed the client on the website, deploy the gateway on App Engine, deploy the database on Cloud Bigtable for writing and for reading the user's navigation context, and then deploy the model on the Vertex AI Prediction.

   D. Embed the client on the website, deploy the gateway on App Engine, deploy the database on Memorystore for writing and for reading the user's navigation context, and then deploy the model on Google Kubernetes Engine (GKE).

2. You are training a TensorFlow model on a structured dataset with 100 billion records stored in several CSV files. You need to improve the input/output execution performance. What should you do?

   A. Load the data into BigQuery and read the data from BigQuery.

   B. Load the data into Cloud Bigtable, and read the data from Bigtable.

   C. Convert the CSV files into shards of TFRecords, and store the data in Google Cloud Storage.

   D. Convert the CSV files into shards of TFRecords, and store the data in the Hadoop Distributed File System (HDFS).

3. You are a data engineer who is building an ML model for a product recommendation system in an e-commerce site that's based on information about logged-in users. You will use Pub/Sub to handle incoming requests. You want to store the results for analytics and visualizing. How should you configure the pipeline?

   Pub/Sub -> Preprocess(1) -> ML training/serving(2) -> Storage(3) -> Data studio/Looker studio for visualization

   A. 1 = Dataflow, 2 = Vertex Al platform, 3 = Cloud BigQuery

   B. 1 = Dataproc, 2 = AutoML, 3 = Cloud Memorystore

   C. 1 = BigQuery, 2 = AutoML, 3 = Cloud Functions

   D. 1 = BigQuery, 2 = Vertex Al platform, 3 = Google Cloud Storage

4. You are developing models to classify customer support emails. You created models with TensorFlow Estimator using small datasets on your on-premises system, but you now need to train the models using large datasets to ensure high performance. You will port your models to Google Cloud and want to minimize code refactoring and infrastructure overhead for easier migration from on-prem to cloud. What should you do?

   A. Use the Vertex AI platform for distributed training.

   B. Create a cluster on Dataproc for training.

   C. Create a managed instance group with autoscaling.

   D. Use Kubeflow Pipelines to train on a Google Kubernetes Engine cluster.

5. You are a CTO wanting to implement a scalable solution on Google Cloud to digitize documents such as PDF files and Word DOC files in various silos. You are also looking for storage recommendations for storing the documents in a data lake. Which options have the least infrastructure efforts? (Choose two.)

   A. Use the Document AI solution.

   B. Use Vision AI OCR to digitize the documents.

   C. Use Google Cloud Storage to store documents.

   D. Use Cloud Bigtable to store documents.

   E. Use a custom Vertex AI model to build a document processing pipeline.

6. You work for a public transportation company and need to build a model to estimate delay for multiple transportation routes. Predictions are served directly to users in an app in real time. Because different seasons and population increases impact the data relevance, you will retrain the model every month. You want to follow Google-recommended best practices. How should you configure the end-to-end architecture of the predictive model?

   A. Configure Kubeflow Pipelines to schedule your multistep workflow from training to deploying your model.

   B. Use a model trained and deployed on BigQuery ML and trigger retraining with the scheduled query feature in BigQuery.

   C. Write a Cloud Functions script that launches a training and deploying job on the Vertex AI platform that is triggered by Cloud Scheduler.

   D. Use Cloud Composer to programmatically schedule a Dataflow job that executes the workflow from training to deploying your model.

7. You need to design a customized deep neural network in Keras that will predict customer purchases based on their purchase history. You want to explore model performance using multiple model architectures, store training data, and be able to compare the evaluation metrics in the same dashboard. What should you do?

   A. Create multiple models using AutoML Tables.

   B. Automate multiple training runs using Cloud Composer.

   C. Run multiple training jobs on the Vertex AI platform with similar job names.

   D. Create an experiment in Kubeflow Pipelines to organize multiple runs.

8. You work with a data engineering team that has developed a pipeline to clean your dataset and save it in a Google Cloud Storage bucket. You have created an ML model and want to use the data to refresh your model as soon as new data is available. As part of your CI/CD workflow, you want to automatically run a Kubeflow Pipelines training job on Google Kubernetes Engine (GKE). How should you architect this workflow?

    A. Configure your pipeline with Dataflow, which saves the files in Google Cloud Storage. After the file is saved, start the training job on a GKE cluster.

    B. Use App Engine to create a lightweight Python client that continuously polls Google Cloud Storage for new files. As soon as a file arrives, initiate the training job.

    C. Configure a Google Cloud Storage trigger to send a message to a Pub/Sub topic when a new file is available in a storage bucket. Use a Pub/Sub–triggered Cloud Function to start the training job on a GKE cluster.

    D. Use Cloud Scheduler to schedule jobs at regular intervals. For the first step of the job, check the time stamp of objects in your Google Cloud Storage bucket. If there are no new files since the last run, abort the job.

9. Your data science team needs to rapidly experiment with various features, model architectures, and hyperparameters. They need to track the accuracy metrics for various experiments and use an API to query the metrics over time. What should they use to track and report their experiments while minimizing manual effort?

    A. Use Kubeflow Pipelines to execute the experiments. Export the metrics file, and query the results using the Kubeflow Pipelines API.

    B. Use Vertex AI Platform Training to execute the experiments. Write the accuracy metrics to BigQuery, and query the results using the BigQuery API.

    C. Use Vertex AI Platform Training to execute the experiments. Write the accuracy metrics to Cloud Monitoring, and query the results using the Monitoring API.

    D. Use Vertex AI Workbench Notebooks to execute the experiments. Collect the results in a shared Google Sheets file, and query the results using the Google Sheets API.

10. As the lead ML Engineer for your company, you are responsible for building ML models to digitize scanned customer forms. You have developed a TensorFlow model that converts the scanned images into text and stores them in Google Cloud Storage. You need to use your ML model on the aggregated data collected at the end of each day with minimal manual intervention. What should you do?

    A. Use the batch prediction functionality of the Vertex AI platform.

    B. Create a serving pipeline in Compute Engine for prediction.

    C. Use Cloud Functions for prediction each time a new data point is ingested.

    D. Deploy the model on the Vertex AI platform and create a version of it for online inference.

11. As the lead ML architect, you are using TensorFlow and Keras as the machine learning framework and your data is stored in disk files as block storage. You are migrating to Google Cloud and you need to store the data in BigQuery as tabular storage. Which of the following techniques will you use to store TensorFlow storage data from block storage to BigQuery?

    A. tf.data.dataset reader for BigQuery

    B. BigQuery Python Client library

    C. BigQuery I/O Connector

    D. tf.data.iterator

12. As the CTO of the financial company focusing on building AI models for structured datasets, you decide to store most of the data used for ML models in BigQuery. Your team is currently working on TensorFlow and other frameworks. How would they modify code to access Big-Query data to build their models? (Choose three.)

    A. tf.data.dataset reader for BigQuery

    B. BigQuery Python Client library

    C. BigQuery I/O Connector

    D. BigQuery Omni

13. As the chief data scientist of a retail website, you develop many ML models in PyTorch and TensorFlow for Vertex AI Training. You also use Bigtable and Google Cloud Storage. In most cases, the same data is used for multiple models and projects and also updated. What is the best way to organize the data in Vertex AI?

    A. Vertex AI–managed datasets

    B. BigQuery

    C. Vertex AI Feature Store

    D. CSV

14. You are the data scientist team lead and your team is working for a large consulting firm. You are working on an NLP model to classify customer support requests. You are working on data storage strategy to store the data for NLP models. What type of storage should you avoid in a managed GCP environment in Vertex AI? (Choose two.)

    A. Block storage

    B. File storage

    C. BigQuery

    D. Google Cloud Storage

Chapter 6

Building Secure ML Pipelines

GOOGLE CLOUD PROFESSIONAL MACHINE LEARNING ENGINEER EXAM OBJECTIVES COVERED IN THIS CHAPTER:

✓ **2.1 Exploring and preprocessing organization-wide data (e.g., Cloud Storage, BigQuery, Cloud Spanner, Cloud SQL, Apache Spark, Apache Hadoop). Considerations include:**

- Privacy implications of data usage and/or collection (e.g., handling sensitive data such as personally identifiable information [PII] and protected health information [PHI])

✓ **2.2 Model prototyping using Jupyter notebooks. Considerations include:**

- Applying security best practices in Vertex AI Workbench

✓ **4.2 Scaling online model serving. Considerations include:**

- Vertex AI public and private endpoints

✓ **6.1 Identifying risks to ML solutions. Considerations include:**

- Building secure ML systems (e.g., protecting against unintentional exploitation of data or models, hacking)

In this chapter, first we will talk about secure strategies to manage your data on Google Cloud Platform, from storage to processing and ML model development. We will also briefly talk about how you can use identity and access management (IAM) best practices to provide your data science team with secure access to the Vertex AI environment.

In addition, we will talk about Google Cloud services and best practices for managing sensitive data such as personally identifiable information (PII) and protected health information (PHI). We will also cover an architecture to manage PII data at scale using the Google Cloud Data Loss Prevention (DLP) API.

Building Secure ML Systems

One of the key tasks of any enterprise is to help ensure the security of its users' and employees' data. Google Cloud provides built-in security measures to facilitate data security, including encryption of stored data and encryption of data in transit. Let's look at what encryption at rest and encryption in transit are for cloud systems.

Encryption at Rest

For machine learning models, your data will be in either Cloud Storage or BigQuery tables. Google encrypts data stored at rest by default for both Cloud Storage and BigQuery. By default, Google manages the encryption keys used to protect your data. You can also use customer-managed encryption keys. You can encrypt individual table values in BigQuery using Authenticated Encryption with Associated Data (AEAD) encryption functions. Please refer to https://cloud.google.com/bigquery/docs/reference/standard-sql/ aead-encryption-concepts to understand AEAD BigQuery encryption functions.

Table 6.1 shows the difference between server-side encryption and client-side encryption in terms of cloud storage and BigQuery.

To protect data from corruption, Google Cloud Storage supports two types of hashes you can use to check the integrity of your data: CRC32C and MD5.

TABLE 6.1   Difference between server-side and client-side encryption

Server-Side Encryption	Client-Side Encryption
Encryption that occurs after the cloud storage receives your data, but before the data is written to disk and stored.	Encryption that occurs before data is sent to Cloud Storage and BigQuery. Such data arrives at Cloud Storage and BigQuery already encrypted but also undergoes server-side encryption.
You can create and manage your encryption keys using a Google Cloud Key Management Service.	You are responsible for the client-side keys and cryptographic operations.

Encryption in Transit

To protect your data as it travels over the Internet during read and write operations, Google Cloud uses Transport Layer Security (TLS).

Encryption in Use

Encryption in use protects your data in memory from compromise or data exfiltration by encrypting data while it's being processed. Confidential Computing is an example. Confidential Computing protects your data in memory from compromise by encrypting it while it is being processed. You can encrypt your data in use with Confidential VMs and Confidential GKE Nodes. Read this blog for more details on data security concepts: https://cloud.google.com/blog/topics/developers-practitioners/data-security-google-cloud.

Identity and Access Management

Identity and Access Management is the way to manage access to data and resources in Google Cloud. (For more information about IAM, see https://cloud.google.com/vertex-ai/docs/general/access-control.) Vertex AI uses IAM to manage access to resources. You can manage access at the project level or resource level:

- **Project-level roles:** To grant access to resources at the project level, assign one or more roles to a principal (user, group, or service account). A service account is an account for an application or compute workload instead of an individual end user. Mostly, service accounts are used for creating Vertex AI Workbench, Vertex AI custom training, and Vertex AI predictions.
- **Resource-level roles:** To grant access to a specific resource, set an IAM policy on that resource; the resource must support resource-level policies. The policy defines which roles are assigned to which principals.

You can use these two levels of granularity to customize permissions. For example, you can grant all Vertex AI Feature Store users read permission to all feature stores by setting a project-level policy. Vertex AI Feature Store stores features in a centralized way. For a subset of users, you grant write permissions to particular feature stores by using a resource-level policy.

 Currently, Vertex AI supports resource-level access control for Vertex AI Feature Store and entity type resources only. Setting a policy at the resource level does not affect project-level policies.

The following are the IAM roles that can be used in Vertex AI:

- **Predefined roles** allow you to grant a set of related permissions to your Vertex AI resources at the project level. Two of the common predefined roles for Vertex AI are Vertex AI Administrator and Vertex AI User.

- **Basic roles** such as Owner, Editor, and Viewer provide access control to your Vertex AI resources at the project level. These roles are common to all Google Cloud services.

- **Custom roles** allow you to choose a specific set of permissions, create your own role with those permissions, and grant the role to users in your organization.

Not all Vertex AI predefined roles and resources support resource-level policies.

IAM Permissions for Vertex AI Workbench

Vertex AI Workbench is a data science service offered by Google Cloud Platform (GCP) that leverages JupyterLab to explore and access data. While setting up a Vertex AI Workbench notebook and resources such as model jobs, training, and deployment, you can choose which Virtual Private Cloud you want to use. Google provides encryption at rest and in transit for Vertex AI Workbench.

There are two types of Vertex AI notebooks with Vertex AI Workbench:

- **User-managed notebook:** User-managed notebook instances are highly customizable and can be ideal for users who need a lot of control over their environment. Therefore, user-managed notebook instances can require more time to set up and manage than a managed notebook instance. You can use a tag in the Metadata section of a user-managed notebook to control the instances; however, this option is not available in managed notebooks. Figure 6.1 shows how to create a user-managed notebook.

- **Managed notebooks:** Managed notebook instances are Google Cloud–managed and therefore less customizable than Vertex AI Workbench user-managed notebook instances. Some of the advantages of managed notebooks are integration with Cloud Storage and BigQuery in JupyterLab and automatic shutdown of the notebook instances when they're not in use. In Figure 6.2, you see the created managed notebooks on the MANAGED NOTEBOOKS tab. You can also find user-managed notebooks on the USER-MANAGED NOTEBOOKS tab.

FIGURE 6.1   Creating a user-managed Vertex AI Workbench notebook

FIGURE 6.2   Managed Vertex AI Workbench notebook

There are two ways to set up user access modes (permission) for both user-managed and managed notebooks:

- **Single User Only:** The Single User Only access mode grants access only to the user that you specify.

- **Service Account:** The Service Account access mode grants access to a service account. You can grant access to one or more users through this service account. To use service accounts with the Google Cloud CLI, you need to set up an environment variable where your code runs.

Figure 6.3 shows the permissions for setting up a managed notebook.

FIGURE 6.3   Permissions for a managed Vertex AI Workbench notebook

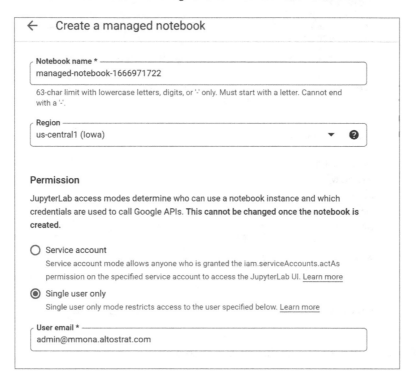

 If you are using Google Colab, you would need to create a service account key with access to the Vertex AI administrator and Cloud Storage owner permission. Then you can provide the location of the JSON key file to the GOOGLE_APPLICATION_CREDENTIALS environment variable to authenticate your Google Colab project to run Vertex AI APIs. Creating a service account key is a security risk that should be avoided if possible. If you must create a service account key, make sure you keep it secure.

In this section, we covered IAM (Identity and Access Management) roles and permissions needed to configure for Vertex AI Workbench. We also covered how you can access the JupyterLab notebooks using a service account and single user access for Vertex AI Workbench. Now let's discuss how we can secure the network with Vertex AI.

Securing a Network with Vertex AI

Before we get into securing a network with Vertex AI, you should understand the Google Cloud shared responsibility and shared fate models. Understanding this terminology is important when determining how to best protect your data and workloads on Google Cloud.

Shared responsibility model: According to the Google shared responsibility model, the cloud provider must monitor and respond to security threats related to the cloud itself and its underlying infrastructure. Meanwhile, end users, including individuals and companies, are responsible for protecting data and other assets they store in any cloud environment.

Shared fate model: This model was started to address the challenges that the shared responsibility model doesn't address. Shared fate focuses on how all parties can better interact to continuously improve security. Shared fate builds on the shared responsibility model because it views the relationship between cloud provider and customer as an ongoing partnership to improve security. There are several components of shared fate:

- **Help getting started:** Secure blueprints that let you deploy and maintain secure solutions using infrastructure as code (IaC). Blueprints have security recommendations enabled by default, such as the Vertex AI Workbench notebooks blueprint.

- **Risk protection program**

- **Assured workloads and governance**

To read more about these concepts, refer to:

```
https://cloud.google.com/architecture/framework/security/
shared-responsibility-shared-fate
```

For the exam, you will not be tested on these concepts. However, basic understanding of these concepts helps you to understand how data and access are controlled in Google Cloud.

Now we will cover how you can secure the following:

- Vertex AI Workbench notebook environment

- Vertex AI endpoints (public vs. private endpoints)

- Vertex AI training jobs

Securing Vertex AI Workbench

By default, your managed notebooks instance uses a Google-managed network. (We covered securing the Vertex AI Workbench with IAM in the previous section.) Some of the best practices to secure your workbench are as follows:

Use a private IP address   Vertex AI Workbench by default has public IP addresses assigned, which can increase your attack surface and expose sensitive data. The best practice is to use a private IP address while creating a workbench. To create a private Vertex AI Workbench, you'll need to specify the `--no-public-ip` command. The following is the Google CLI command to create a workbench with a private IP address:

```
gcloud beta notebooks instances create example-instance  \
  --vm-image-project=deeplearning-platform-release  \
  --vm-image-name=tf2-2-1-cu101-notebooks-20200110  \
  --machine-type=n1-standard-4  \
  --location=us-central1-b  \
  --no-public-ip
```

Connect your instance to a VPC network in the same project   To connect a managed notebooks instance to a VPC network in the same project as your managed notebooks instance, you need to configure private services access. Private services access enables you to reach internal IP addresses hosted in a VPC network. This is useful if you want your VM instances in your VPC network to use internal IP addresses instead of external IP addresses. Refer to this link to learn more:

https://cloud.google.com/vpc/docs/private-services-access

Shared VPC network   You can also specify a VPC network located within your project or a shared VPC network that you have access to. If you specify a VPC or shared VPC network, the network requires a private services access connection. Shared VPC allows an organization to connect resources from multiple projects to a common virtual private cloud (VPC) network so that they can communicate with each other securely and efficiently by using internal IP addresses from that network.

VPC Service Controls   This is a feature that allows you to control the services that are available in your VPC. You can use VPC Service Controls to allow or deny access to specific services or limit the amount of traffic that can be generated by specific services. When you use VPC Service Controls to protect Vertex AI, the following artifacts can't leave your service perimeter:

- Training data for an AutoML model or custom model
- Models that you created
- Requests for online predictions
- Results from a batch prediction request

Securing Vertex AI Endpoints

Vertex AI provides options to host your models by creating an endpoint through Vertex AI prediction, covered in Chapter 10, "Scaling Models in Production." There are public endpoints and private endpoints.

Public endpoint   This endpoint is publicly accessible to the Internet. By default, this option is available when creating an endpoint with Vertex AI.

Private endpoints   In Vertex AI Prediction through VPC Peering, you can set up a private connection to talk to your endpoint without your data ever traversing the public Internet, resulting in increased security and lower latency for online predictions. Before you make use of a private endpoint, you'll first need to create connections between your VPC network and Vertex AI.

It's very easy to set up a private endpoint from the Vertex AI console. Go to Endpoint and select Create Endpoint. You will see an option to select Private. Figure 6.4 shows how you can create a private endpoint in Vertex AI.

FIGURE 6.4   Creating a private endpoint in the Vertex AI console

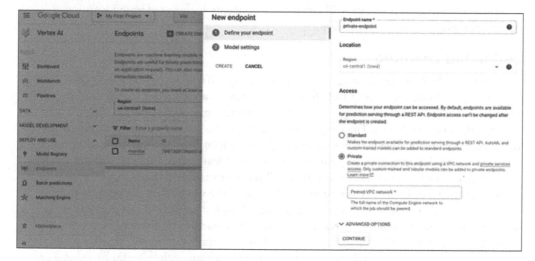

To set up VPC Network Peering, you can configure Vertex AI to peer with a VPC to connect directly with certain resources in Vertex AI, such as custom training jobs that were covered in Chapter 8, "Model Training and Hyperparameter Tuning," private prediction endpoints, and Vertex AI Matching Engine.

Vertex AI Matching Engine is used to build use cases that match semantically similar items such as a recommendation engine, search engine, etc. Vertex AI Matching Engine is a high-scale, low-latency vector database that is referred to as vector similarity-matching or an approximate nearest neighbor (ANN) service.

Securing Vertex AI Training Jobs

Using private IP addresses to connect to your training jobs provides more network security and lower network latency than using public IP addresses. To use private IP addresses, you use VPC to peer your network with any type of Vertex AI custom training job. This allows your training code to access private IP addresses inside your Google Cloud or on-premises networks. See https://cloud.google.com/vertex-ai/docs/training/using-private-ip for more information.

It is recommended that you use both VPC Service Controls and IAM for defense in depth. VPC Service Controls prevents service operations such as a `gsutil cp` command copying to a public Cloud Storage bucket or a `bq mk` command copying to a permanent external BigQuery table.

In the following sections, we will cover some concepts such as federated learning, differential privacy, and tokenization.

Federated Learning

According to the Google AI blog, `https://ai.googleblog.com/2017/04/federated-learning-collaborative.html`, *federated learning* is a technique that is used to enable mobile phones to collaboratively learn a shared prediction model while keeping all the training data on the device. The device downloads the model and learns from the device data. This updated model is then sent to the cloud with encrypted communication. Since all the training data remains on your device, federated learning allows for smarter models, lower latency, and less power consumption, all while ensuring privacy.

An example would be a group of hospitals around the world that are participating in the same clinical trial. The data that an individual hospital collects about patients is not shared outside the hospital. As a result, hospitals can't transfer or share patient data with third parties. Federated learning lets affiliated hospitals train shared ML models while still retaining security, privacy, and control of patient data within each hospital by using a centralized model shared by all the hospitals. This model trains local data in the hospital, and only the model update is sent back to the centralized cloud server. The model updates are decrypted, averaged, and integrated into the centralized model. Iteration after iteration, the collaborative training continues until the model is fully trained. This way federated learning decouples the ability to do machine learning from the need to store the data in the cloud. Refer to this link for more information: `https://cloud.google.com/architecture/federated-learning-google-cloud`.

Differential Privacy

According to `https://en.wikipedia.org/wiki/Differential_privacy`, *differential privacy (DP)* is a system for publicly sharing information about a dataset by describing the patterns within groups of individuals within the dataset while withholding information about each individual in the dataset. For example, training a machine learning model for medical diagnosis, we would like to have machine learning algorithms that do not memorize sensitive information about the training set, such as the specific medical histories of individual patients. Differential privacy is a notion that allows quantifying the degree of privacy protection provided by an algorithm for the underlying (sensitive) dataset it operates on. Through differential privacy, we can design machine learning algorithms that responsibly train models on private data.

You can use both the techniques together, federated learning with differential privacy, to securely train a model with PII data sitting in distributed silos.

Format-Preserving Encryption and Tokenization

Format-Preserving Encryption, or *FPE*, is an encryption algorithm that preserves the format of information while it is being encrypted. It is the process of encrypting data in such a way that the output (ciphertext) remains in the same format as the input (plain text). See `https://en.wikipedia.org/wiki/Format-preserving_encryption` for more information.

Two use cases for this are as follows:

- **Payment Card Verification:** In the retail and e-commerce sector, payment card data must be collected and stored to make payments. Additionally, employees may need to see and verify the last four digits of a customer's payment card information. FPE makes it easier to expose only the required information to employees while leaving the other 12 digits protected.

- **Legacy Databases:** A telecommunications system may have a multitude of legacy systems that require the use of encrypted data for security. However, it might not be an option for the organization to restructure its databases to store encrypted data. With FPE, the structure of the databases can remain unchanged. (For more information, see `www.ubiqsecurity.com/what-is-format-preserving-encryption-fpe-and-its-benefits`.)

Tokenization refers to a process by which a piece of sensitive data, such as a credit card number, is replaced by a surrogate value known as a token. The sensitive data still generally needs to be stored securely at one centralized location for subsequent reference and requires strong protections around it. The security of a tokenization approach depends on the security of the sensitive values and the algorithm and process used to create the surrogate value and map it back to the original value.

FPE obfuscates sensitive information, while tokenization removes it entirely (to another location).

Privacy Implications of Data Usage and Collection

In the following sections, we will cover *personally identifiable information (PII)* and *protected health information (PHI)* in the data and how Google Cloud recommends strategies to deal with sensitive data.

PII is a type of data that allows for an individual to be identified. It includes any information relating to a specific individual, such as name, address, Social Security number (SSN), date of birth, financial information, passport number, telephone numbers, and email addresses.

The Health Insurance Portability and Accountability Act (HIPAA) Privacy Rule provides federal protections for PHI held by covered entities and gives patients an array of rights with respect to that information. At the same time, the Privacy Rule is balanced so that it permits the disclosure of personal health information needed for patient care and other important purposes.

Google Cloud Data Loss Prevention

The Google Cloud Data Loss Prevention (DLP) API can de-identify sensitive data in text content, including text stored in container structures such as tables. *De-identification* is the process of removing identifying information from data. The API detects sensitive data such as PII and then uses a de-identification transformation to mask, delete, or otherwise obscure the data.

The de-identification techniques used are as follows:

- Masking sensitive data by partially or fully replacing characters with a symbol, such as an asterisk (*) or hash (#)

- Replacing each instance of sensitive data with a token using a technique such as cryptographic hashing

- Encrypting and replacing sensitive data using a randomly generated or predetermined key

- Using bucketing, which replaces a more identifiable value with a less distinguishing value

The following are some of the key concepts associated with DLP:

- **Data profiles:** The data profiler lets you protect data across your organization by identifying where sensitive and high-risk data reside. When you turn on data profiling, Cloud DLP automatically scans all BigQuery tables and columns across the entire organization, individual folders, and projects. It then creates data profiles at the table, column, and project levels.

- **Risk analysis:** You can use risk analysis methods before de-identification to help determine an effective de-identification strategy or after de-identification to monitor for any changes or outliers. Cloud DLP can compute four re-identification risk metrics: k-anonymity, l-diversity, k-map, and δ-presence. (For more information, see https://cloud.google.com/dlp/docs/concepts-risk-analysis.)

- **Inspection (jobs and triggers):** A *job* is an action that Cloud Data Loss Prevention runs to either scan content for sensitive data or calculate the risk of re-identification. Cloud DLP creates and runs a job resource whenever you tell it to inspect your data. You can schedule when Cloud DLP runs jobs by creating job triggers. A *job trigger* is an event that automates the creation of DLP jobs to scan Google Cloud Storage repositories, including Cloud Storage buckets, BigQuery tables, and Datastore. You can also trigger a DLP scan job by using Cloud Functions every time a file is uploaded to Cloud Storage.

DLP provides templates that are configurations to help you set up DLP jobs; see Figure 6.5.

FIGURE 6.5 Architecture for de-identification of PII on large datasets using DLP

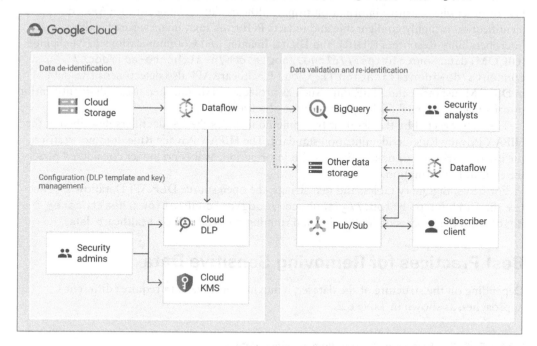

The architecture consists of the following:

- **Data de-identification streaming pipeline:** De-identifies sensitive data in text using Dataflow. If you have streaming data coming, you can use Dataflow to trigger a DLP job to de-identify data and store it in Google Cloud Storage or populate the de-identified data in a BigQuery table. You can also run a DLP job on batch data stored in Cloud Storage.

- **Configuration (DLP template and key) management:** You can manage the templates and configuration for your DLP jobs with a small group of people as security admins and use Cloud KMS (key management service) to avoid exposing de-identification methods and encryption keys.

- **Data validation and re-identification pipeline:** You can have batch and streaming data de-identified and stored in BigQuery as a DLP job output. You can also choose to store this in other types of storage. You can validate copies of the de-identified data and use a Dataflow pipeline to re-identify data at a large scale.

Google Cloud Healthcare API for PHI Identification

Under the U.S. Health Insurance Portability and Accountability Act (HIPAA), PHI that is linked based on the list of 18 identifiers such as name, medical record number, Social Security number, IP address, and so on must be treated with special care. For the complete list of identifiers, refer to this Wikipedia page: https://en.wikipedia.org/wiki/Protected_health_information.

The Google Cloud Healthcare API has the de-identify operation, which removes PHI or otherwise sensitive information from healthcare data. The healthcare API's de-identification is highly configurable and redacts PHI from text, images, Fast Healthcare Interoperability Resources (FHIR), and Digital Imaging and Communications in Medicine (DICOM) data. Source `https://cloud.google.com/healthcare-api/docs/concepts/de-identification` The Cloud Healthcare API also detects sensitive data in DICOM instances and FHIR data, such as protected PHI, and then uses a de-identification transformation to mask, delete, or otherwise obscure the data.

The PHI targeted by the de-identify command includes the 18 identifiers described in the HIPAA Privacy Rule de-identification standard. The HIPAA Privacy Rule does not restrict the use or disclosure of de-identified health information, as it is no longer considered protected health information.

For CSVs, BigQuery tables, and text strings, the open source DLP API Dataflow pipeline (see the GitHub repo `https://github.com/GoogleCloudPlatform/healthcare-deid`) eases the process of configuring and running the DLP API on healthcare data.

Best Practices for Removing Sensitive Data

Depending on the structure of the dataset, removing sensitive data requires different approaches, as shown in Table 6.2.

TABLE 6.2   Strategies for handling sensitive data

Type of Data	Strategy Used
Data is restricted to specific columns in structured datasets.	You can create a view that doesn't provide access to the columns in question. The data engineers cannot view the data, but at the same time the data is live and doesn't require human intervention to de-identify it for continuous training.
Sensitive data is part of unstructured content, but it's identifiable using known patterns or regex.	You can use Cloud DLP to address this type of data.
Sensitive data exists within images, videos, audio, or unstructured free-form data.	Use NLP API, Cloud Speech API, and Vision AI and Video Intelligence API to identify the sensitive data such as email and location out of box and then mask or remove it.

Refer to `https://cloud.google.com/architecture/sensitive-data-and-ml-datasets` for more details.

One of the methods of protecting data with multiple columns is to use an ML algorithm such as Principal Component Analysis (PCA) or other dimension-reducing techniques to combine several features and then carry out ML training only on the resulting PCA vectors, according to `https://medium.com/lizuna/beacon-the-use-of-principal-components-analysis-to-mask-sensitive-data-in-machine-learning-7904b01445d0`. For example, given three different fields of age, smoker (represented as 1 or 0), and body weight, the data might get condensed into a single PCA column that uses the following equation:

1.5age + 30smoker + 0.2 * body-weight

Somebody who is 20 years old, smokes, and weighs 140 pounds generates a value of 88. This is the same value generated by someone who is 30 years old, doesn't smoke, and weighs 215 pounds.

This method can be quite robust because even if one identifies individuals who are unique in some way, it is hard to determine without an explanation of the PCA vector formula what makes them unique.

Coarsening is another technique used to decrease the granularity of data in order to make it more difficult to identify sensitive data within the dataset while still giving comparable benefits versus a training model with the pre-coarsened data. The fields in Table 6.3 are particularly well-suited to this approach.

TABLE 6.3   Techniques to handle sensitive fields in data

Field	Description
IP addresses	Zero out the last octet of IPv4 addresses (the last 80 bits if using IPv6).
Numeric quantities	Numbers can be binned to make them less likely to identify an individual; for example, age and birthdays can be changed into ranges.
Zip codes	Can be coarsened to include just the first three digits.
Location	Use location identifiers such as city, state, or zip code, or use a large range to obfuscate the unique characteristics of one row.

Summary

In this chapter, we discussed some of the security best practices used to manage data for machine learning in Google Cloud, such as encryption at rest and encryption in transit.

We also covered IAM briefly and how to use IAM to provide and manage access to Vertex AI Workbench for your data science team. We covered some secure ML development techniques such as federated learning and differential privacy.

Last, we covered how you can manage PII and PHI data using the Cloud DLP and Cloud Healthcare APIs. We also covered an architecture pattern on how you can scale the PII identification and de-identification on a large dataset.

Exam Essentials

Build secure ML systems.   Understand encryption at rest and encryption in transit for Google Cloud. Know how encryption at rest and in transit works for storing data for machine learning in Cloud Storage and BigQuery. Know how you can set up IAM roles to manage your Vertex AI Workbench and how to set up network security for your Vertex AI Workbench. Last, understand some concepts such as differential privacy, federated learning, and tokenization.

Understand the privacy implications of data usage and collection.   Understand the Google Cloud Data Loss Prevention (DLP) API and how it helps identify and mask PII type data. Also, understand the Google Cloud Healthcare API to identify and mask PHI type data. Finally, understand some of the best practices for removing sensitive data.

Review Questions

1. You are an ML security expert at a bank that has a mobile application. You have been asked to build an ML-based fingerprint authentication system for the app that verifies a customer's identity based on their fingerprint. Fingerprints cannot be downloaded into and stored in the bank databases. Which learning strategy should you recommend to train and deploy this ML model and make sure the fingerprints are secure and protected?

    A. Differential privacy

    B. Federated learning

    C. Tokenization

    D. Data Loss Prevention API

2. You work on a growing team of more than 50 data scientists who all use Vertex AI Workbench. You are designing a strategy to organize your jobs, models, and versions in a clean and scalable way. Which strategy is the most managed and requires the least effort?

    A. Set up restrictive IAM permissions on the Vertex AI platform notebooks so that only a single user or group can access a given instance.

    B. Separate each data scientist's work into a different project to ensure that the jobs, models, and versions created by each data scientist are accessible only to that user.

    C. Use labels to organize resources into descriptive categories. Apply a label to each created resource so that users can filter the results by label when viewing or monitoring the resources.

    D. Set up a BigQuery sink for Cloud Logging logs that is appropriately filtered to capture information about AI Platform resource usage. In BigQuery, create a SQL view that maps users to the resources they are using.

3. You are an ML engineer of a Fintech company working on a project to create a model for document classification. You have a big dataset with a lot of PII that cannot be distributed or disclosed. You are asked to replace the sensitive data with specific surrogate characters. Which of the following techniques is best to use?

    A. Format-preserving encryption or tokenization

    B. K-anonymity

    C. Replacement

    D. Masking

4. You are a data scientist of an EdTech company, and your team needs to build a model on the Vertex AI platform. You need to set up access to a Vertex AI Python library on Google Colab Jupyter Notebook. What choices do you have? (Choose three.)

    A. Create a service account key.

    B. Set the environment variable named GOOGLE_APPLICATION_CREDENTIALS.

    C. Give your service account the Vertex AI user role.

    D. Use console keys.

    E. Create a private account key.

5. You are a data scientist training a deep neural network. The data you are training contains PII. You have two challenges: first you need to transform the data to hide PII, and you also need to manage who has access to this data in various groups in the GCP environment. What are the choices provided by Google that you can use? (Choose two.)

    A. Network firewall

    B. Cloud DLP

    C. VPC security control

    D. Service keys

    E. Differential privacy

6. You are a data science manager and recently your company moved to GCP. You have to set up a JupyterLab environment for 20 data scientists on your team. You are looking for a least-managed and cost-effective way to manage the Vertex AI Workbench so that your instances are only running when the data scientists are using the notebook. How would you architect this on GCP?

    A. Use Vertex AI–managed notebooks.

    B. Use Vertex AI user-managed notebooks.

    C. Use Vertex AI user-managed notebooks with a script to stop the instances when not in use.

    D. Use a Vertex AI pipeline.

7. You have Fast Healthcare Interoperability Resources (FHIR) data and you are building a text classification model to detect patient notes. You need to remove the PHI from the data. Which service you would use?

    A. Cloud DLP

    B. Cloud Healthcare API

    C. Cloud NLP API

    D. Cloud Vision AI

8. You are an ML engineer of a Fintech company building a real-time prediction engine that streams files that may contain personally identifiable information (PII) to GCP. You want to use the Cloud Data Loss Prevention (DLP) API to scan the files. How should you ensure that the PII is not accessible by unauthorized individuals?

    A. Stream all files to Google Cloud, and then write the data to BigQuery. Periodically conduct a bulk scan of the table using the DLP API.

    B. Stream all files to Google Cloud, and write batches of the data to BigQuery. While the data is being written to BigQuery, conduct a bulk scan of the data using the DLP API.

    C. Create two buckets of data: sensitive and nonsensitive. Write all data to the Nonsensitive bucket. Periodically conduct a bulk scan of that bucket using the DLP API, and move the sensitive data to the Sensitive bucket.

    D. Periodically conduct a bulk scan of the Google Cloud Storage bucket using the DLP API, and move the data to either the Sensitive or Nonsensitive bucket.

Chapter

7

Model Building

GOOGLE CLOUD PROFESSIONAL MACHINE
LEARNING ENGINEER EXAM OBJECTIVES
COVERED IN THIS CHAPTER:

✓ **3.1 Building models. Considerations include:**

- Choosing ML framework and model architecture

- Modeling techniques given interpretability requirements

✓ **3.2 Training models. Considerations include:**

- Using distributed training to organize reliable pipelines

In this chapter, we will talk about data parallel and model parallel strategies to use while training a large neural network. Then we will cover some of the modeling techniques by defining some important concepts such as gradient descent, learning, rate, batch size, and epoch in a neural network. Then you will learn what happens when we change these hyperparameters (batch size, learning rate) while training a neural network.

We are going to discuss transfer learning and how pretrained models are used to kickstart training when you have limited datasets.

Then we are going to cover semi-supervised learning and when to use this technique. We will also cover data augmentation techniques and how they can be used in an ML pipeline. Last, we will cover key concepts such as bias and variance and then discuss how they can lead to underfit and overfit models. We will also cover strategies for underfit models and overfit models and detail the regularization strategy used for overfit models.

Choice of Framework and Model Parallelism

The number of parameters in modern deep learning models is becoming larger and larger, and the size of the dataset is also increasing dramatically. To train a sophisticated modern deep learning model on a large dataset, you have to use multinode training; otherwise, it just takes forever. You may always see data parallelism and model parallelism in distributed deep learning training.

Data Parallelism

Data parallelism is when the dataset is split into parts and then assigned to parallel computational machines or graphics processing units (GPUs). For every GPU or node, the same parameters are used for the forward propagation. A small batch of data is sent to every node, and the gradient is computed normally and sent back to the main node. There are two strategies when distributed training is practiced, *synchronous* and *asynchronous*. For data parallelism, we have to reduce the learning rate to keep a smooth training process if there are too many computational nodes. Refer to https://analyticsindiamag.com/data-parallelism-vs-model-parallelism-how-do-they-differ-in-distributed-training for more details.

Synchronous Training

In synchronous training, the model sends different parts of the data into each accelerator or GPU. Every GPU has a complete copy of the model and is trained solely on a part of the data. Every single part starts a forward pass simultaneously and computes a different output and gradient. Synchronous training uses an all-reduce algorithm, which collects all the trainable parameters from various workers and accelerators.

Asynchronous Training

Synchronous training can be harder to scale and can result in workers staying idle at times. In asynchronous training, workers don't have to wait for each other during downtime in maintenance, and all workers are independently training over the input data and updating variables asynchronously. An example is the parameter server strategy for TensorFlow distributed training. See Figure 7.1 to understand data parallelism with a parameter server.

FIGURE 7.1   Asynchronous data parallelism

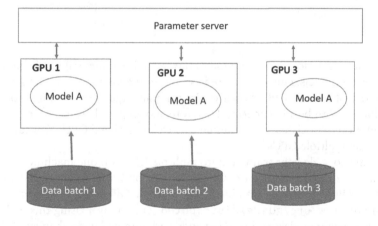

 The "all-reduce sync" strategy is great for Tensor Processing Unit (TPU) and one-machine multi-GPUs.

Model Parallelism

In *model parallelism*, every model is partitioned into parts, just as with data parallelism. Each model is then placed on an individual GPU.

Model parallelism has some obvious benefits. It can be used to train a model such that it does not fit into just a single GPU. For example, say we have 10 GPUs and we want to train a simple ResNet50 model. We could assign the first five layers to GPU 1, the second five layers to GPU 2, and so on, and the last five layers to GPU 10. During the training, in each iteration, the forward propagation has to be done in GPU 1 first and GPU 2 is waiting for the output from GPU 1. Once the forward propagation is done, we calculate the gradients for the last layers that reside in GPU 10 and update the model parameters for those layers in GPU 10. Then the gradients back propagate to the previous layers in GPU 9. Each GPU/node is like a compartment in the factory production line; it waits for the products from its previous compartment and sends its own products to the next compartment. See Figure 7.2 where the model is split into various GPUs.

FIGURE 7.2   Model parallelism

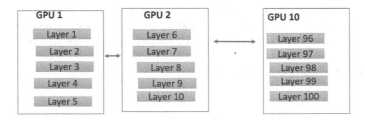

Increasing the size of deep learning models (layers and parameters) yields better accuracy for complex vision models. However, there is a limit to the maximum model size you can fit in the memory of a single GPU. When you're training large deep learning models, GPU memory limitations can be a bottleneck. Therefore, model parallelism can be used to overcome the limitations associated with training a model on a single GPU. You can split the model (layers) on multiple GPUs.

You may want to scale your training onto multiple GPUs on one machine, or multiple machines in a network (with 0 or more GPUs each), or on Cloud TPUs. tf.distribute.Strategy is a TensorFlow API to distribute training across multiple GPUs, multiple machines, or TPUs. (See www.tensorflow.org/guide/distributed_training.) Using this API, you can distribute your existing models and training code with minimal code changes. Table 7.1 explains which of these are supported in which scenarios in TensorFlow.

TABLE 7.1   Distributed training strategies using TensorFlow

Strategy	Description
MirroredStrategy	Synchronous distributed training on multiple GPUs on one machine.
CentralStorageStrategy	Synchronous training but no mirroring.
MultiWorkerMirroredStrategy	Synchronous distributed training across multiple workers, each with potentially multiple GPUs or multiple machines.

Strategy	Description
TPUStrategy	Synchronous distributed training on multiple TPU cores.
ParameterServer-Strategy	Some machines are designated as workers and some as parameter servers.

Typically sync training is supported via all-reduce and async through parameter server architecture for TensorFlow.

After you have trained your TF model using the appropriate distribution strategy, you can deploy the model using either tf.serving or TFLite on mobile devices and TensorFlow.js for browsers. Figure 7.3 shows training and serving with TensorFlow.

FIGURE 7.3   Training strategy with TensorFlow

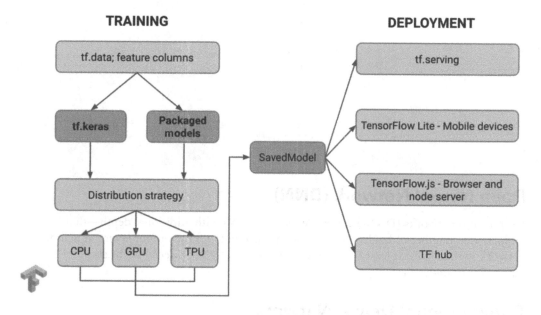

Modeling Techniques

Let's go over some basic terminology in neural networks that you might see in exam questions.

Artificial Neural Network

Artificial neural networks (ANNs) are the simplest type of neural network; they have one hidden layer. A feedforward neural network is a classic example of an ANN. They are mainly used for supervised learning where the data is mostly numerical and structured, such as, for example, regression problems. See Figure 7.4.

FIGURE 7.4   Artificial or feedforward neural network

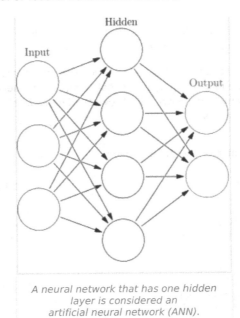

A neural network that has one hidden layer is considered an artificial neural network (ANN).

Deep Neural Network (DNN)

Deep neural networks (DNNs) can be defined as ANNs with additional depth—that is, an increased number of hidden layers between the input and the output layers. A neural network with usually at least two layers qualifies as a DNN, or *deep net* for short. See Figure 7.5 to understand DNN.

Convolutional Neural Network

Convolutional neural networks (CNNs) are a type of DNN network designed for image input. CNNs are most well-suited to image classification tasks, although they can be used on a wide array of tasks that take images as input.

FIGURE 7.5   Deep neural network

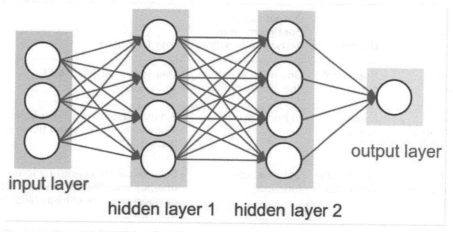

output layer

input layer

hidden layer 1   hidden layer 2

Two or more hidden layers comprise a deep neural network

Recurrent Neural Network

Recurrent neural networks (RNNs) are designed to operate upon sequences of data. They have proven to be very effective for natural language processing problems where sequences of text are provided as input to the model. RNNs have also seen some modest success for time-series forecasting and speech recognition. The most popular type of RNN is the long short-term memory (LSTM) network. LSTMs can be used in a model to accept a sequence of input data and make a prediction, such as to assign a class label or predict a numerical value like the next value or values in the sequence.

Neural networks are trained using stochastic gradient descent and require that you choose a loss function when designing and configuring your model. A loss is a number indicating how bad the model's prediction was on a single example. If the model's prediction is perfect, the loss is zero; otherwise, the loss is greater. The goal of training a model is to find a set of weights and biases that have low loss, on average, across all examples. The loss function is one of the important components of neural networks. Loss is nothing but a prediction error of neural net. And the method to calculate the loss is called loss function. In simple words, the loss is used to calculate the gradients. And gradients are used to update the weights of the neural net.

What Loss Function to Use

Importantly, the choice of loss function is directly related to the activation function used in the output layer of your neural network. These two design elements are connected. Table 7.2 summarizes the loss functions based on ML problems.

TABLE 7.2 Summary of loss functions based on ML problems

	Output	Output Layer Configuration or Activation Function	Loss Functions
Regression problem	Numerical output	One node with a linear activation unit	Mean squared error (MSE)
Binary classification problem	Binary outcome	Sigmoid activation unit	Binary cross-entropy, categorical hinge loss, and squared hinge loss (Keras)
Multiclass classification problem	Single label multiclass	Softmax activation function	Categorical cross-entropy (on one-hot encoded data) and sparse categorical cross-entropy (apply on integers)

 Use sparse categorical cross-entropy when your classes are mutually exclusive (when each sample belongs exactly to one class) and categorical cross-entropy when one sample can have multiple classes or labels. Look at the list of loss functions supported by tf.keras: www.tensorflow.org/api_docs/python/tf/keras/losses.

The following is an example code snippet of TensorFlow multiclass classification. The model must have one node for each class in the output layer and use the softmax activation function. The loss function sparse_categorical_crossentropy is appropriate for integer encoded class labels (e.g., 0 for one class, 1 for the next class, etc.).

```
# define model
model = Sequential()
model.add(Dense(10, activation='relu', kernel_initializer='he_normal',
input_shape=(n_features,)))
model.add(Dense(8, activation='relu', kernel_initializer='he_normal'))
model.add(Dense(3, activation='softmax'))
# compile the model
model.compile(optimizer='adam', loss='sparse_categorical_crossentropy',
metrics=['accuracy'])
```

Gradient Descent

The gradient descent algorithm calculates the gradient of the loss curve at the starting point. The gradient of the loss is equal to the derivative (slope) of the curve. The gradient has both magnitude and direction (vector) and always points in the direction of the steepest increase in the loss function. The gradient descent algorithm takes a step in the direction of the negative gradient in order to reduce loss as quickly as possible.

Learning Rate

As we know, the gradient vector has both a direction and a magnitude. Gradient descent algorithms multiply the gradient by a scalar known as the learning rate (also sometimes called *step size*) to determine the next point. For example, if the gradient magnitude is 2.5 and the learning rate is 0.01, then the gradient descent algorithm will pick the next point 0.025 away from the previous point.

Batch

In gradient descent, a batch is the total number of examples you use to calculate the gradient in a single iteration. So far, we've assumed that the batch has been the entire dataset. A very large batch may cause even a single iteration to take a very long time to compute.

Batch Size

Batch size is the number of examples in a batch. For example, the batch size of SGD is 1, while the batch size of a mini-batch is usually between 10 and 1,000. Batch size is usually fixed during training and inference; however, TensorFlow does permit dynamic batch sizes.

Epoch

An epoch means an iteration for training the neural network with all the training data. In an epoch, we use all of the data exactly once. A forward pass and a backward pass together are counted as one pass. An epoch is made up of one or more batches.

Hyperparameters

We covered loss, learning rate, batch size, and epoch. These are the hyperparameters that you can change while training your ML model. Most machine learning programmers spend a fair amount of time tuning the learning rate.

- If you pick a learning rate that is too small, learning will take too long.

- Conversely, if you specify a large batch size, the model might take more time to compute.

Tuning Batch Size

The following are the best practices for tuning batch size:

- A smaller mini-batch size (not too small) usually leads not only to a smaller number of iterations of a training algorithm than a large batch size but also to a higher accuracy overall; that is, a neural network that performs better, in the same amount of training time. Our parallel coordinate plot also makes a key trade-off very evident: larger batch sizes take less time to train but are less accurate.

- If batch size is too small, training will bounce around; if it's too large, training will take a very long time.

- However, using a smaller batch size lets your gradient update more often per epoch, which can result in a larger decrease in loss per epoch. Furthermore, models trained using smaller batches generalize better.

 Large batch size can lead to out of memory error while training neural networks.

Tuning Learning Rate

It is important to achieve a desirable learning rate for the following reasons:

- Both low and high learning rates result in wasted time and resources.

- A lower learning rate means more training time.

- More time results in increased cloud GPU costs.

- A higher rate could result in a model that might not be able to predict anything accurately.

- If the learning rate is too small, training will take ages; if it's too large, training will bounce around and ultimately diverge.

Transfer Learning

According to a Wiki definition, *transfer learning* (https://en.wikipedia.org/wiki/Transfer_learning) is a research problem in machine learning (ML) that focuses on storing knowledge gained while solving one problem and applying it to a different but related problem. For example, knowledge gained while learning to recognize cars could apply when trying to recognize trucks. In deep learning, transfer learning is a technique whereby a neural network model is first trained on a problem similar to the problem that is being solved. One or more layers from the trained model are then used in a new model trained on the problem of interest.

Transfer learning is an optimization to save time or get better performance.

- You can use an available pretrained model, which can be used as a starting point for training your own model.

- Transfer learning can enable you to develop models even for problems where you may not have very much data.

Semi-supervised Learning

Semi-supervised learning (SSL) is a third type of learning. It is a machine learning problem that involves a small number of labeled examples and a large number of unlabeled examples. Semi-supervised learning is an approach to machine learning that combines a small amount of labeled data with a large amount of unlabeled data during training. It falls between unsupervised learning (with no labeled training data) and supervised learning (with only labeled training data).

When You Need Semi-supervised Learning

When you don't have enough labeled data to produce an accurate model and you don't have the resources to get more data, you can use semi-supervised techniques to increase the size of your training data.

For example, imagine you are developing a model intended to detect fraud for a large bank. Some fraud you know about, but other instances of fraud are slipping by without your knowledge. You can label the dataset with the fraud instances you're aware of, but the rest of your data will remain unlabeled. You can use a semi-supervised learning algorithm to label the data and retrain the model with the newly labeled dataset. Then, you apply the retrained model to new data, more accurately identifying fraud using supervised machine learning techniques. However, there is no way to verify that the algorithm has produced labels that are 100 percent accurate, resulting in less trustworthy outcomes than traditional supervised techniques.

The following are some use cases:

- Fraud detection or anomaly detection
- Clustering
- Speech recognition
- Web content classification
- Text document classification

Limitations of SSL

With a minimal amount of labeled data and plenty of unlabeled data, semi-supervised learning shows promising results in classification tasks. But it doesn't mean that semi-supervised learning is applicable to all tasks. If the portion of labeled data isn't representative of the entire distribution, the approach may fall short.

Data Augmentation

Neural networks typically have a lot of parameters. You would need to show your machine learning model a proportional number of examples to get good performance. Also, the number of parameters you need is proportional to the complexity of the task your model has to perform.

You need a large amount of data examples to train neural networks. In most of the use cases, it's difficult to find a relevant dataset with a large number of examples. So, to get more data or examples to train the neural networks, you need to make minor alterations to your existing dataset—minor changes such as flips or translations or rotations. Our neural network would think these are distinct images. This is *data augmentation*, where we train our neural network with synthetically modified data (orientation, flips, or rotation) in the case of limited data.

Even if you have a large amount of data, it can help to increase the amount of relevant data in your dataset. There are two ways you can apply augmentation in your ML pipeline: offline augmentation and online augmentation.

Offline Augmentation

In offline augmentation, you perform all the necessary transformations beforehand, essentially increasing the size of your dataset. This method is preferred for relatively smaller datasets because you would end up increasing the size of the dataset by a factor equal to the number of transformations you perform. For example, by rotating all images, you can increase the size of the dataset by a factor of 2.

Online Augmentation

In online augmentation, you perform data augmentation transformations on a mini-batch, just before feeding it to your machine learning model. This is also known as *augmentation on the fly*. This method is preferred for large datasets as mini-batches you would feed into the model.

The following list includes some of the data augmentation techniques for images:

- Flip
- Rotate
- Crop
- Scale
- Gaussian noise (adding just the right amount of noise to enhance the learning capability)
- Translate
- Conditional generative adversarial networks (GANs) to transform an image from one domain to an image in another domain
- Transfer learning to give the models a better chance with the scarce amount of data

Model Generalization and Strategies to Handle Overfitting and Underfitting

While training neural network models, there are two important things that exist:

- **Bias:** Bias is the difference between the average prediction of our model and the correct value we are trying to predict. It is actually the error rate of the training data. When the error rate has a high value, bias is high, and when error is low, its bias is low. A model with high bias pays very little attention to the training data and oversimplifies the model.

- **Variance:** The error rate of the testing data is called variance. When the error rate has a high value, we call it high variance, and when the error rate has a low value, we call it low variance. A model with high variance pays a lot of attention to training data and does not generalize on the data it hasn't seen before. As a result, such models perform very well on training data but have high error rates on test data.

Training a deep neural network that can generalize well to new data is a challenging problem. A model with too little capacity cannot learn the problem, whereas a model with too much capacity can learn it too well and overfit the training dataset. Both cases result in a model that does not generalize well.

Bias Variance Trade-Off

You need to find the right balance without overfitting or underfitting the data. If your model is too simple and has very few parameters, then it may have high bias and low variance. If our model has a large number of parameters, then it's going to have high variance and low bias. This trade-off in complexity is why there is a trade-off between bias and variance.

Underfitting can easily be addressed by increasing the capacity (weights) of the network, but overfitting requires the use of specialized techniques. Refer to `www.geeksforgeeks` `.org/underfitting-and-overfitting-in-machine-learning` to learn more.

Underfitting

An underfit model fails to sufficiently learn the problem and performs poorly on a training dataset and does not perform well on a test or validation dataset. In the context of the bias variance trade-off, an underfit model has high bias and low variance. Regardless of the specific samples in the training data, it cannot learn the problem. There are a couple of reasons for model underfitting:

- Data used for training is not cleaned.
- The model has a high bias.

The overfit model performance varies widely with unseen examples in the training dataset. Here are some of the ways to reduce underfitting:

- Increase model complexity.
- Increase the number of features by performing feature engineering.
- Remove noise from the data.
- Increase the number of epochs or increase the duration of training to get better results.

Overfitting

The model learns the training data too well and performance varies widely with new unseen examples or even statistical noise added to examples in the training dataset. An overfit model has low bias and high variance. There are two ways to approach an overfit model:

- Reduce overfitting by training the network on more examples.
- Reduce overfitting by changing the complexity of network structure and parameters.

  Here are some of the ways to avoid overfitting:
- Regularization technique: explained in next section.
- Dropout: Probabilistically remove inputs during training.
- Noise: Add statistical noise to inputs during training.
- Early stopping: Monitor model performance on a validation set and stop training when performance degrades.
- Data augmentation.
- Cross-validation.

 BigQuery ML supports two methods for preventing overfitting: early stopping and regularization. Refer to https://cloud.google.com/bigquery-ml/docs/preventing-overfitting.

Refer to this link to learn 10 ways to avoid overfitting: www.v7labs.com/blog/overfitting.

Regularization

Regularization comes into play and shrinks the learned estimates toward 0. In other words, it tunes the loss function by adding a penalty term that prevents excessive fluctuation of the coefficients, thereby reducing the chances of overfitting.

L1 and L2 are two common regularization methods. You will use L1 when you are trying to reduce features and L2 when you are looking for a stable model. Table 7.3 summarizes the difference between the two techniques.

TABLE 7.3 Differences between L1 and L2 regularization

L1 Regularization	L2 Regularization
L1 regularization, also known as L1 norm or lasso (in regression problems), combats overfitting by shrinking the parameters toward 0. This makes some features obsolete. So, this works well for feature selection in case you have a huge number of features.	L2 regularization, or the L2 norm or ridge (in regression problems), combats overfitting by forcing weights to be small but not making them exactly 0.
L1 regularization penalizes the sum of absolute values of the weights.	L2 regularization penalizes the sum of squares of the weights.
L1 regularization has built-in feature selection.	L2 regularization doesn't perform feature selection.
L1 regularization is robust to outliers.	L2 regularization is not robust to outliers.
L1 regularization helps with feature selection and reducing model size or leading to smaller models.	L2 regularization always improves generalization in linear models.

We covered regularization in this section. Now we will cover some of the common ways backpropagation can go wrong while training neural networks and ways to regularize:

- **Exploding gradients:** If the weights in a network are very large, then the gradients for the lower layers involve products of many large terms leading to gradients that get too large to converge. Batch normalization and lower learning rate can help prevent exploding gradients.

- **Dead ReLU units:** Rectified linear activation function, or ReLU for short, is a linear function that will output the input directly if it is positive; otherwise, it will output 0. Networks that use the rectifier function for the hidden layers are referred to as rectified networks. Once the weighted sum for a ReLU unit falls below 0, the ReLU unit can get stuck. It outputs 0 activation, contributing nothing to the network's output, and gradients can no longer flow through it during backpropagation. With a source of gradients cut off, the input to the ReLU may not ever change enough to bring the weighted sum back above 0. Lowering the learning rate can help keep ReLU units from dying.

- **Vanishing gradients:** The gradients for the lower layers (closer to the input) can become very small. When the gradients vanish toward 0 for the lower layers, these layers train very slowly or they do not train at all. The ReLU activation function can help prevent vanishing gradients.

- **Dropout regularization:** This type of regularization is useful for neural networks. It works by randomly "dropping out" unit activations in a network for a single gradient step. The more you drop out, the stronger the regularization:

  - 0.0 = No dropout regularization.
  - 1.0 = Drop out everything. The model learns nothing.
  - Values between 0.0 and 1.0 = More useful.

For vanishing gradients, using ReLU instead of sigmoid can help. For exploding gradients, batch normalization, grading, and clipping can help. Lowering your learning rate can help with both exploding gradients and dead ReLU units.

Losses are good now, but in case you want to reduce your training loss further, you can try the following techniques:

- Increase the depth and width of your neural network.
- If the features don't add information relative to existing features, try a different feature.
- Decrease the learning rate.
- Increase the depth and width of your layers (to increase predictive power).
- If you have lots of data, use held-out test data.
- If you have little data, use cross-validation or bootstrapping.

The model you have trained is not converging and it is bouncing around. This can be due to the following:

- Features might not have predictive power.
- Raw data might not comply with the defined schema.
- Learning rate seems high, and you need to decrease it.
- Reduce your training set to few examples to obtain a very low loss.
- Start with one or two features (and a simple model) that you know have predictive power and see if the model overperforms your baseline.

Summary

In this chapter, we discussed model parallelism and data parallelism and some strategies to use while training a TensorFlow model with a model and data parallel approach.

You learned about modeling techniques such as what loss function to choose while training a neural network. We covered important concepts related to training neural networks such as gradient descent, learning rate, batch size, epoch, and hyperparameters.

We also covered the importance of these hyperparameters when training a neural network—for example, what happens when we decrease learning rate or increase the epoch while training the network.

We discussed transfer learning and the advantages of using it. We also covered semi-supervised learning: when you need semi-supervised learning along with its limitations.

We discussed data augmentation techniques. You use online augmentation when you have a large dataset and offline augmentation when you have a small dataset. We also covered techniques such as rotation and flipping to augment your existing dataset.

Finally, we discussed model underfitting, model overfitting, and regularization concepts.

Exam Essentials

Choose either framework or model parallelism.   Understand multinode training strategies to train a large neural network model. The strategy can be data parallel or model parallel. Also, know what strategies can be used for distributed training of TensorFlow models.

Understand modeling techniques.   Understand when to use which loss function (sparse cross-entropy versus categorical cross-entropy). Understand important concepts such as gradient descent, learning rate, batch size, and epoch. Also understand that these are hyperparameters and know some strategies to tune these hyperparameters to minimize loss or error rate while training your model.

Understand transfer learning.   Understand what transfer learning is and how it can help with training neural networks with limited data as these are pretrained models trained on large datasets.

Use semi-supervised learning (SSL).   Understand semi-supervised learning and when you need to use this method. Also know the limitations of SSL.

Use data augmentation.   You need to understand data augmentation and how you can apply it in your ML pipeline (online versus offline). You also need to learn some key data augmentation techniques such as flipping, rotation, GANs, and transfer learning.

Understand model generalization and strategies to handle overfitting and underfitting.   You need to understand bias variance trade-off while training a neural network. Know the strategies to handle underfitting as well as strategies to handle overfitting, such as regularization. You need to understand the difference between L1 and L2 regularization and when to apply which approach.

Review Questions

1. Your data science team trained and tested a deep neural net regression model with good results in development. In production, six months after deployment, the model is performing poorly due to a change in the distribution of the input data. How should you address the input differences in production?

   A. Perform feature selection on the model using L1 regularization and retrain the model with fewer features.

   B. Retrain the model, and select an L2 regularization parameter with a hyperparameter tuning service.

   C. Create alerts to monitor for skew, and retrain the model.

   D. Retrain the model on a monthly basis with fewer features.

2. You are an ML engineer of a start-up and have trained a deep neural network model on Google Cloud. The model has low loss on the training data but is performing worse on the validation data. You want the model to be resilient to overfitting. Which strategy should you use when retraining the model?

   A. Optimize for the L1 regularization and dropout parameters.

   B. Apply an L2 regularization parameter of 0.4, and decrease the learning rate by a factor of 10.

   C. Apply a dropout parameter of 0.2.

   D. Optimize for the learning rate, and increase the number of neurons by a factor of 2.

3. You are a data scientist of a Fintech company training a computer vision model that predicts the type of government ID present in a given image using a GPU-powered virtual machine on Compute Engine. You use the following parameters:

   Optimizer: SGD, Image shape = 224x224, Batch size = 64, Epochs = 10, and Verbose = 2.

   During training you encounter the following error: "ResourceExhaustedError: out of Memory (oom) when allocating tensor." What should you do?

   A. Change the optimizer.

   B. Reduce the batch size.

   C. Change the learning rate.

   D. Reduce the image shape.

4. You are a data science manager of an EdTech company and your team needs to build a model that predicts whether images contain a driver's license, passport, or credit card. The data engineering team already built the pipeline and generated a dataset composed of 20,000 images with driver's licenses, 2,000 images with passports, and 2,000 images with credit cards. You now have to train a model with the following label map: ['drivers_license', 'passport', 'credit_card']. Which loss function should you use?

   A. Categorical hinge

   B. Binary cross-entropy

C.   Categorical cross-entropy

D.   Sparse categorical cross-entropy

5.   You are a data scientist training a deep neural network. During batch training of the neural network, you notice that there is an oscillation in the loss. How should you adjust your model to ensure that it converges?

A.   Increase the size of the training batch.

B.   Decrease the size of the training batch.

C.   Increase the learning rate hyperparameter.

D.   Decrease the learning rate hyperparameter.

6.   You have deployed multiple versions of an image classification model on the Vertex AI platform. You want to monitor the performance of the model versions over time. How should you perform this comparison?

A.   Compare the loss performance for each model on a held-out dataset.

B.   Compare the loss performance for each model on the validation data.

C.   Compare the mean average precision across the models using the Continuous Evaluation feature.

D.   Compare the ROC curve for each model.

7.   You are training an LSTM-based model to summarize text using the following hyperparameters: epoch = 20, batch size =32, and learning rate = 0.001. You want to ensure that training time is minimized without significantly compromising the accuracy of your model. What should you do?

A.   Modify the epochs parameter.

B.   Modify the batch size parameter.

C.   Modify the learning rate parameter.

D.   Increase the number of epochs.

8.   Your team needs to build a model that predicts whether images contain a driver's license or passport. The data engineering team already built the pipeline and generated a dataset composed of 20,000 images with driver's licenses and 5,000 images with passports. You have transformed the features into one-hot encoded value for training. You now have to train a model to classify these two classes; which loss function should you use?

A.   Sparse categorical cross-entropy

B.   Categorical cross-entropy

C.   Categorical hinge

D.   Binary cross-entropy

9. You have developed your own DNN model with TensorFlow to identify products for an industry. During training, your custom model converges but the tests are giving unsatisfactory results. What do you think is the problem and how can you fix it? (Choose two.)

   A. You have to change the algorithm to XGBoost.

   B. You have an overfitting problem.

   C. You need to increase your learning rate hyperparameter.

   D. The model is complex and you need to regularize the model using L2.

   E. Reduce the batch size.

10. As the lead ML engineer for your company, you are building a deep neural network TensorFlow model to optimize customer satisfaction. Your focus is to minimize bias and increase accuracy for the model. Which other parameter do you need to consider so that your model converges while training and doesn't lead to underfit or overfit problems?

   A. Learning rate

   B. Batch size

   C. Variance

   D. Bagging

11. As a data scientist, you are working on building a DNN model for text classification using Keras TensorFlow. Which of the following techniques should not be used? (Choose two.)

   A. Softmax function

   B. Categorical cross-entropy

   C. Dropout layer

   D. L1 regularization

   E. K-means

12. As the ML developer for a gaming company, you are asked to create a game in which the characters look like human players. You have been asked to generate the avatars for the game. However, you have very limited data. Which technique would you use?

   A. Feedforward neural network

   B. Data augmentation

   C. Recurrent neural network

   D. Transformers

13. You are working on building a TensorFlow model for binary classification with a lot of categorical features. You have to encode them with a limited set of numbers. Which activation function will you use for the task?

   A. One-hot encoding

   B. Sigmoid

   C. Embeddings

   D. Feature cross

14. You are the data scientist working on building a TensorFlow model to optimize the level of customer satisfaction for after-sales service. You are struggling with learning rate, batch size, and epoch to optimize and converge your model. What is your problem in ML?

A. Regularization

B. Hyperparameter tuning

C. Transformer

D. Semi-supervised learning

15. You are a data scientist working for a start-up on several projects with TensorFlow. You need to increase the performance of the training and you are already using caching and prefetching. You want to use GPU for training but you have to use only one machine to be cost-effective. Which of the following tf distribution strategies should you use?

A. MirroredStrategy

B. MultiWorkerMirroredStrategy

C. TPUStrategy

D. ParameterServerStrategy

Chapter

8

Model Training and Hyperparameter Tuning

GOOGLE CLOUD PROFESSIONAL MACHINE LEARNING ENGINEER EXAM OBJECTIVES COVERED IN THIS CHAPTER:

✓ **2.1 Exploring and preprocessing organization-wide data (e.g., Cloud Storage, BigQuery, Cloud Spanner, Cloud SQL, Apache Spark, Apache Hadoop). Considerations include:**

- Organizing different types of data (e.g., tabular, text, speech, images, videos) for efficient training

- Data preprocessing (e.g., Dataflow, TensorFlow Extended [TFX], BigQuery)

✓ **2.2 Model prototyping using Jupyter notebooks. Considerations include:**

- Choosing the appropriate Jupyter backend on Google Cloud (e.g., Vertex AI Workbench notebooks, notebooks on Dataproc)

- Using Spark kernels

- Integration with code source repositories

- Developing models in Vertex AI Workbench by using common frameworks (e.g., TensorFlow, PyTorch, sklearn, Spark, JAX)

✓ **3.2 Training models. Considerations include:**

- Organizing training data (e.g., tabular, text, speech, images, videos) on Google Cloud (e.g., Cloud Storage, BigQuery)

- Ingestion of various file types (e.g., CSV, JSON, images, Hadoop, databases) into training

- Training using different SDKs (e.g., Vertex AI custom training, Kubeflow on Google Kubernetes Engine, AutoML, tabular workflows)

- Using distributed training to organize reliable pipelines
- Hyperparameter tuning
- Troubleshooting ML model training failures

✓ **3.3 Choosing appropriate hardware for training. Considerations include:**

- Distributed training with TPUs and GPUs (e.g., Reduction Server on Vertex AI, Horovod)

In this chapter, we will talk about various file types and how they can be stored and ingested for AI/ML workloads in GCP. Then we will talk about how you can train your model using Vertex AI training. Vertex AI training supports frameworks such as scikit-learn, TensorFlow, PyTorch, and XGBoost. We will talk about how you can train a model using prebuilt containers and custom containers. We will also cover why and how you can unit test the data and model for machine learning. Then, we will cover hyperparameter tuning and various search algorithms for hyperparameter tuning available in Google Cloud. We will also cover Vertex AI Vizier and how it's different than hyperparameter tuning. We will talk about how you can track and debug your training model in Vertex AI metrics using the Vertex AI interactive shell, TensorFlow Profiler, and What-If Tool. Last, we are going to talk about data drift, concept drift, and when you should retrain your model to avoid drift.

Ingestion of Various File Types into Training

Data for training can be in various types, such as, for example, the following:

- Structured data such as tables from an on-premise database or CSV files
- Semi-structured data such as PDFs or JSON files
- Unstructured data such as chats, emails, audio, images, or videos

Also, this data can be either batch data or real-time streaming data—for example, data streamed from Internet of Things (IoT) sensors. Moreover, the data can be small, such as a few megabytes, or it can be petabyte scale. As you learned in previous chapters, before training the data, it's important to clean and transform it so that you can apply ML training on it. The Google Cloud analytics portfolio provides tools to collect, store, process, and analyze this data, as shown in Figure 8.1.

Let's look at the various steps.

FIGURE 8.1 Google Cloud data and analytics overview

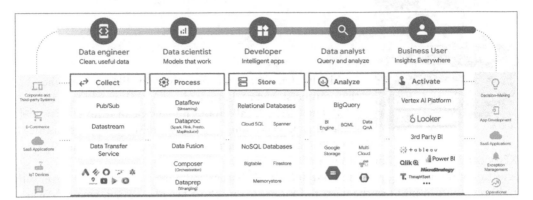

Collect

If you need to collect batch or streaming data from various sources such as IoT devices, e-commerce websites, or any third-party applications, this can be done by Google Cloud services.

- **Pub/Sub and Pub/Sub Lite for real-time streaming:** Pub/Sub is a serverless scalable service (1 KB to 100 GB with consistent performance) for messaging and real-time analytics. Pub/Sub can both publish and subscribe across the globe, regardless of where your ingestion or processing applications live. It has deep integration with processing services (Dataflow) and analytics services (BigQuery). You can directly stream data from a third party to BigQuery using Pub/Sub. Pub/Sub Lite is also a serverless offering that optimizes for cost over reliability. Pub/Sub Lite is good for workloads with more predictable and consistent load.

- **Datastream for moving on premise Oracle and MySQL databases to Google Cloud data storage:** Datastream is a serverless and easy-to-use change data capture (CDC) and replication service. It allows you to synchronize data across heterogeneous databases and applications reliably and with minimal latency and downtime. Datastream supports streaming from Oracle and MySQL databases into Cloud Storage. Datastream is integrated with Dataflow, and it leverages Dataflow templates to load data into BigQuery, Cloud Spanner, and Cloud SQL.

- **BigQuery Data Transfer Service:** You can load data from the following sources to BigQuery using the BigQuery Data Transfer Service:

  - Data warehouses such as Teradata and Amazon Redshift

  - External cloud storage provider Amazon S3

  - Google software as a service (SaaS) apps such as Cloud Storage, Google Ads, etc.

After you configure a data transfer, the BigQuery Data Transfer Service automatically loads data into BigQuery on a regular basis.

Process

Once you have collected the data from various sources, you need tools to process or transform the data before it is ready for ML training. The following sections cover some of the tools that can help.

Cloud Dataflow

Cloud Dataflow is a serverless, fully managed data processing or ETL service to process streaming and batch data. Dataflow used Apache Beam before open-sourcing its SDK. Apache Beam offers exactly-once streaming semantics, which means it has mechanisms in place to process each message not only at least once, but exactly one time. This simplifies your business logic because you don't have to worry about handling duplicates or errors.

Data flows are processing pipelines that perform a set of actions, and this allows you to build pipelines, monitor their execution, and transform and analyze data. It aims to address the performance issues of MapReduce when building pipelines. Many Hadoop workloads can be done easily and be more maintainable with Dataflow. Cloud Dataflow allows you to process and read data from source Google Cloud data services to sinks as shown in Figure 8.2.

FIGURE 8.2   Cloud Dataflow source and sink

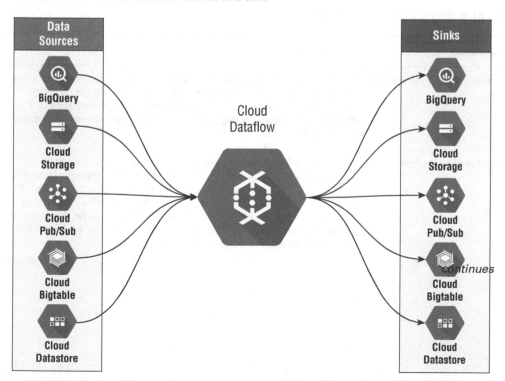

continues

For example, you can process and transform data from Cloud Pub/Sub (Source) to BigQuery (Sink) using Cloud Dataflow.

Cloud Data Fusion

We covered Cloud Data Fusion in Chapter 3, "Feature Engineering." Cloud Data Fusion is a UI-based ETL tool with no code implementation.

Cloud Dataproc

Dataproc is a fully managed and highly scalable service for running Apache Spark, Apache Flink, Presto, and 30+ open-source tools and frameworks. Dataproc lets you take advantage of open-source data tools for batch processing, querying, streaming, and machine learning. Dataproc automation helps you create clusters quickly, manage them easily, and save money by turning them off when you do not need them.

Dataproc has built-in integration with other Google Cloud Platform services such as Big-Query, Cloud Storage, Cloud Bigtable, Cloud Logging, and Cloud Monitoring, which provides a complete data platform. For example, you can use Dataproc to effortlessly ETL (Extract Transform Load) terabytes of raw log data directly into BigQuery for business reporting. Dataproc uses the Hadoop Distributed File System (HDFS) for storage. Additionally, Dataproc automatically installs the HDFS-compatible Cloud Storage connector, which enables the use of Cloud Storage in parallel with HDFS. Data can be moved in and out of a cluster through upload/download to HDFS or Cloud Storage. Table 8.1 summarizes connectors with Dataproc.

TABLE 8.1   Dataproc connectors

Connector	Description
Cloud Storage connector	This is by default available on Dataproc and this connector helps run Apache Hadoop or Apache Spark jobs directly on data in Cloud Storage. Store your data in Cloud Storage and access it directly with Cloud Storage connector. You do not need to transfer it into HDFS first.
BigQuery connector	You can use BigQuery connector to enable programmatic read/write access to BigQuery. This is an ideal way to process data that is stored in BigQuery as command-line access is not exposed. The BigQuery connector is a library that enables Spark and Hadoop applications to process data from BigQuery and write data to Big-Query. BigQuery Spark connector is used for Spark and BigQuery Hadoop connector is used for Hadoop.

continues

TABLE 8.1   Dataproc connectors *(continued)*

Connector	Description
BigQuery Spark connector	Apache Spark SQL connector for Google BigQuery. The connector supports reading Google BigQuery tables into Spark's DataFrames, and writing DataFrames back into BigQuery. This is done by using the Spark SQL Data Source API to communicate with BigQuery.
Cloud Bigtable with Dataproc	Bigtable is an excellent option for any Apache Spark or Hadoop uses that require Apache HBase. Bigtable supports the Apache HBase APIs so it is easy to use Bigtable with Dataproc.
Pub/Sub Lite Spark connector	The Pub/Sub Lite Spark connector supports Pub/Sub Lite as an input source to Apache Spark Structured Streaming in the default micro-batch processing and experimental continuous processing modes.

All Cloud Dataproc clusters come with the BigQuery connector for Hadoop built in so that you can easily and quickly read and write BigQuery data to and from Cloud Dataproc.

Cloud Composer

There are multiple ways of creating, running, and managing workflows such as running Cron tasks, using Cron jobs, and scripting and creating custom applications. Each approach has pros and cons. More importantly, there is management overhead in all the approaches here. That is why we have Cloud Composer, which is a fully managed data workflow orchestration service that allows you to author, schedule, and monitor pipelines. Cloud Composer is built on Apache Airflow, and pipelines are configured as directed acyclic graphs (DAGs) using Python.

It supports hybrid and multicloud architecture to manage your workflow pipelines whether it's on-premises, in multiple clouds, or fully within Google Cloud.

Cloud Composer provides end-to-end integration with Google Cloud products including BigQuery, Dataflow, Dataproc, Datastore, Cloud Storage, Pub/Sub, and Vertex AI Platform, which gives users the freedom to fully orchestrate their pipeline.

Cloud Dataprep

We covered Cloud Dataprep in Chapter 3. Cloud Dataprep is a UI-based ETL tool to visually explore, clean, and prepare structured and unstructured data for analysis, reporting, and machine learning at any scale.

Summary of Processing Tools

A summary of all the tools we have covered so far is shown in Figure 8.3.

FIGURE 8.3   Summary of processing tools on GCP

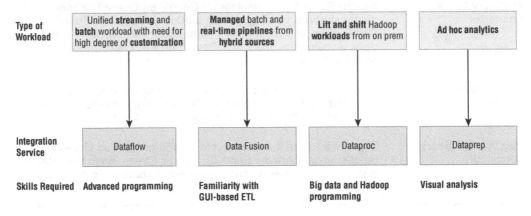

Store and Analyze

After you use tools to collect and process data, you need scalable storage to store various types of data. Table 8.2 shows the Google Cloud Storage options for various types of data for machine learning. Refer to Table 8.2 for data storage guidance on GCP for machine learning.

TABLE 8.2   Data storage guidance on GCP for machine learning

Type of Data	Product
Tabular data	BigQuery, BigQuery ML
Image, video, audio, and unstructured data	Google Cloud Storage
Unstructured data	Vertex Data Labeling
Structured data	Vertex AI Feature Store
For AutoML image, video, text	Vertex AI Managed Datasets

Avoid storing data in block storage like Network File System (NFS) and VMs. Similarly, avoid reading data directly from databases like Cloud SQL.

Store image, video, audio, and unstructured data in large container formats on Cloud Storage. Also, combine many individual images, videos, and audio clips into large files because this will improve your read and write throughput to Google Cloud Storage. Aim for files of at least 100 MB, and between 100 and 10,000 shard.

For TensorFlow workloads, store data as sharded TFRecord files, and for any other framework, store as Avro files in Google Cloud Storage. You can also use TF I/O to manage data in Parquet format for TensorFlow training. TensorFlow I/O is a collection of file systems and file formats that are not available in TensorFlow's built-in support. It provides useful extra dataset, streaming, and file system extensions.

Developing Models in Vertex AI Workbench by Using Common Frameworks

In this section, we will cover how you can create a Jupyter Notebook environment to train, tune, and deploy your model using Vertex AI Workbench.

Vertex AI Workbench is a Jupyter Notebook–based development environment for the entire data science workflow. You can interact with Vertex AI and other Google Cloud services from within a Vertex AI Workbench instance's Jupyter Notebook. We introduced Vertex AI Workbench in Chapter 6, "Building Secure ML Pipelines," when we covered the security aspect of creating an instance and the two types of notebooks:

User-managed notebook   The oldest version of Jupyter Notebooks within the Vertex AI platform (previously the AI platform). They have more control and fewer features compared to managed notebooks. See Table 8.3 for the feature differences.

Managed notebook   The latest offering. These come with features such as automatic shutdown, integration with data storage, and the ability to schedule the notebook for an execution.

Both notebook options are prepackaged with JupyterLab and have a preinstalled suite of deep learning packages such as TensorFlow and PyTorch frameworks as well as other packages such as R, Spark, and Python. You can use CPU-only or GPU-enabled instances. Both notebook instances also integrate with GitHub so that you can sync your notebook with a GitHub repository.

First we'll go over some of the feature differences between managed notebooks and user-managed notebooks and then we will cover how to create and use these notebooks for model development.

TABLE 8.3   Differences between managed and user-managed notebooks

Managed notebook	User-managed notebook
Automated shutdown for idle instances: Choosing a managed notebook will shut down your Jupyter Notebooks when not in use. This feature helps save costs because the instances will shut down when not in use automatically.	**Automated shutdown for idle instances:** This feature is not supported out of the box. However, you can create a monitor to see when instances are idle using Cloud Monitoring and Cloud Functions and shut them down when not in use.
UI integration with Cloud Storage and Big-Query: From within JupyterLab's navigation menu on a managed notebooks instance, you can use the Cloud Storage and Big-Query integration to browse data and other files that you have access to and load data into your notebook.	**UI integration with Cloud Storage and Big-Query:** There is no UI integration. However, you can use the BigQuery connector to connect to BigQuery data using code or you can also use the BigQuery magic (%%) command to run BigQuery SQLl commands on a Jupyter Notebook. For Cloud Storage, you can use gsutil commands to write and read data in user-managed notebooks.
Automated notebook runs: You can set a notebook to run on a recurring schedule. Even while your instance is shut down, Vertex AI Workbench will run your notebook file and save the results for you to look at and share with others.	**Automated notebook runs:** This feature is not supported. You would use Cloud Scheduler to schedule the training jobs or the notebook.
Custom containers: You can add your own custom container images to a managed notebook Jupyter instance.	**Custom containers:** You have the choice to add custom containers.
Dataproc or Serverless Spark integration: You can process data quickly by running a notebook on a Dataproc cluster or Serverless Spark. This feature is in private preview now. After your cluster is set up, you can run a notebook file on it without leaving the JupyterLab interface.	**Dataproc or Serverless Spark integration:** This feature is not supported.
Frameworks: All the frameworks are already preinstalled when you create the managed notebook. You can choose any framework supported once you have created a managed notebook.	**Frameworks:** You have the choice to create only one framework from all the supported frameworks. For example, TensorFlow, R, and PyTorch are supported by the user-managed notebook, but while creating, you can only choose one framework for your JupyterLab environment.

continues

TABLE 8.3   Differences between managed and user-managed notebooks *(continued)*

Managed notebook	User-managed notebook
Network and security: You can run this in the VPC in the same project. Shared VPC control is not yet supported for managed notebooks.	**Network and security:** For users who have specific networking and security needs, user-managed notebooks can be the best option. You can use VPC Service Controls to set up a user-managed notebooks instance within a service perimeter and implement other built-in networking and security features.

Next we explore the features of each type of notebook by creating a notebook in the Vertex AI GCP console.

Creating a Managed Notebook

Go to Vertex AI and choose Enable All APIs. By default in the GCP, all the service APIs are disabled. After enabling the APIs, click on Workbench, go to the Managed Notebooks tab, and choose New Notebook. Click the Create button to create the notebook using the default settings (Figure 8.4).

Notice that there is a monthly billing estimate for running the notebook at the right-hand side.

FIGURE 8.4   Creating a managed notebook

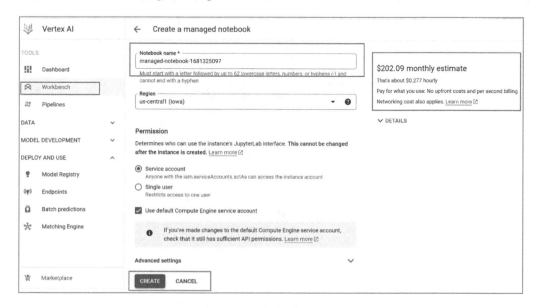

After some time, you will find that the notebook is created and the Open JupyterLab button is enabled (see Figure 8.5). Click on the Open JupyterLab button to get inside your managed JupyterLab environment.

FIGURE 8.5   Opening the managed notebook

Notice the Upgrade available option with managed notebooks in Figure 8.5. Managed notebook instances are dual-disk, with one boot disk and one data disk. The upgrade process upgrades the boot disk to a new image while preserving your data on the data disk. It's a manual upgrade process you have a choice to do. To learn more about how it works, check out https://cloud.google.com/vertex-ai/docs/workbench/managed/upgrade.

Exploring Managed JupyterLab Features

After you click Open JupyterLab, you are redirected to the screen shown in Figure 8.6. You will find that you have all the frameworks available to use in this environment, including Serverless Spark as well as PySpark installed locally. The Serverless Spark feature is to run the Dataproc cluster within the notebook.

FIGURE 8.6   Exploring frameworks available in a managed notebook

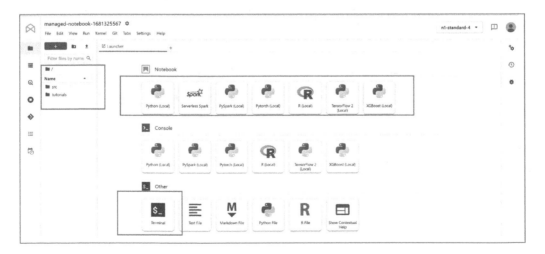

In the tutorials folder, you will find existing notebooks to help you get started with building and training your models on this JupyterLab environment. JupyterLab also comes with a terminal option to run terminal commands on the entire notebook.

Next, let's explore features supported by this type of notebook.

Data Integration

Click the Browse GCS icon on the left navigation bar (Figure 8.7) to browse and load data from cloud storage folders.

FIGURE 8.7   Data integration with Google Cloud Storage within a managed notebook

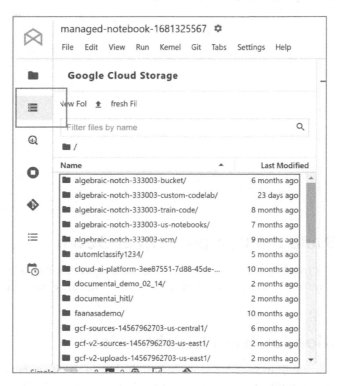

BigQuery Integration

Click the BigQuery icon on the left as shown in Figure 8.8 to get data from your BigQuery tables. The interface also has an Open SQL editor option to query these tables without leaving the JupyterLab interface.

FIGURE 8.8   Data Integration with BigQuery within a managed notebook

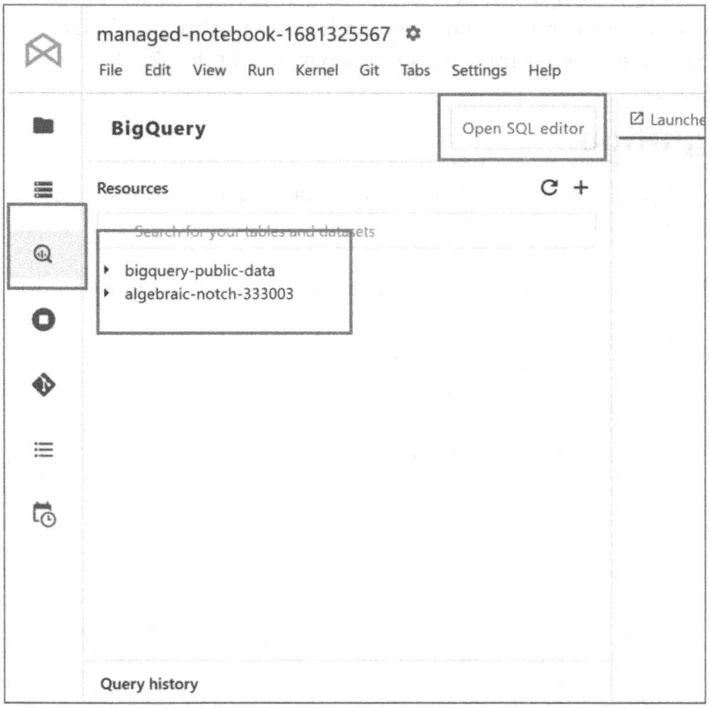

Ability to Scale the Compute Up or Down

Click n1-standard-4 (see Figure 8.9). You will get the option to modify the hardware of the Jupyter environment. You can also attach a GPU to this instance without leaving the environment.

Git Integration for Team Collaboration

Click the left navigation branch icon and you get to the screen to integrate your existing git repository or clone a repository for project collaboration (see Figure 8.10). Alternatively, you can use the terminal and run the command `git clone <your-repository name>` to clone your repository.

FIGURE 8.9   Scaling up the hardware from a managed notebook

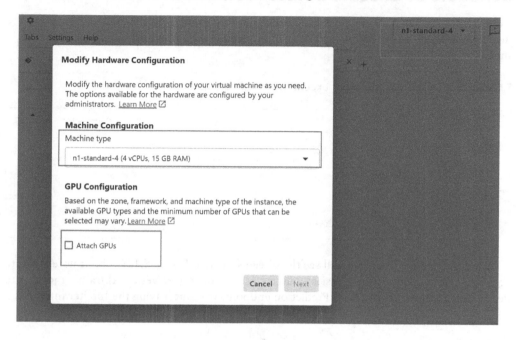

FIGURE 8.10   Git integration within a managed notebook

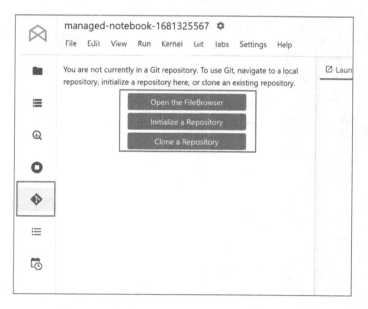

Schedule or Execute a Notebook Code

Click Python, write "hello world," and click run cell to execute the cell manually using the triangle black arrow. In order to execute this notebook automatically, click Execute as shown in Figure 8.11.

FIGURE 8.11   Scheduling or executing code in the notebook

After clicking Execute, you will see the screen shown in Figure 8.12: Submit notebooks to Executor. This functionality is basically used to set up or trigger Vertex AI training jobs or to deploy scheduling of a Vertex AI Prediction endpoint without leaving the Jupyter interface.

FIGURE 8.12   Submitting the notebook for execution

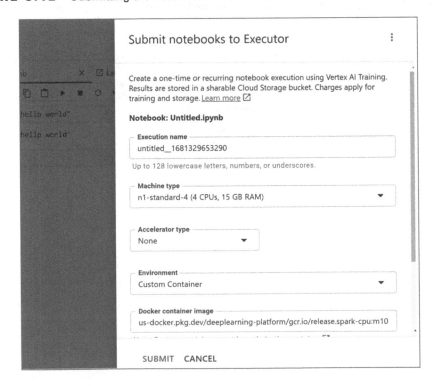

Scroll down to the Type option to schedule the notebook run as shown in Figure 8.13.

FIGURE 8.13 Scheduling the notebook for execution

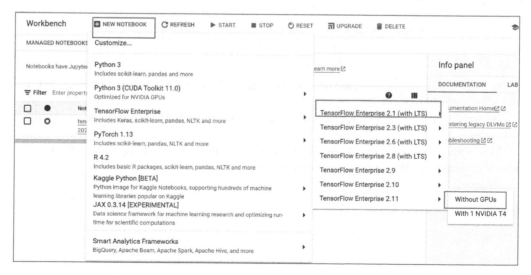

We covered all the features of managed notebooks such as integration with Cloud Storage/BigQuery, the ability to scale up or scale down the notebook hardware, git integration, and the ability to schedule the notebook either for a onetime run or at a scheduled time.

Creating a User-Managed Notebook

With user-managed notebooks, you need to choose the execution environment during the creation of the notebook, as shown in Figure 8.14.

FIGURE 8.14 Choosing TensorFlow framework to create a user-managed notebook

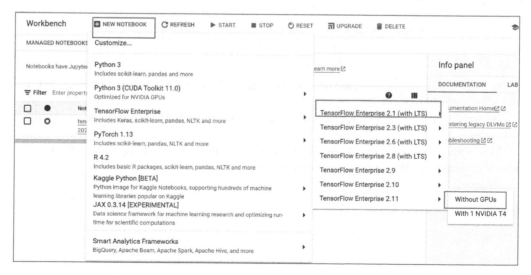

You need to pick a specific framework from options such as Python 3, TensorFlow, R, JAX, Kaggle, PyTorch, and so on. Let's go ahead and create a TensorFlow notebook without GPUs by following the path shown in Figure 8.14. Then click Create to create a user-managed notebook (see Figure 8.15).

FIGURE 8.15 Create a user-managed TensorFlow notebook

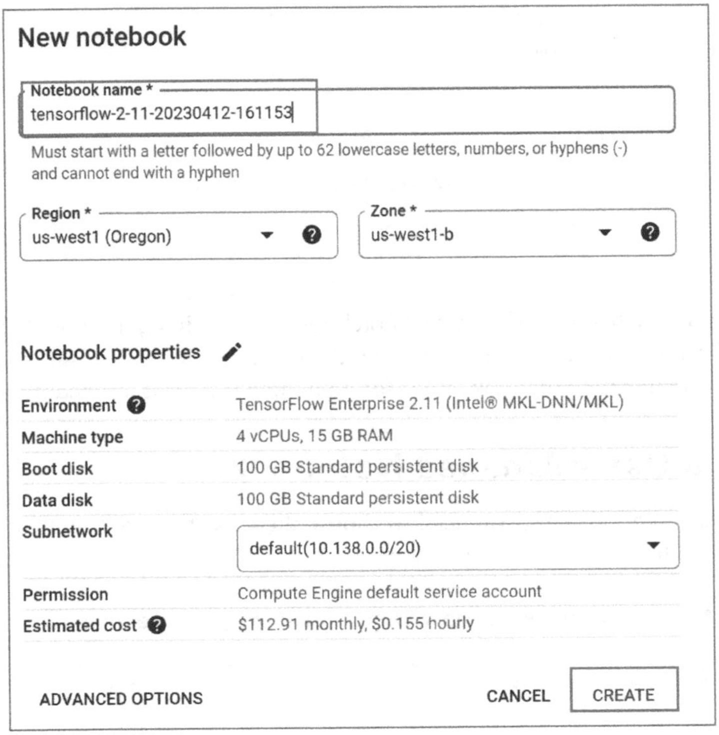

You can see that user-managed notebooks come with advanced options to configure networking with shared VPCs.

Once the notebook is active, you will see the Open JupyterLab option. Click it to explore the notebook (see Figure 8.16).

This notebook comes with TensorFlow already installed. You have git integration and terminal access available with user-managed notebooks.

FIGURE 8.16   Exploring the network

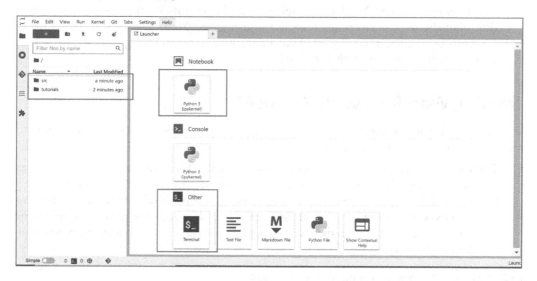

You can use both managed and user-managed notebooks to trigger Vertex AI training using the Vertex AI Python SDK or to run predictions using the Vertex AI Training Python SDK.

You do not need a large hardware or compute instance to develop the code in JupyterLab because the hardware is not used for training. You perform training using Vertex AI Training or Prediction SDKs. These APIs or SDKs create a training container outside the JupyterLab environment that shuts down automatically when training is over. Similarly, the prediction SDKs or APIs start the prediction container and host it and give you an endpoint to get predictions outside the notebook hardware environment.

In this section we covered some feature differences between user-managed and managed notebooks. We also covered how to create them.

In the next section, you will learn how to train a model using Vertex AI Training.

Training a Model as a Job in Different Environments

Vertex AI supports two types of training:

- **AutoML:** AutoML lets you create and train a model with minimal technical effort. We covered AutoML in detail in Chapter 4, "Choosing the Right ML Infrastructure."

- **Custom training:** Custom training lets you create a training application optimized for your targeted outcome. You have complete control over training application functionality. Namely, you can target any objective, use any algorithm, develop your own loss functions or metrics, or do any other customization. In the following sections, we will focus on custom training with Vertex AI.

Training Workflow with Vertex AI

With Vertex AI, you can use the following options to create training jobs or resources for training either AutoML or custom models:

- **Training pipelines:** Training pipelines are the primary model training workflow in Vertex AI. You can use training pipelines to create an AutoML-trained model or a custom-trained model. For custom-trained models, training pipelines orchestrate custom training jobs and hyperparameter tuning with additional steps like adding a dataset or uploading the model to Vertex AI for prediction serving. Figure 8.17 shows the training pipeline in the Vertex AI console.

FIGURE 8.17 Training in the Vertex AI console

Source: Google LLC.

- **Custom jobs:** Custom jobs specify how Vertex AI runs your custom training code, including worker pools, machine types, and settings related to your Python training application and custom container. Custom jobs are only used by custom-trained models and not AutoML models. When you create a custom job, you specify settings that Vertex AI needs to run your training code.

- **Hyperparameter tuning jobs:** Hyperparameter tuning searches for the best combination of hyperparameter values by optimizing metric values across a series of trials. Hyperparameter tuning is only used by custom-trained models and not AutoML models. We will cover this later in this chapter in the section "Hyperparameter Tuning."

For prebuilt container training, Vertex AI supports PyTorch, TensorFlow, Scikit, and XGBoost framework. For TensorFlow models, you can use TensorFlow Hub to choose a model to deploy on GCP. TensorFlow Hub is a repository of trained models that is optimized to use on GCP.

Training Dataset Options in Vertex AI

Training starts with a dataset. In Vertex AI you have two choices for storing and managing datasets:

- **No Managed Dataset:** You can use data stored in Google Cloud Storage or data stored in BigQuery for training. Vertex AI managed notebooks integrates with Cloud Storage and BigQuery. So that you can directly use data for training from these sources, you can use Google Cloud Storage FUSE in Vertex AI Workbench to specify datasets in GCS buckets for the No Managed Dataset option. GCS FUSE provides a way for applications to upload and download Cloud Storage objects using standard file system semantics.

- **Managed dataset:** This is the preferred way to train machine learning models on Vertex AI. The following are some of the advantages of using a managed dataset for training on Vertex AI:

  - Manage your datasets in a central location.

  - Easily create labels and multiple annotation sets.

  - Create tasks for human labeling using integrated data labeling.

  - Track lineage to models for governance and iterative development.

  - Compare model performance by training AutoML and custom models using the same datasets.

  - Generate data statistics and visualizations.

  - Automatically split data into training, test, and validation sets.

You can configure your custom training jobs to mount NFS shares to the container where your code is running. This allows your jobs to access remote files as though they are local with high throughput and low latency.

Vertex AI training provides two choices for training: prebuilt containers and custom containers. Let's go over each in detail.

Pre-built Containers

Vertex AI supports scikit-learn, TensorFlow, PyTorch, and XGBoost containers hosted on the container registry for prebuilt training. Google manages all the container images and their versions. In order to set up a training with prebuilt container, please follow the steps below:

1. You need to organize your code according to the application structure as shown in Figure 8.18. You should have a root folder with `setup.py` and a trainer folder with `task.py` (training code), which is the entry point for a Vertex AI training job. You can

use standard dependencies or libraries not in the prebuilt container by specifying it in `setup.py`.

2. You need to upload your training code as Python source distribution to a Cloud Storage bucket before you start training with a prebuilt container. You use the `sdist` command to create a source distribution—for example, `python setup.py sdist --formats=gztar,zip`. Figure 8.18 shows the folder structure and architecture for a prebuilt container.

Figure 8.19 shows how the GCP console looks to set up a Vertex AI training pipeline for a prebuilt container.

FIGURE 8.18 Vertex AI training architecture for a prebuilt container

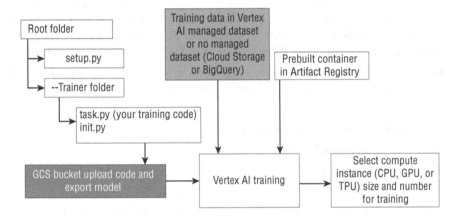

After choosing the training container, you can choose what type of compute instances you want to train.

The following command builds a Docker image based on a prebuilt training container image and your local Python code, pushes the image to Container Registry, and creates a custom job.

```
gcloud ai custom-jobs create \
  --region=LOCATION \
  --display-name=JOB_NAME \
  --worker-pool-spec=machine-type=MACHINE_TYPE,replica-count=REPLICA_
COUNT,executor-image-uri=EXECUTOR_IMAGE_URI,local-package-path=WORKING_
DIRECTORY,script=SCRIPT_PATH
```

```
LOCATION: The region where the container or Python package will be run.
JOB_NAME: Required. A display name for the CustomJob.
MACHINE_TYPE: The type of machine. Refer to available machine types for
training.
REPLICA_COUNT: The number of worker replicas to use. In most cases, set this
to 1 for your first worker pool.
EXECUTOR_IMAGE_URI: The URI of the container image that runs the provided
code. Refer to the available pre-built containers for training.
```

This image acts as the base image for the new Docker image that you are building with this command.

WORKING_DIRECTORY: A directory in your local file system containing the entry point script that runs your training code (see the following list item).

The path relative to WORKING_DIRECTORY on your local file system, to the script that is the entry point for your training code. For example, if you want to run /custom job/trainer/task.py and WORKING_DIRECTORY is /custom job, then use trainer/task.py for this value.

FIGURE 8.19   Vertex AI training console for pre-built containers

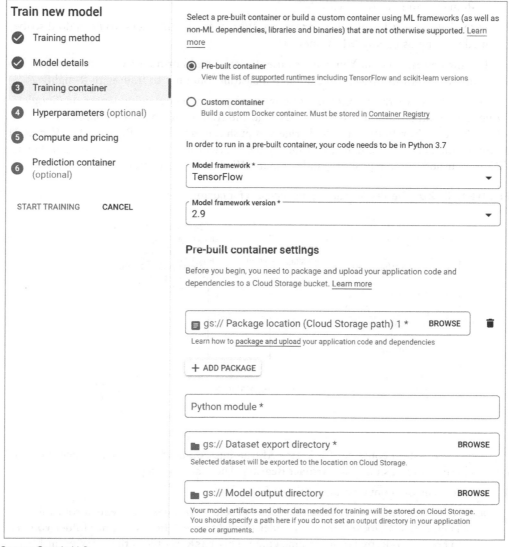

Custom Containers

A custom container is a Docker image that you create to run your training application. The following are some of the benefits of using custom container versus prebuilt:

- **Faster start-up time.** If you use a custom container with your dependencies preinstalled, you can save the time that your training application would otherwise take to install dependencies when starting up.

- **Use the ML framework of your choice.** If you can't find a Vertex AI prebuilt container with the ML framework you want to use, you can build a custom container with your chosen framework and use it to run jobs on Vertex AI. For example, you can use a custom container to train with PyTorch.

- **Extended support for distributed training.** With custom containers, you can do distributed training using any ML framework.

- **Use the newest version.** You can also use the latest build or minor version of an ML framework. For example, you can build a custom container to train with tf-nightly.

Figure 8.20 shows the architecture of how custom container training works on Google Cloud. You build a container using a Dockerfile and training file with a recommended folder structure. You build your Dockerfile and push it to an Artifact Registry. For Vertex AI training with a custom container, you specify the dataset (managed), custom container image URI you pushed to the repository, and compute (VM) instances to train on.

FIGURE 8.20   Vertex AI training architecture for custom containers

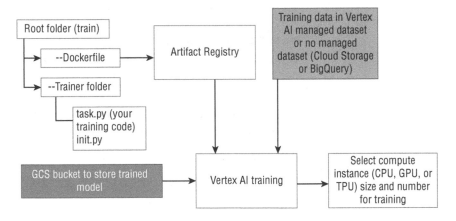

To create a custom container for Vertex AI training, you need to create a Dockerfile, build the Dockerfile, and push it to an Artifact Registry. These are the steps:

1. Create a custom container and training file.

   a. Set up your files as per required folder structure: you need to create a root folder. Then create a Dockerfile and a folder named trainer/. In that trainer folder you need to create `task.py` (your training code). This `task.py` file is the entry point file.

b. Create a Dockerfile. Your Dockerfile needs to include commands as shown in the following code that includes tasks such as choose a base image, install additional dependencies, copy your training code to the image, and configure the entry point to invoke your training code.

```
# Specifies base image and tag
FROM image:tag
WORKDIR /root
# Installs additional packages
RUN pip install pkg1 pkg2 pkg3
# Downloads training data
RUN curl https://example-url/path-to-data/data-filename --output /root/
data-filename
# Copies the trainer code to the docker image
COPY your-path-to/model.py /root/model.py
COPY your-path-to/task.py /root/task.py
# Sets up the entry point to invoke the trainer
ENTRYPOINT ["python", "task.py"]
```

2. Build and run your Docker container.

You can use the following code to build the docker image:

```
export PROJECT_ID=$(gcloud config list project --format "value(core.project)")
export REPO_NAME=REPOSITORY_NAME
export IMAGE_NAME=IMAGE_NAME
export IMAGE_TAG=IMAGE_TAG
export IMAGE_URI=us-central1-docker.pkg
.dev/${PROJECT_ID}/${REPO_NAME}/${IMAGE_NAME}:${IMAGE_TAG}
docker build -f Dockerfile -t ${IMAGE_URI} ./
```

For local run, use the following command:

```
docker run ${IMAGE_URI}
```

3. Push the container image to Artifact Registry.

If the Docker build works, you can push the container to Artifact Registry by running the following command.

```
docker push ${IMAGE_URI}
```

 By running your training job in a custom container, you can use ML frameworks, non-ML dependencies, libraries, and binaries that are not otherwise supported on Vertex AI.

4. After pushing the image to the repository, you can start training by creating a custom job using the following command:

```
gcloud ai custom-jobs create \
  --region=LOCATION \
  --display-name=JOB_NAME \
```

```
--worker-pool-spec=machine-type=MACHINE_TYPE,replica-count=REPLICA_
COUNT,container-image-uri=CUSTOM_CONTAINER_IMAGE_URI
```

Distributed Training

You need to specify multiple machines (nodes) in a training cluster in order to run a distributed training job with Vertex. The training service allocates the resources for the machine types you specify. The running job on a given node is called a *replica*. A group of replicas with the same configuration is called a worker pool. You can configure any custom training job as a distributed training job by defining multiple worker pools. You can also run distributed training within a training pipeline or a hyperparameter tuning job. Use an ML framework that supports distributed training. In your training code, you can use the CLUSTER_SPEC or TF_CONFIG environment variables to reference specific parts of your training cluster. Please refer to Table 8.4 to understand worker pool tasks in distributed training.

TABLE 8.4   Worker pool tasks in distributed training

Position in workerPoolSpecs[]	Task Performed in Cluster
First (workerPoolSpecs[0])	Primary, chief, scheduler, or "master." Exactly -one replica is designated the *primary replica*. This task manages the others and reports status for the job as a whole.
Second (workerPoolSpecs[1])	Secondary, replicas, workers. One or more replicas may be designated as *workers*. These replicas do their portion of the work as you designate in your job configuration.
Third (workerPoolSpecs[2])	Parameter servers and Reduction Server • Parameter servers: If supported by your ML framework, one or more replicas may be designated as parameter servers. These replicas store model parameters to coordinate shared model state between the workers. • *Reduction Server* is an all-reduce algorithm that can increase throughput and reduce latency for distributed training. You can use this option if you are doing distributed training with GPU workers. Your training code uses TensorFlow or PyTorch and is configured for multi-host data-parallel training with GPUs using NCCL all-reduce. For TensorFlow, you can also use Horovod, which supports Tensor Fusion to batch small tensors for all-reduce.
Fourth (workerPoolSpecs[3])	Evaluators: These replicas can be used to evaluate your model. If you are using TensorFlow, note that TensorFlow generally expects that you use no more than one evaluator.

Setting up Vertex AI Reduction Server distributed training: Vertex AI makes Reduction Server available in a Docker container image that you can use for one of your worker pools during distributed training. You need to follow some prerequisites mentioned in this link: `https://cloud.google.com/vertex-ai/docs/training/distributed-training` before you set up a Reduction Server container in your workerpoolspec[2].

The following command provides an example of how to create a `CustomJob` resource that uses Reduction Server for distributed training by setting up workerpool:

```
gcloud ai custom-jobs create \
  --region=LOCATION \
  --display-name=JOB_NAME \
  --worker-pool-spec=machine-type=n1-highmem-96,replica-count=1,accelerator-type=NVIDIA_TESLA_V100,accelerator-count=8,container-image-uri=CUSTOM_CONTAINER_IMAGE_URI \
  --worker-pool-spec=machine-type=n1-highmem-96,replica-count=4,accelerator-type=NVIDIA_TESLA_V100,accelerator-count=8,container-image-uri=CUSTOM_CONTAINER_IMAGE_URI \
  --worker-pool-spec=machine-type=n1-highcpu-16,replica-count=16,container-image-uri=us-docker.pkg.dev/vertex-ai-restricted/training/reductionserver:latest
```

We covered distributed training strategies using TensorFlow in Chapter 7, "Model Building." In order to learn more how Reduction Server works, refer to this deep-dive blog, `https://cloud.google.com/blog/topics/developers-practitioners/optimize-training-performance-reduction-server-vertex-ai`

HyperparameterTuning

Hyperparameters are parameters of the training algorithm itself that are not learned directly from the training process. Let us look at an example of a simple feed-forward neural network trained DNN model using gradient descent. One of the hyperparameters in the gradient descent is the learning rate, which we covered in Chapter 7. The learning rate must be set up front before any learning can begin. Therefore, finding the right learning rate involves choosing a value, training a model, evaluating it, and trying again.

Figure 8.21 summarizes the difference between a parameter and hyperparameter.

FIGURE 8.21   ML model parameter and hyperparameter

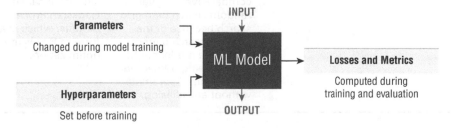

Why Hyperparameters Are Important

Hyperparameter selection is crucial for the success of your neural network architecture because hyperparameters heavily influence the behavior of the learned model. For instance, if the learning rate is set too low, the model will miss important patterns in the data, but if it's too large, the model will find patterns in accidental coincidences too easily. Finding good hyperparameters involves solving two problems:

- **How to efficiently search the space of possible hyperparameters:** There are algorithms to help with hyperparameter search space optimization. The Vertex AI default algorithm applies Bayesian optimization to arrive at the optimal solution. Table 8.5 is a summary of the search algorithms supported by Vertex AI hyperparameter tuning.

TABLE 8.5   Search algorithm options for hyperparameter tuning on GCP

Grid Search	Random Search	Bayesian Search
Grid search is essentially an exhaustive search through a manually specified set of hyperparameters. For example, a model with hyperparameters learning_rate and num_layers.	Random search is a technique where random combinations of the hyperparameters are used to find the best solution for the built model. This works best under the assumption that not all hyperparameters are equally important. In this search pattern, random combinations of parameters are considered in every iteration.	This is the Vertex AI default search algorithm. Bayesian optimization in turn takes into account past evaluations when choosing the hyperparameter set to evaluate next.
Learning_rate = [0.1,0.5,1]		
Num_layers = [5,10,20]		
Grid search will train on each pair [learning rate, num_layers] for each training, for example, [0.1,5] and measures performance either using cross-validation on the training set or a separate validation set. The hyperparameter setting that gives the maximum score is the final output.		
One of the drawbacks of grid search is that when it comes to dimensionality, it suffers when evaluating the number of hyperparameters grows exponentially.	The downside of random search, however, is that it doesn't use information from prior experiments to select the next setting.	It uses past evaluations.
To use grid search, all parameters must be of type INTEGER, CATEGORICAL, or DISCRETE.	The chances of finding the optimal parameter are comparatively higher in random search than grid search because of the random search pattern where the model might end up being trained on the optimized parameters without any aliasing.	Hyperparameter tuning uses an algorithm called Gaussian Process Bandits, which is a form of Bayesian optimization.

- **How to manage a large set of experiments for hyperparameter tuning:** Without an automated technology like Vertex AI hyperparameter tuning, you would need to make manual adjustments to the hyperparameters over the course of many training runs to arrive at the optimal values. Hyperparameter tuning makes the process of determining the best hyperparameter settings easier and less tedious. Hyperparameter tuning takes advantage of the compute infrastructure of Google Cloud to test different hyperparameter configurations when training your model. It can give you optimized values for hyperparameters, which maximizes your model's predictive accuracy.

Techniques to Speed Up Hyperparameter Optimization

There are several techniques to speed up hyperparameter optimization:

- If you have a large dataset, use a simple validation set instead of cross-validation. This will increase the speed by a factor of ~k, compared to k-fold cross-validation. This approach won't work well if you don't have enough data.

- Parallelize the problem across multiple machines by using distributed training with hyperparameter optimization. Each machine can fit models with different choices of hyperparameters. This will increase the speed by a factor of ~n for n machines.

- Avoid redundant computations by pre-computing or caching the results of computations that can be reused for subsequent model fits.

- If using grid search, decrease the number of hyperparameter values you are willing to consider. This can lead to potentially large speedups because the total number of combinations scales multiplicatively.

 You can improve performance by using the random search algorithm since it uses fewer trails.

To learn more, visit the following pages:

```
https://cloud.google.com/blog/products/ai-machine-learning/
hyperparameter-tuning-cloud-machine-learning-engine-using-bayesian-
optimization
    https://cloud.google.com/ai-platform/training/docs/
hyperparameter-tuning-overview
```

How Vertex AI Hyperparameter Tuning Works

Hyperparameter tuning works by running multiple trials of your training application with values for the hyperparameters you specify and set within limits. Hyperparameter tuning requires communication between the Vertex AI and training application. The training application defines all the information that your model needs. You define the hyperparameters (variables) that you want to adjust and target variables that are used to evaluate each trial.

Hyperparameter tuning optimizes target variables that you specify, called hyperparameter metrics. Metrics must be numeric.

When configuring a hyperparameter tuning job, you define the name and goal of each metric. The goal specifies whether you want to tune your model to maximize or minimize the value of this metric.

Follow these steps to configure hyperparameter tuning jobs using gcloud CLI commands with custom jobs:

1. For a custom container, install the `cloud-ml hypertune` Python package in your Dockerfile.

2. In `trainer/task.py`, add hyperparameter tuning code in main function and add arguments as shown in the code below.

```
Def main():
  args = get_args()
  train_data, validation_data = create_dataset()
  model = create_model(args.num_units, args.learning_rate, args.momentum)
  history = model.fit(train_data, epochs=NUM_EPOCHS,
validation_data=validation_data)
  # DEFINE METRIC
  hp_metric = history.history['val_accuracy'][-1]
  hpt = hypertune.HyperTune()
  hpt.report_hyperparameter_tuning_metric(
      hyperparameter_metric_tag='accuracy',
      metric_value=hp_metric,
      global_step=NUM_EPOCHS)
```

3. Build and push this container to Artifact Registry. After setting the training, you can configure a hyperparameter tuning job using a training pipeline or a custom job.

FIGURE 8.22   Configure hyperparameter tuning by training the pipeline UI

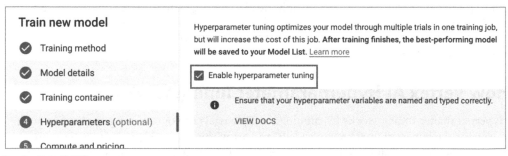

Source: Google LLC.

You can create a hyperparameter tuning job using the console, gcloud, command line, Java, or Python for a prebuilt container or a custom container. The following steps walk you through setting the hyperparameter tuning by a custom job using gcloud CLI commands:

1. Create a YAML file named `config.yaml` with some API fields that you want to specify for your new `HyperparameterTuningJob`:

```
studySpec:
  metrics:
  - metricId: METRIC_ID
    goal: METRIC_GOAL
  parameters:
  - parameterId: HYPERPARAMETER_ID
    doubleValueSpec:
      minValue: DOUBLE_MIN_VALUE
      maxValue: DOUBLE_MAX_VALUE
trialJobSpec:
  workerPoolSpecs:
    - machineSpec:
        machineType: MACHINE_TYPE
      replicaCount: 1
      containerSpec:
        imageUri: CUSTOM_CONTAINER_IMAGE_URI
```

`METRIC_ID`: The name of a hyperparameter metric to optimize. Your training code must report this metric when it runs.

`METRIC_GOAL`: The goal for your hyperparameter metric, either `MAXIMIZE` or `MINIMIZE`.

`HYPERPARAMETER_ID`: The name of a hyperparameter to tune. Your training code must parse a command-line flag with this name. For this example, the hyperparameter must take floating-point values.

`DOUBLE_MIN_VALUE`: The minimum value (a number) that you want Vertex AI to try for this hyperparameter.

`DOUBLE_MAX_VALUE`: The maximum value (a number) that you want Vertex AI to try for this hyperparameter.

`MACHINE_TYPE`: The type of VM to use for training.

`CUSTOM_CONTAINER_IMAGE_URI`: The URI of a Docker container image with your training code.

Note: You can also specify a search algorithm. If one is not specified, Google Cloud picks up a Bayesian algorithm by default.

2. In the same directory as your `config.yaml` file, run the following shell command to create a custom job to start hyperparameter tuning:

```
gcloud ai hp-tuning-jobs create \
    --region=LOCATION \
    --display-name=DISPLAY_NAME \
```

```
    --max-trial-count=MAX_TRIAL_COUNT \
    --parallel-trial-count=PARALLEL_TRIAL_COUNT \
    --config=config.yaml
LOCATION: The region where you want to create the HyperparameterTuningJob.
DISPLAY_NAME: A display name of your choice.
MAX_TRIAL_COUNT: The maximum number of trials to run.
PARALLEL_TRIAL_COUNT: The maximum number of trials to run in parallel.
```

You can track the progress of this job on a Vertex AI console in Vertex AI Training.

Vertex AI Vizier

Vertex AI Vizier is a black-box optimization service that helps you tune hyperparameters in complex ML models. Below are the criteria to use Vertex AI Vizier to train ML models:

- Vertex AI Vizier doesn't have a known objective function to evaluate.

- Vertex AI Vizier is too costly to evaluate by using the objective function, usually due to the complexity of the system.

- Vertex AI Vizier optimizes hyperparameters of ML models, but it can also perform other optimization tasks such as tuning model parameters and works with any system that you can evaluate.

Some of the examples or use cases where you can use Vertex AI Vizier for hyperparameter tuning are as follows:

- Optimize the learning rate, batch size, and other hyperparameters of a neural network recommendation engine.

- Optimize usability of an application by testing different arrangements of user interface elements.

- Minimize computing resources for a job by identifying an ideal buffer size and thread count.

- Optimize the amounts of ingredients in a recipe to produce the most delicious version.

How Vertex AI Vizier Differs from Custom Training

Vertex AI Vizier is an independent service for optimizing complex models with many parameters. It can be used for both ML and non-ML use cases. It can be used with training jobs or with other systems (even multicloud). Hyperparameter tuning for custom training is a built-in feature that uses Vertex AI Vizier for training jobs. It helps determine the best hyperparameter settings for an ML model. By default, it uses Bayesian optimization.

For more info, see

```
https://cloud.google.com/vertex-ai/docs/training/using-
hyperparameter-tuning#aiplatform_create_hyperparameter_tuning_job_
python_package_sample-gcloud
```

Tracking Metrics During Training

In the following sections, we will cover how you can track and debug machine learning model metrics by using tools such as an interactive shell, the TensorFlow Profiler, and the What-If Tool.

Interactive Shell

Using an interactive shell to inspect your training container can help you debug problems with your training code or your Vertex AI configuration. You can browse the file system and run debugging utilities in each prebuilt container or custom container running on Vertex AI. You can use an interactive shell to run tracing and profiling tools, analyze GPU usage, and check Google Cloud permissions available to the container. You can enable an interactive shell for a custom training resource by setting the enableWebAccess API field to true while setting up custom jobs programmatically or checking Enable training debugging in the Vertex AI console training pipeline, as shown in Figure 8.23.

FIGURE 8.23   Enabling an interactive shell in the Vertex AI console

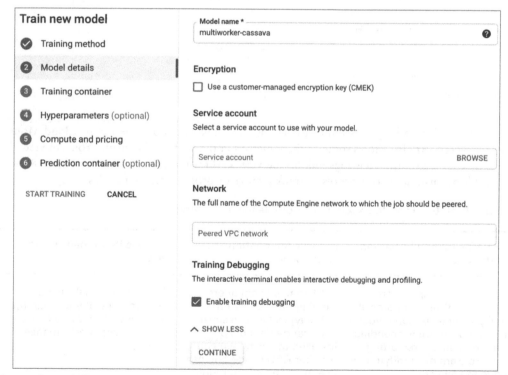

Source: Google LLC.

When Vertex AI finishes running your job or trial or changes from RUNNING state to COMPLETED state, you will lose access to your interactive shell. The interactive shell is only available while the job is in the RUNNING state. Once the job is running, you will see links to the interactive shell web page on the job details page. The Launch Web Terminal link is created for each node for the job, as shown in Figure 8.24.

FIGURE 8.24   Web terminal to access an interactive shell

Accelerator (Worker pool 0)	NVIDIA_TESLA_P100
Accelerator count (Worker pool 0)	1
Container Location (Worker pool 0)	gcr.io/$PROJECT_ID/multiworker:cassava
Machine type (Worker pool 1)	n1-standard-8
Machine count (Worker pool 1)	2
Accelerator (Worker pool 1)	NVIDIA_TESLA_P100
Accelerator count (Worker pool 1)	2
Container Location (Worker pool 1)	gcr.io/$PROJECT_ID/multiworker:cassava
Training Debugging	Launch web terminal ⬀ for worker pool 0, node 0
	Launch web terminal ⬀ for worker pool 1, node 0
	Launch web terminal ⬀ for worker pool 1, node 1
Dataset	No managed dataset
Algorithm	Custom training
Objective	Custom
Container (Training)	Custom
Logs	View logs
VIEW CUSTOM JOB INPUTS IN JSON	

Source: Google LLC.

You can also find logs in Cloud Monitoring as Vertex AI exports metrics to Cloud Monitoring. Vertex AI also shows some of these metrics in the Vertex AI console. You can view the logs by clicking on the View logs link on the Vertex AI training page, shown in Figure 8.24.

Table 8.6 lists some other tools to track metrics or profile training metrics.

TABLE 8.6   Tools to track metric or profile training metrics

Visualize Python Execution with py-spy	Retrieve Information about GPU Usage	Analyze Performance with Perf
py-spy is a sampling profiler for Python programs. It lets you visualize what your Python program is spending time on without restarting the program or modifying the code in any way.	GPU-enabled containers running on nodes with GPUs typically have several command-line tools pre-installed that can help you monitor GPU usage. You can use `nvidia-smi` to monitor GPU utilization of various processes or use `nvprof` to collect a variety of GPU profiling information.	Perf lets you analyze the performance of your training node. It's a way to do Linux profiling with performance counters.

TensorFlow Profiler

Vertex AI TensorBoard is an enterprise-ready managed version of TensorBoard. Vertex AI TensorBoard Profiler lets you monitor and optimize your model training performance by helping you understand the resource consumption of training operations. This can pinpoint and fix performance bottlenecks to train models faster and cheaper. There are two ways to access the Vertex AI TensorBoard Profiler dashboard from the Google Cloud console:

- From the custom jobs page
- From the experiments page

To capture a profiling session, your training job must be in the RUNNING state.

TF Profiler allows you to profile your remote Vertex AI training jobs on demand and visualize the results in Vertex TensorBoard. For details, see Profile model training performance using Profiler at `https://cloud.google.com/vertex-ai/docs/experiments/tensorboard-profiler`.

What-If Tool

You can use the What-If Tool (WIT) within notebook environments to inspect AI Platform Prediction models through an interactive dashboard. The What-If Tool integrates with TensorBoard, Jupyter Notebooks, Colab notebooks, and JupyterHub. It is also preinstalled on Vertex AI Workbench user-managed notebooks and TensorFlow instances.

To use WIT, you need to install the witwidget library, which is already installed in Vertex AI Workbench. Then configure WitConfigBuilder to either inspect a model or compare two models. The following is some example code to inspect a model:

```
PROJECT_ID = 'YOUR_PROJECT_ID'
MODEL_NAME = 'YOUR_MODEL_NAME'
VERSION_NAME = 'YOUR_VERSION_NAME'
TARGET_FEATURE = 'mortgage_status'
LABEL_VOCAB = ['denied', 'approved']
config_builder = (WitConfigBuilder(test_examples.tolist(), features.columns
.tolist() + ['mortgage_status'])
  .set_ai_platform_model(PROJECT_ID, MODEL_NAME, VERSION_NAME,
adjust_prediction=adjust_prediction)
  .set_target_feature(TARGET_FEATURE)
  .set_label_vocab(LABEL_VOCAB)
```

Then pass the config builder to WitWidget, and set a display height.

```
WitWidget(config_builder, height=800)
```

The What-If Tool displays an interactive visualization within your notebook. Try this Colab notebook to explore how the What-If Tool works:

https://colab.research.google.com/github/pair-code/what-if-tool/blob/master/What_If_Tool_Notebook_Usage.ipynb

Retraining/Redeployment Evaluation

After the model is trained and deployed in the real world, over time model performance changes; your model is sensitive to change as user behavior and training data keeps changing with time. Although all machine learning models decay, the speed of decay varies with time. Data drift, concept drift, or both mostly cause this. Let us understand these terms.

Data Drift

Data drift is a change in the statistical distribution of production data from the baseline data used to train or build the model. You can detect data drift if the feature attribution of your model changes or the data itself changes. For example, suppose you built a model with temperature data collected from an IoT sensor in Fahrenheit degrees but the unit changed to Celsius. This means there has been a change in your input data, so the data has drifted. You can detect data drift by examining the feature distribution or correlation between features or checking the data schema over baseline using a monitoring system.

Concept Drift

Concept drift is a phenomenon where the statistical properties of the target variable you're trying to predict change over time. For example, say you build a model to classify positive and negative sentiment of Reddit feed around certain topics. Over time, people's sentiments about these topics change. Tweets belonging to a positive sentiment may evolve over time to be negative.

In order to detect drift, you need to monitor your deployed model, which can be done by Vertex AI Model Monitoring. We will cover this topic in detail in Chapter 12, "Model Monitoring, Tracking and Auditing Metadata."

When Should a Model Be Retrained?

Decide on a retraining strategy based on Table 8.7. We will discuss how you can use Vertex AI pipelines and Vertex AI Model Monitoring to set up retraining in Chapter 12.

TABLE 8.7   Retraining strategies

Periodic training	You can choose an interval such as weekly, monthly, or yearly for retraining your model. It depends on how frequently your training data gets updated. Retraining your model based on an interval only makes sense if it aligns with your business use case. The selection of a random period for model retraining can give you a worse model than the previous model.
Performance-based trigger	If your model performance falls below your set threshold, which is the ground truth or baseline data, this automatically triggers the retraining pipeline. This approach assumes that you have implemented a sophisticated monitoring system in production.
Data changes trigger	If data drift happens, that should trigger a build for model retraining. Usually model performance changes in production, which can lead to data drift.
Retraining on demand	This is a manual and traditional way of retraining your models that employs traditional techniques.

Unit Testing for Model Training and Serving

Testing machine learning systems is hard because the code, model, and data all control the behavior of the system. Testing ML models means testing the model code as well as testing the data and the model. Unit tests allow us to test whether a unit of code is functioning as we expect it to.

Model testing involves explicit checks for behaviors that we expect our model to follow. Testing allow us to identify some bugs early. We can run some tests without needing trained parameters. These tests include the following:

- Checking the shape of your model output and ensuring it aligns with the labels in your dataset.
- Checking the output ranges and ensuring it aligns with your expectations (e.g., the output of a classification model should be a distribution with class probabilities that sum to 1).
- Making sure a single gradient step on a batch of data yields a decrease in your loss.
- Making assertions about your datasets.
- Checking for label leakage between your training and validation datasets.

Testing for Updates in API Calls

You can test updates to an API call by retraining your model, but that would be resource intensive. Rather, you can write a unit test to generate random input data and run a single step of gradient descent to complete without runtime errors.

Testing for Algorithmic Correctness

To check your model for algorithmic correctness, follow these steps:

1. Train your model for a few iterations and verify that the loss decreases.

2. Train your algorithm without regularization. If your model is complex enough, it will memorize the training data and your training loss will be close to 0.

3. Test specific subcomputations of your algorithm. For example, you can test that a part of CNN runs once per element of the input data.

Summary

In this chapter, we discussed various file types such as structured, unstructured, and semi-structured and how they can be stored and ingested for AI/ML workloads in GCP. We divided the file ingestion into Google Cloud Platform into stages such as collect, process, store, and analyze and discussed services that can help at each stage. We covered Pub/Sub and Pub/Sub Lite to collect real-time data and BigQuery Data Transfer Service and Datastream to migrate data from third-party sources and databases to Google Cloud. In the process phase, we covered how we can transform the data using services such as Cloud Dataflow, Cloud Data Fusion, Cloud Dataproc, Cloud Composer, and Cloud Dataprep.

Then we talked about how you can train your model using Vertex AI training. Vertex AI training supports frameworks such as scikit-learn, TensorFlow, PyTorch, and XGBoost. We talked about how you can train a model using prebuilt containers and custom containers.

We also covered why and how you can unit test the data and model for machine learning.

Then we covered hyperparameter tuning and various search algorithms for hyperparameter tuning available in Google Cloud, as well as Vertex AI Vizier and how it's different than hyperparameter tuning.

You learned how you can track and debug your training model in Vertex AI metrics using Vertex AI interactive shell, TensorFlow Profiler, and the What-If Tool.

You also learned about data drift and concept drift and when you should retrain your model to avoid drift.

Exam Essentials

Know how to ingest various file types into training.   Understand the various file types, such as structured (for example, CSV), unstructured (for example, text files), and semi-structured (for example, JSON files). Know how these file types can be stored and ingested for AI/ML workloads in GCP. Understand how the file ingestion into Google Cloud works by using a Google Cloud data analytics platform into stages such as collect, process, store, and analyze. For collecting data into Google Cloud Storage, you can use Pub/Sub and Pub/Sub Lite to collect real-time data as well as BigQuery Data Transfer Service and Datastream to migrate data from third-party sources and databases to Google Cloud. In the process phase, understand how we can transform the data or run Spark/Hadoop jobs for ETL using services such as Cloud Dataflow, Cloud Data Fusion, Cloud Dataproc, Cloud Composer, and Cloud Dataprep. know how to use Vertex AI Workbench environment by using common frameworks: understand the feature differences and framework supported by both managed and user managed notebooks. Understand when you should use user managed notebook vs managed notebook. Understand how to create these notebooks and what features they support out of the box.

Know how to use the Vertex AI Workbench environment by using common frameworks.   Understand the feature differences and framework supported by both managed and user-managed notebooks. Understand when you should use user-managed notebooks versus managed notebooks. Understand how to create these notebooks and what features they support out of the box.

Know how to train a model as a job in different environments.   Understand options for Vertex AI training such as AutoML and custom training. Then understand how you can perform custom training by using either a prebuilt container or a custom container using Vertex AI training along with architecture. Understand using a training pipeline versus custom jobs to set up training in Vertex AI. Vertex AI training supports frameworks such as scikit-learn, TensorFlow, PyTorch, and XGBoost. Also, understand how to set up distributed training using Vertex AI custom jobs.

Be able to unit test for model training and serving.   Understand why and how you can unit test the data and model for machine learning. Understand how to test for updates in APIs after model endpoints are updated and how to test for algorithm correctness.

Understand hyperparameter tuning.   Understand hyperparameter tuning and various search algorithms for hyperparameter tuning such as grid search, random search, and Bayesian search. Understand when to use which search algorithm to speed up performance. Know how to set up hyperparameter tuning using custom jobs. Last, also understand Vertex AI Vizier and how it's different from setting up hyperparameter tuning.

Track metrics during training.   You can use Interactive shell, Tensorflow Profiler and What-If tool to track metrics during model training.

Conduct a retraining/redeployment evaluation.   Understand bias variance trade-off while training a neural network. Then you need to understand strategies to handle underfitting and strategies to handle overfitting, such as regularization. Know the difference between L1 and L2 regularization and when to apply which approach.

Review Questions

1. You are a data scientist for a financial firm who is developing a model to classify customer support emails. You created models with TensorFlow Estimators using small datasets on your on-premises system, but you now need to train the models using large datasets to ensure high performance. You will port your models to Google Cloud and want to minimize code refactoring and infrastructure overhead for easier migration from on-prem to cloud. What should you do?

   A. Use Vertex AI custom jobs for training.

   B. Create a cluster on Dataproc for training.

   C. Create an AutoML model using Vertex AI training.

   D. Create an instance group with autoscaling.

2. You are a data engineer building a demand-forecasting pipeline in production that uses Dataflow to preprocess raw data prior to model training and prediction. During preprocessing, you perform z-score normalization on data stored in BigQuery and write it back to BigQuery. Because new training data is added every week, what should you do to make the process more efficient by minimizing computation time and manual intervention?

   A. Translate the normalization algorithm into SQL for use with BigQuery.

   B. Normalize the data with Apache Spark using the Dataproc connector for BigQuery.

   C. Normalize the data with TensorFlow data transform.

   D. Normalize the data by running jobs in Google Kubernetes Engine clusters.

3. You are an ML engineer for a fashion apparel company designing a customized deep neural network in Keras that predicts customer purchases based on their purchase history. You want to explore model performance using multiple model architectures, to store training data, and to compare the evaluation metric while the job is running. What should you do?

   A. Create multiple models using AutoML Tables.

   B. Create an experiment in Kubeflow Pipelines to organize multiple runs.

   C. Run multiple training jobs on the Vertex AI platform with an interactive shell enabled.

   D. Run multiple training jobs on the Vertex AI platform with hyperparameter tuning.

4. You are a data scientist who has created an ML pipeline with hyperparameter tuning jobs using Vertex AI custom jobs. One of your tuning jobs is taking longer than expected and delaying the downstream processes. You want to speed up the tuning job without significantly compromising its effectiveness. Which actions should you take? (Choose three.)

   A. Decrease the number of parallel trials.

   B. Change the search algorithm from grid search to random search.

   C. Decrease the range of floating-point values.

   D. Change the algorithm to grid search.

   E. Set the early stopping parameter to TRUE.

5. You are a data engineer using PySpark data pipelines to conduct data transformations at scale on Google Cloud. However, your pipelines are taking over 12 hours to run. In order to expedite pipeline runtime, you do not want to manage servers and need a tool that can run SQL. You have already moved your raw data into Cloud Storage. How should you build the pipeline on Google Cloud while meeting speed and processing requirements?

   A. Use Data Fusion's GUI to build the transformation pipelines, and then write the data into BigQuery.

   B. Convert your PySpark commands into Spark SQL queries to transform the data and then run your pipeline on Dataproc to write the data into BigQuery using BigQuery Spark connector.

   C. Ingest your data into BigQuery from Cloud Storage, convert your PySpark commands into BigQuery SQL queries to transform the data, and then write the transformations to a new table.

   D. Ingest your data into Cloud SQL, convert your PySpark commands into Spark SQL queries to transform the data, and then use SQL queries from BigQuery for machine learning.

6. You are a lead data scientist manager who is managing a team of data scientists using a cloud-based system to submit training jobs. This system has become very difficult to administer. The data scientists you work with use many different frameworks such as Keras, PyTorch, Scikit, and custom libraries. What is the most managed way to run the jobs in Google Cloud?

   A. Use the Vertex AI training custom containers to run training jobs using any framework.

   B. Use the Vertex AI training prebuilt containers to run training jobs using any framework.

   C. Configure Kubeflow to run on Google Kubernetes Engine and receive training jobs through TFJob.

   D. Create containerized images on Compute Engine using GKE and push these images on a centralized repository.

7. You are training a TensorFlow model on a structured dataset with 500 billion records stored in several CSV files. You need to improve the input/output execution performance. What should you do?

   A. Load the data into HDFS.

   B. Load the data into Cloud Bigtable, and read the data from Bigtable using a TF Bigtable connector.

   C. Convert the CSV files into shards of TFRecords, and store the data in Cloud Storage.

   D. Load the data into BigQuery using Dataflow jobs.

8. You are the senior solution architect of a gaming company. You have to design a streaming pipeline for ingesting player interaction data for a mobile game. You want to perform ML on the streaming data. What should you do to build a pipeline with the least overhead?

   A. Use Pub/Sub with Cloud Dataflow streaming pipeline to ingest data.

   B. Use Apache Kafka with Cloud Dataflow streaming pipeline to ingest data.

   C. Use Apache Kafka with Cloud Dataproc to ingest data.

   D. Use Pub/Sub Lite streaming connector with Cloud Data Fusion.

9. You are a data scientist working on a smart city project to build an ML model to detect anomalies in real-time sensor data. You will use Pub/Sub to handle incoming requests. You want to store the results for analytics and visualization. How should you configure the below pipeline:

   Ingest data using Pub/Sub-> 1. Preprocess -> 2. ML training

   -> 3. Storage -> Visualization in Data Studio

   A. 1. Dataflow, 2. Vertex AI Training, 3. BigQuery

   B. 1. Dataflow, 2. Vertex AI AutoML, 3. Bigtable

   C. 1. BigQuery, 2. Vertex AI Platform, 3. Cloud Storage

   D. 1. Dataflow, 2. Vertex AI AutoML, 3. Cloud Storage

10. You are a data scientist who works for a Fintech company. You want to understand how effective your company's latest advertising campaign for a financial product is. You have streamed 900 MB of campaign data into BigQuery. You want to query the table and then manipulate the results of that query with a pandas DataFrame in a Vertex AI platform notebook. What will be the least number of steps needed to do this?

    A. Download your table from BigQuery as a local CSV file, and upload it to your AI platform notebook instance. Use pandas `read_csv` to ingest the file as a pandas DataFrame.

    B. Export your table as a CSV file from BigQuery to Google Drive, and use the Google Drive API to ingest the file into your notebook instance.

    C. Use the Vertex AI platform notebook's BigQuery cell magic to query the data, and ingest the results as a pandas DataFrame using pandas BigQuery client.

    D. Use the `bq extract` command to export the table as a CSV file to Cloud Storage, and then use `gsui cp` to copy the data into the notebook Use pandas `read_csv` to ingest the file.

11. You are a data scientist working on a fraud detection model. You will use Pub/Sub to handle incoming requests. You want to store the results for analytics and visualization. How should you configure the following pipeline:

    1. Ingest data -> 2. Preprocess -> 3. ML training and visualize in Data/Looker Studio

    A. 1. Dataflow, 2. Vertex AI Training, 3. BigQuery

    B. 1. Pub/Sub, 2. Dataflow, 3. BigQuery ML

    C. 1. Pub/Sub, 2. Dataflow, 3. Vertex AI Training

    D. 1. Dataflow, 2. Vertex AI AutoML, 3. Cloud Storage

12. You are an ML engineer working for a public health team to create a pipeline to classify support tickets on Google Cloud. You analyzed the requirements and decided to use TensorFlow to build the classifier so that you have full control of the model's code, serving, and deployment. You will use Kubeflow Pipelines for the ML platform. To save time, you want to build on existing resources and use managed services instead of building a completely new model. How should you build the classifier?

    A. Use an established text classification model and train using Vertex AI Training as is to classify support requests.

    B. Use an established text classification model and train using Vertex AI Training to perform transfer learning.

    C. Use AutoML Natural Language to build the support requests classifier.

    D. Use the Natural Language API to classify support requests.

13. You are training a TensorFlow model for binary classification with a lot of categorical features using Vertex AI custom jobs. You are looking for UI tools to track metrics of your model such as CPU utilization and network I/O and features used while training. Which tools will you pick? (Choose two.)

    A. Interactive shell

    B. TensorFlow Profiler

    C. Jupyter Notebooks

    D. Looker Studio

    E. Looker

14. You are training a TensorFlow model to identify semi-finished products using Vertex AI custom jobs. You want to monitor the performance of the model. Which of the following can you use?

    A. TensorFlow Profiler

    B. TensorFlow Debugger

    C. TensorFlow Trace

    D. TensorFlow Checkpoint

15. You are a data scientist working for a start-up on several projects with TensorFlow. Your data is in Parquet format and you need to manage input and output. You are looking for the most cost-effective solution to manage the input while training TensorFlow models on Google Cloud. Which of the following should you use?

    A. TensorFlow I/O

    B. Cloud Dataproc

    C. Cloud Dataflow

    D. BigQuery to TFRecords

16. You are training a TensorFlow model for binary classification with many categorical features using Vertex AI custom jobs. Your manager has asked you about the classification metric and also to explain the inference. You would like to show them an interactive demo with visual graphs. Which tool should you use?

A. TensorBoard

B. What-If Tool

C. Looker

D. Language Interpretability Tool (LIT)

Chapter

9

Model Explainability on Vertex AI

GOOGLE CLOUD PROFESSIONAL MACHINE LEARNING ENGINEER EXAM OBJECTIVES COVERED IN THIS CHAPTER:

✓ **6.1 Identifying risks to ML solutions. Considerations include:**

- Building secure ML systems (e.g., protecting against unintentional exploitation of data or models, hacking)
- Aligning with Google's Responsible AI practices (e.g., biases)
- Assessing ML solution readiness (e.g., data bias, fairness)
- Model explainability on Vertex AI (e.g., Vertex AI Prediction)

In this chapter, we will cover what explainable AI is and why it's important in machine learning. We will talk about the details of model explainability techniques on the Vertex AI platform and use cases to apply.

Model Explainability on Vertex AI

For a team developing ML models, the responsibility to explain model predictions increases as the impact of predictions on business outcomes increases. For example, consumers are likely to accept a movie recommendation from an ML model without needing an explanation. The consumer may or may not agree with the recommendation, but the need to justify the prediction is relatively low on the model developers.

On the contrary, if an ML model predicts whether a credit loan application is approved or a patient's drug dosage is correct, the model developers are responsible for explaining the prediction. They need to address questions such as "Why was my loan rejected?" or "Why should I take 10 mg of this drug?" For this reason, gaining visibility into the training process and developing human-explainable ML models is important.

Explainable AI

Explainability is the extent to which you can explain the internal mechanics of an ML or deep learning system in human terms. It is in contrast to the concept of the black box, in which even designers cannot explain why an AI arrives at a specific decision.

There are two types of explainability, global and local:

- *Global explainability* aims at making the overall ML model transparent and comprehensive.

- *Local explainability* focuses on explaining the model's individual predictions.

The ability to explain an ML model and its predictions builds trust and improves ML adoption. The model is no longer a black box. This increases the comfort level of the consumers of model predictions. For model owners, the ability to understand the uncertainty inherent in ML models helps with debugging the model when things go wrong and improving the model for better business outcomes.

Debugging machine learning models is complex because of deep neural nets. As the number of variables increases, it becomes really hard to see what feature contributed to which outcome. Linear models are easily explained and interpreted since the input parameters have a linear relationship with the output: (X = ax + y), where X is the predicted output depending on x and y (input parameters). With models based on decision trees such as XGBoost and deep neural nets, this mathematical relationship to determine the output from a set of inputs gets complex, leading to difficulty in debugging these models. That is why explainable techniques are needed to explain the model.

Interpretability and Explainability

Interpretability and *explainability* are often used interchangeably. However, there is a slight difference in what they mean. Interpretability has to do with how accurately a machine learning model can associate a cause to an effect. Explainability has to do with explaining the ability of the parameters hidden in deep neural nets (which we covered in Chapter 7, "Model Building") to justify the results.

Feature Importance

Feature importance is a technique that explains the features that make up the training data using a score (importance). It indicates how useful or valuable the feature is relative to other features. In the use case of individual income prediction using XGBoost, the importance score indicates the value of each feature in the construction of the boosted decision trees within the model. The more a model uses an attribute to make key decisions with decision trees, the higher the attribute's relative importance.

The following are the most important benefits of using feature importance:

- **Variable selection:** Suppose you are training with 1,000 variables. You can easily figure out which variables are not important or contributing less to your model prediction and easily remove those variables before deploying the model in production. This can save a lot of compute and infrastructure costs and training time.

- **Target/label or data leakage in your model:** Data leakage occurs when by mistake you have added your target variable (the feature you are trying to predict) in your training dataset as a feature. We covered this in Chapter 2, "Exploring Data and Building Data Pipelines."

Vertex Explainable AI

Vertex Explainable AI integrates feature attributions into Vertex AI and helps you understand your model's outputs for classification and regression tasks. Vertex AI tells you how much each feature in the data contributed to the predicted result. You can then use this information to verify that the model is behaving as expected, recognize bias in your model, and get ideas for ways to improve your model and your training data. These are supported services for Vertex Explainable AI:

- AutoML image models (classification models only)
- AutoML tabular models (classification and regression models only)
- Custom-trained TensorFlow models based on tabular data
- Custom-trained TensorFlow models based on image data

Feature Attribution

Google Cloud's current offering in Vertex AI is centered around instance-level feature attributions, which provide a signed per-feature attribution score proportional to the feature's contribution to the model's prediction. Feature attributions indicate how much each feature in your model contributed to the predictions for each given instance. When you request predictions, you get the predicted values as appropriate for your model. When you request explanations, you get the predictions along with feature attribution information.

For more information, refer to `https://cloud.google.com/vertex-ai/docs/explainable-ai/overview#feature-based_explanations`.

Feature attribution functionality to get explainability is integrated into the Google Cloud console for AutoML Tables and AutoML Images. You can set feature attribution while training custom TensorFlow models using the Vertex AI Explainable SDK with Vertex AI Prediction.

The Vertex Explainable AI offers three methods to use for feature attributions: sampled Shapley, integrated gradients, and XRAI.

- **Sampled Shapley:** This assigns credit for the outcome to each feature and considers different permutations of the features. This method provides a sampling approximation of exact Shapley values. Figure 9.1 shows how you can use Shapley plots to determine the black box feature importance (`https://github.com/slundberg/shap`). You have four input variables in the model that is giving you an output. Using Shapley values, you can know which of these four features (age, sex, BP, BMI) contributed positively or negatively to the output or prediction.

FIGURE 9.1   SHAP model explainability

- **Integrated gradients:** There is a gradients-based method to efficiently compute feature attributions. This is mostly used in deep neural networks with image use cases. The gradient is calculated, which informs which pixel has the strongest effect on the model's predicted class probabilities. For example, an image classification model is trained to predict whether a given image contains a dog or a cat. If you request predictions from this model on a new set of images, then you receive a prediction for each image ("dog" or "cat"). If you request explanations, you get the predicted class along with an overlay for the image, showing which pixels in the image contributed most strongly to the resulting prediction, as shown in Figure 9.2. For more information, see `https://cloud.google.com/vertex-ai/docs/explainable-ai/overview#integrated-gradients`.

FIGURE 9.2   Feature attribution using integrated gradients for cat image

Source: Google LLC / `www.tensorflow.org/tutorials/interpretability/integrated_gradients` last accessed November 21, 2022.

Integrated gradients provide feature importance on individual examples; however, they do not provide global feature importance across an entire dataset. Also they do not explain feature interactions and combinations.

- **XRAI (eXplanation with Ranked Area Integrals):** Based on the integrated gradients method, XRAI assesses overlapping regions of the image to create a saliency map, which highlights relevant regions of the image rather than pixels. The XRAI method combines the integrated gradients method with additional steps to determine which *regions* of the image contribute the most to a given class prediction. XRAI does pixel-level segmentation, oversegmentation, and region selection to provide explanations in images. For more information, see `https://cloud.google.com/vertex-ai/docs/explainable-ai/overview#xrai`.

You do not need to understand the details of these methods for the exam. However, you would need to know when to use which technique for the use cases and data types in Vertex AI; see Table 9.1.

TABLE 9.1   Explainable techniques used by Vertex AI

Method	Supported Data Types	Model Types	Use Case	Vertex AI–Equivalent Model
Sampled Shapley	Tabular	Nondifferentiable models (explained after the table), such as ensembles of trees and neural networks.	Classification and regression on tabular data	Custom-trained models (any prediction container) AutoML tabular models
Integrated gradients	Image and tabular data	Differentiable models (explained after the table), such as neural networks. Recommended especially for models with large feature spaces. Recommended for low-contrast images, such as X-rays.	Classification and regression on tabular data Classification on image data	Custom-trained TensorFlow models that use a TensorFlow pre-built container to serve predictions AutoML image models
XRAI (eXplanation with Ranked Area Integrals)	Image data	Models that accept image inputs. Recommended especially for natural images, which are any real-world scenes that contain multiple objects.	Classification on image data	Custom-trained TensorFlow models that use a TensorFlow pre-built container to serve predictions AutoML image models

Source: `https://cloud.google.com/vertex-ai/docs/explainable-ai/overview#compare-methods`

We mention differentiable models and nondifferentiable models in Table 9.1. Let's talk about the basic difference between them:

- **Differentiable models:** You can calculate the derivative of all the operations in your TensorFlow graph. This property helps to make backpropagation possible in such models. For example, neural networks are differentiable. To get feature attributions for differentiable models, use the integrated gradients method.

- **Nondifferentiable models:** These include nondifferentiable operations in the TensorFlow graph, such as operations that perform decoding and rounding tasks. For example, a model built as an ensemble of trees and neural networks is nondifferentiable. To get feature attributions for nondifferentiable models, use the sampled Shapley method.

The integrated gradients method does not work for nondifferentiable models. Sampled Shapley works on differentiable and nondifferentiable models, but it's more compute intensive.

For an in-depth explanation, refer to the *AI Explanations Whitepaper* at `https://cloud.google.com/blog/products/ai-machine-learning/example-based-explanations-to-build-better-aiml-models`.

Vertex AI Example–Based Explanations

Example-based explanations are used for misclassification analysis and can enable active learning so that data can be selectively labeled. For instance, if out of 10 total explanations for an image, 5 are from class "bird" and five are from class "plane," the image can be a candidate for human annotation, further enriching the data.

Example-based explanations are not limited to images. They can generate embeddings for multiple types of data such as images, text, and table. Refer to this blog to learn more about this: `https://cloud.google.com/blog/products/ai-machine-learning/example-based-explanations-to-build-better-aiml-models`.

This feature is in public preview, and you might not get questions from this topic on the exam. However, it's a good topic to understand for the Explainable AI options provided by Google Cloud.

Data Bias and Fairness

Data can be biased when certain parts of the data are not collected or are misrepresented. This might happen using data collected through surveys, data that is based on systemic or historical beliefs, or a data sample that is not random or is too small. Any of these can lead to skewed outcomes, as biased data does not accurately represent the machine learning model use case. It also presents another problem of system prejudice or fairness in the data.

ML fairness ensures that biases in the data and model inaccuracies do not lead to models that treat individuals unfavorably on the basis of characteristics such as race, gender, disabilities, or sexual or political orientation—for example, granting a credit card based on gender or denying an application based on race.

The following list includes some of the ways you can detect bias and fairness in data in Vertex AI:

- The Explainable AI feature attributions technique, which is already present in AutoML tables, helps detect bias and fairness in the tabular or structured dataset.

- Use Vertex AI to inspect models through an interactive dashboard with the integrated What-If Tool. (We covered the What-If Tool in Chapter 8, "Model Training and Hyperparameter Tuning.") This tool can be used to detect bias in the dataset using the features overview functionality, which automatically detects bias from the data. You can refer to this link for more details: `https://pair-code.github.io/what-if-tool/learn/tutorials/features-overview-bias`.

- Alternatively, for detecting bias and fairness in NLP (natural language processing) models, you can utilize the open source Language Interpretability Tool.

By using these tools and techniques, you can detect bias and fairness in your dataset before training models on them during the data exploration or data preprocessing phase, which we covered in Chapter 2, "Exploring Data and Building Data Pipelines," and Chapter 3, "Feature Engineering."

ML Solution Readiness

We will talk about ML solution readiness in terms of these two concepts:

- Responsible AI
- Model governance

Google believes in Responsible AI principles, which we covered in Chapter 1, "Framing ML Problems." Google shares best practices with customers through Google Responsible AI practices, fairness best practices, technical references, and technical ethics materials.

Responsible AI tools are an increasingly effective way to inspect and understand AI models. Some of the tools are listed here:

- Explainable AI, which we covered earlier in this chapter—how you can have Explainable AI in your models using Vertex AI offerings.
- Model cards, which explain what a model does, its intended audience, and who maintains it. A model card also provides insight into the construction of the model, including its architecture and the training data used. Refer to this link to learn more about model cards: `https://modelcards.withgoogle.com/about`.
- TensorFlow open source toolkit to provide model transparency in a structured, accessible way.

Model governance is a core function in companies that provides guidelines and processes to help employees implement the company's AI principles. These principles can include avoiding models that create or enforce bias and being able to justify AI-made decisions.

Some of the ways you can achieve model governance are as follows:

- Make sure there is a human in the loop to review model output or prediction for sensitive and high-impact workloads.
- Have a responsibility assignment matrix for each model by task.
- Maintain model cards to track model versioning and data lineage.
- Evaluate the model on benchmark datasets that cover both standard cases and edge cases and validate the model against fairness indicators to help detect implicit bias.
- Use what-if analysis tools to understand the importance of different data features.

- All the model readiness best practices from data cleaning, training, and tuning to deploying the model are mentioned in this Google Cloud documentation: `https://cloud.google.com/architecture/guidelines-for-developing-high-quality-ml-solutions`.

How to Set Up Explanations in the Vertex AI

If you are using a custom-trained model (TensorFlow, Scikit, or XGBoost), which we covered in Chapter 8, you need to configure explanations for custom-trained models (`https://cloud.google.com/vertex-ai/docs/explainable-ai/configuring-explanations-feature-based`) to create a model that supports Vertex Explainable AI. For an AutoML tabular classification or regression, you do not need any specific configuration to use Vertex Explainable AI (`https://cloud.google.com/vertex-ai/docs/explainable-ai/getting-explanations`).

After having a model resource with Explainable AI created, you can perform the following explanations:

- **Online explanations:** Synchronous requests to the Vertex AI API, similar to online predictions that return predictions with feature attributions. For online explanations, instead of sending a `projects.locations.endpoints.predict` request to the Vertex AI API, send a `projects.locations.endpoints.explain` request.

- **Batch explanations:** Asynchronous requests to the Vertex AI API that return predictions with feature attributions. Batch explanations are an optional part of batch prediction requests. To get batch explanations, set the generateExplanation field to true when you create a batch prediction job.

- **Local kernel explanations:** Perform these in the User-Managed Vertex AI Workbench notebook we covered in Chapter 6, "Building Secure ML Pipelines." You can generate explanations for your custom-trained model by running the Vertex Explainable AI within your notebook's local kernel or runtime without deploying the model to Vertex AI to get explanations. Using local explanations allows you to try different Vertex Explainable AI settings without adjusting your Vertex AI model deployment for each change.

 The Explainable AI SDK is preinstalled in user-managed notebook instances. Within your notebook, you can use the Explainable AI SDK to save your model artifact and automatically identify metadata about your model's inputs and outputs for the explanation request.

If you're using TensorFlow, you can use the Explainable AI SDK's `save_model_with_metadata()` method to infer your model's inputs and outputs and save this explanation metadata with your model. Next, load the model into the Explainable AI SDK using `load_model_from_local_path()`. Finally, call `explain()` with instances of data, and visualize the feature attributions.

Summary

In this chapter, we discussed what explainable AI is and the difference between explainability and interpretability. Then we covered the term *feature importance* and why it's important to explain the models. We covered data bias and fairness as well as ML solution readiness.

Last, we covered the explainable AI technique on the Vertex AI platform and feature attribution. We covered three primary techniques for model feature attribution used on the Vertex AI platform: sampled Shapley, XRAI, and integrated gradients.

Exam Essentials

Understand model explainability on Vertex AI.   Know what explainability is and the difference between global and local explanations. Why is it important to explain models? What is feature importance? Understand the options of feature attribution on the Vertex AI platform such as Sampled Shapley algorithm, integrated gradients, and XRAI. We covered data bias and fairness and how feature attributions can help with determining bias and fairness from the data. ML Solution readiness talks about Responsible AI and ML model governance best practices. Understand that explainable AI in Vertex AI is supported for the TensorFlow prediction container using the Explainable AI SDK and for the Vertex AI AutoML tabular and AutoML image models.

Review Questions

1. You are a data scientist building a linear model with more than 100 input features, all with values between −1 and 1. You suspect that many features are non-informative. You want to remove the non-informative features from your model while keeping the informative ones in their original form. Which technique should you use?

    A. Use principal component analysis to eliminate the least informative features.

    B. When building your model, use Shapley values to determine which features are the most informative.

    C. Use L1 regularization to reduce the coefficients of noninformative features to 0.

    D. Use an iterative dropout technique to identify which features do not degrade the model when removed.

2. You are a data scientist at a startup and your team is working on a number of ML projects. Your team trained a TensorFlow deep neural network model for image recognition that works well and is about to be rolled out in production. You have been asked by leadership to demonstrate the inner workings of the model. What explainability technique would you use on Google Cloud?

    A. Sampled Shapley

    B. Integrated gradient

    C. PCA

    D. What-If Tool analysis

3. You are a data scientist working with Vertex AI and want to leverage Explainable AI to understand which are the most essential features and how they impact model predictions. Select the model types and services supported by Vertex Explainable AI. (Choose three.)

    A. AutoML Tables

    B. Image classification

    C. Custom DNN models

    D. Decision trees

    E. Linear learner

4. You are an ML engineer working with Vertex Explainable AI. You want to understand the most important features for training models that use image and tabular datasets. Which of the feature attribution techniques can you use? (Choose three.)

    A. XRAI

    B. Sampled Shapley

    C. Minimum likelihood

    D. Interpretability

    E. Integrated gradients

5. You are a data scientist training a TensorFlow model with graph operations as operations that perform decoding and rounding tasks. Which technique would you use to debug or explain this model in Vertex AI?

    A. Sampled Shapley

    B. Integrated gradients

    C. XRAI

    D. PCA

6. You are a data scientist working on creating an image classification model on Vertex AI. You want these images to have feature attribution. Which of the attribution techniques is supported by Vertex AI AutoML images? (Choose two.)

    A. Sampled Shapely

    B. Integrated gradients

    C. XRAI

    D. DNN

7. You are a data scientist working on creating an image classification model on Vertex AI. You want to set up an explanation for testing your TensorFlow code in user-managed notebooks. What is the suggested approach with the least effort?

    A. Set up local explanations using Explainable AI SDK in the notebooks.

    B. Configure explanations for the custom TensorFlow model.

    C. Set up an AutoML classification model to get explanations.

    D. Set the generateExplanation field to true when you create a batch prediction job.

8. You are a data scientist who works in the aviation industry. You have been given a task to create a model to identify planes. The images in the dataset are of poor quality. Your model is identifying birds as planes. Which approach would you use to help explain the predictions with this dataset?

    A. Use Vertex AI example–based explanations.

    B. Use the integrated gradients technique for explanations.

    C. Use the Sampled Shapley technique for explanations.

    D. Use the XRAI technique for explanations.

Chapter

10

Scaling Models in Production

GOOGLE CLOUD PROFESSIONAL MACHINE LEARNING ENGINEER EXAM OBJECTIVES COVERED IN THIS CHAPTER:

✓ **4.1 Serving models. Considerations include:**

- Batch and online inference (e.g., Vertex AI, Dataflow, BigQuery ML, Dataproc)
- Using different frameworks (e.g., PyTorch, XGBoost) to serve models
- Organizing a model registry
- A/B testing different versions of a model

✓ **4.2 Scaling online model serving. Considerations include:**

- Scaling the serving backend based on the throughput (e.g., Vertex AI Prediction, containerized serving)
- Tuning ML models for training and serving in production (e.g., simplification techniques, optimizing the ML solution for increased performance, latency, memory, throughput)

✓ **5.1 Developing end-to-end ML pipelines. Considerations include:**

- Hosting third-party pipelines on Google Cloud (e.g., MLFlow)

In this chapter, we will cover how you can deploy a model and scale it in production using TensorFlow Serving. Then we will cover Google Cloud architecture patterns for serving models online and in batches. We will also cover caching strategies with serving models in Google Cloud. We will talk about how you can set up real-time endpoints and batch jobs using Vertex AI Prediction. We will cover some of the challenges while testing a model for target performance in production. Last, we will cover ways to orchestrate triggers and pipelines for automating model training and prediction pipelines.

Scaling Prediction Service

For the exam, you need to understand how you would deploy a model trained using TensorFlow after training. Figure 10.1 recaps the training option in TensorFlow and various distribution strategies we covered using CPUs, GPUs, and TPUs with TensorFlow. After training, you get a saved model. A saved model contains a complete TensorFlow program, including trained parameters (i.e., `tf.Variables`) and computation. It does not require the original model building code to run, which makes it useful for sharing or deploying with TensorFlow Lite, TensorFlow.js, TensorFlow Serving, or TensorFlow Hub.

FIGURE 10.1 TF model serving options

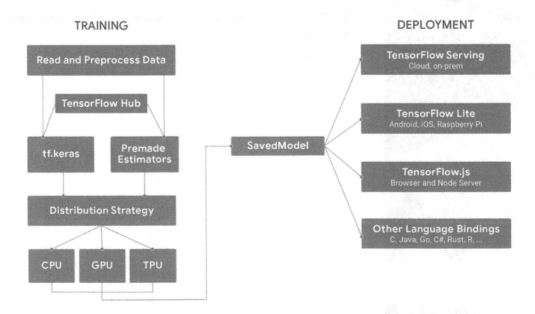

A saved model is what you get when you call `tf.saved_model.save()`. Saved models are stored as a directory on disk. The file, `saved_model.pb`, within that directory is a protocol buffer describing the function `tf.Graph`.

TensorFlow Serving

TensorFlow (TF) Serving allows you to host a trained TensorFlow model as an API endpoint through a model server. TensorFlow Serving handles the model serving and version management and lets you serve models. It allows you to load your models from different sources.

TensorFlow Serving allows two types of API endpoints: REST and gRPC.

These are the steps to set up TF Serving:

1. Install TensorFlow Serving with Docker.

2. Train and save a model with TensorFlow.

3. Serve the saved model using TensorFlow Serving.

See `www.tensorflow.org/tfx/serving/api_rest` for more information.

 You can install TensorFlow Serving without Docker, but using Docker is recommended and is certainly the easiest way to proceed. To manage TensorFlow Serving, you can choose to use a managed TensorFlow pre-built container on Vertex AI.

Serving a Saved Model with TensorFlow Serving

The TensorFlow ModelServer running on host:port accepts the following REST API requests:

```
POST http://host:port/<URI>:<VERB>
```

```
URI: /v1/models/${MODEL_NAME}[/versions/${MODEL_VERSION}]
VERB: classify|regress|predict
```

To call the `predict()` REST endpoint, you need to define a JSON data payload because TF Serving expects data as JSON, as shown here:

```
data = json.dumps({"signature_name": "serving_default",
 "instances": instances.tolist()})
  headers = {"content-type": "application/json"}
  json_response = requests.post(url, data=data, headers=headers)
  predictions = json.loads(json_response.text)['predictions']
```

The `signature_name` specifies the input/output data type. `Instances` is the data/input/instance you want to predict on. You should pass this as a list.

TF Serving handles all the model and API infrastructure for you so that you can focus on model optimization. For the exam, you might be given an instance and signature of a TF Serving JSON load and have to provide the `predict()` function output.

The following is an example of a tensor instance:

```
{
  // List of 2 tensors each of [1, 2] shape
  "instances": [ [[1, 2]], [[3, 4]] ]
}
```

To know what your `predict()` response format will be, you need to look at the Saved-Model's SignatureDef (for more information, see www.tensorflow.org/tfx/serving/signature_defs). You can use the SignatureDef CLI to inspect a saved model. The given SavedModel SignatureDef contains the following output(s):

```
outputs['class_ids'] tensor_info:
dtype: DT_INT64
shape: (-1, 1)
name: dnn/head/predictions/ExpandDims:0
outputs['classes'] tensor_info:
dtype: DT_STRING
shape: (-1, 1)
name: dnn/head/predictions/str_classes:0
outputs['logits'] tensor_info:
dtype: DT_FLOAT
shape: (-1, 3)
name: dnn/logits/BiasAdd:0
outputs['probabilities'] tensor_info:
dtype: DT_FLOAT
shape: (-1, 3)
name: dnn/head/predictions/probabilities:0
Method name is: tensorflow/serving/predict
```

Based on the previous SignatureDef, the `predict()` request returns a JSON object in the response body, as shown in the following code:

```
{
"predictions": [
```

```
{
"class_ids": [3],
"probabilities": [2.0495e-7, 0.0243, 0.9756],
"classes": ["2"],
"logits": [-5.74621, 5.94074, 9.62958]
}
]
}
```

The previous example has a class ID integer with shape (–1,1) classes as strings with shape (–1,1), logits as float with shape (–1,3), and probability as float with shape (–1,3).

Since both the shape of class ID and class is (–1,1), there will be only one value in the prediction for them. Similarly, for both probability and logit, the shape (–1,3) will give three tensor values in response. –1 means we can pass on any size to the saved model.

For the exam, you need to understand what the tensor shape means in the SignatureDef of the saved model and what the predict response can be, based on the shape of tensors in the SignatureDef.

Once the model is available in the model directory or folder, TF Serving automatically loads a new model. Moreover, when a new model version is available, TF Serving automatically unloads the old model and loads the newer version. This technique is very efficient and can be easily added into an MLOps pipeline. This helps you to focus more on model optimization instead of model serving infrastructure. We will cover the topic System design using TFX/Kubeflow in Chapter 11, "Designing ML Training Pipelines."

For more information, see `https://neptune.ai/blog/how-to-serve-machine-learning-models-with-tensorflow-serving-and-docker`.

Serving (Online, Batch, and Caching)

In Chapter 5, "Architecting ML Solutions," we covered two types of serving options in ML systems, batch prediction (or offline serving) and online prediction, and their recommended architectures. In this chapter, we will cover some best practices for your serving and caching strategy.

Real-Time Static and Dynamic Reference Features

There are two types of input features that are fetched in real time to invoke the model for prediction: static reference features and dynamic reference features. Let's look at Table 10.1 to understand the differences.

TABLE 10.1 Static vs. dynamic features

Static Reference Features	Dynamic Real-Time Features
Their values do not change in real time. Instead, the values are usually updated in a batch.	Real-time features are computed on the fly in an event-stream processing pipeline.
These types of features are usually available in a data warehouse—for example, customer ID and movie ID.	For real-time features, you need a list of aggregated values for a particular window (fixed, sliding, or session) in a certain period of time and not an overall aggregation of values within that period of time.
Use cases are estimating the price of a house based on the location of the house or recommending similar products given the attributes of the products that a customer is currently viewing.	Use cases can be predicting whether an engine will fail in the next hour given real-time sensor data. Another use case can be in recommending the next news article to read based on the list of last N viewed articles by the user during the current session.
These types of static reference features are stored in a NoSQL database that *is* optimized for singleton lookup operations, such as Firestore. BigQuery is not optimized for singleton reads, for example, a query like "Select 100 columns from several tables for a specific customer ID," where the result is a single row with many columns.	You can use a Dataflow streaming pipeline to implement this use case for dynamic feature read. For dynamic feature creation, the pipeline captures and aggregates (sum, mean, and so on) the events in real time and stores them in a low-latency read/write database. Cloud Bigtable is a good option for a low-latency read/write database for feature values.
Static reference architecture (see Figure 10.2).	Dynamic reference architecture (see Figure 10.3).

FIGURE 10.2   Static reference architecture

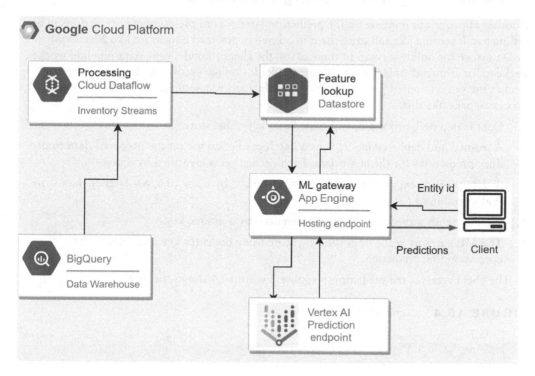

FIGURE 10.3   Dynamic reference architecture

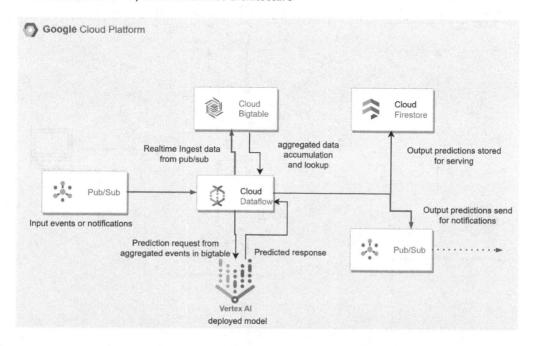

Pre-computing and Caching Prediction

Another approach to improve online prediction latency is to pre-compute predictions in an offline batch scoring job and store them in a low-latency read data store like Memorystore or Datastore for online serving. In these cases, the client (mobile, web, data pipeline worker, backend, or frontend API) doesn't call the model for online prediction. Instead, the client fetches the pre-computed predictions from the data store, assuming the prediction exists. The process works like this:

1. Data is ingested, processed, and stored in a key-value store.

2. A trained and deployed model runs a batch prediction job on the prepared data to produce predictions for the input data. Each prediction is identified by a key.

3. A data pipeline exports the predictions referenced by a key to a low-latency data store that's optimized for singleton reads.

4. A client sends a prediction request referenced by a unique key.

5. The ML gateway reads from the data store using the entry key and returns the corresponding prediction.

   The client receives the prediction response. Figure 10.4 shows the flow.

FIGURE 10.4   Caching architecture

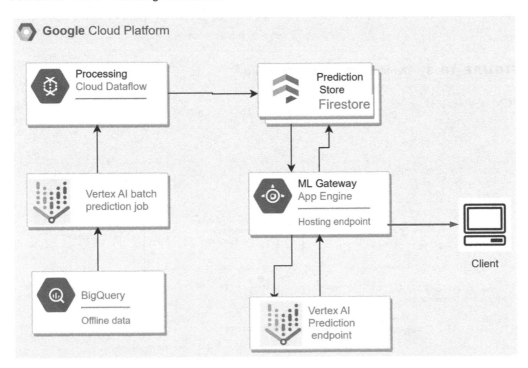

Prediction requests can be used for two categories of lookup keys:

- Specific entity where predictions relate to a single entity based on an ID such as custom-erid, or a deviceid, or a specific combination of input features. If you have too many entities (high cardinality), it can be challenging to precompute prediction in a limited amount of time. An example is forecasting daily sales by item when you have hundreds of thousands or millions of items. In that case, you can use a hybrid approach as per the architecture diagram, where you precompute predictions for the top N entities, such as for the most active customers or the most viewed products. You can then use the model directly for online prediction for the rest of the entities.

- Specific combination of input features to figure out whether an anonymous or a new customer will buy something on your website. When you have a combination of input features, you would create a hashed approach where the key is a hashed combination of all possible input features and the value is the prediction.

Google Cloud Serving Options

In Google Cloud, you can deploy your models for either online predictions or batch predictions. You can perform batch and online predictions for both AutoML and custom models. In the following sections, we will cover how to set up online and batch jobs using Vertex AI.

Online Predictions

To set up a real-time prediction endpoint, you might have these two use cases:

- **Models trained in Vertex AI using Vertex AI training:** This can be AutoML or custom models, as explained in Chapter 8, "Model Training and Hyperparameter Tuning."

- **Model trained elsewhere (on-premise, on another cloud, or in local device):** If you already have a model trained elsewhere, you need to import the model to Google Cloud before deploying and creating an endpoint.

If you are importing as a prebuilt container, ensure that your model artifacts have filenames that exactly match the following examples:

- **TensorFlow SavedModel:** `saved_model.pb`

- **scikit-learn:** `model.joblib` or `model.pkl`

- **XGBoost:** `model.bst`, `model.joblib`, or `model.pkl`

If you are importing a custom container, you need to create a container image and push the image possibly using Cloud Build to Artifact Registry as per the requirements for custom container hosting.

For both options, you need to follow these steps to set up Vertex AI predictions:

1. Deploy the model resource to an endpoint.

2. Make a prediction.

3. Undeploy the model resource if the endpoint is not in use.

Deploying the Model

When you deploy the model using the Vertex AI Prediction endpoint, you specify the auto-scaling for the endpoint's container (TensorFlow, scikit-learn, or XGBoost). Vertex AI automatically provisions the container resources and sets up autoscaling for your endpoint. You can deploy more than one model to an endpoint, and you can deploy a model to more than one endpoint. There are two ways you can deploy the model using an API and using the Google Cloud console.

Deploying a Model Using an API

You can deploy your model by calling the Vertex AI `deploy` function on the `Model` resource. The `deploy` method will create an endpoint and also deploy your model on the endpoint. You need to provide a traffic-split, machine-type GPU and the min nodes to set the `deploy` method. The following `deploy` function returns an `Endpoint` object.

```
Endpoint = model.deploy(
    deployed_model_display_name=DEPLOYED_NAME,
    traffic_split=TRAFFIC_SPLIT,
    machine_type=DEPLOY_COMPUTE,
    accelerator_type=DEPLOY_GPU.name,
    accelerator_count=DEPLOY_NGPU,
    min_replica_count=MIN_NODES,
    max_replica_count=MAX_NODES,
)
```

The previous Vertex AI function takes the following parameters:

`deployed_model_display_name`: A human readable name for the deployed model.

`TRAFFIC_SPLIT`: Percent of traffic at the endpoint that goes to this model, which is specified as a dictionary of one or more key/value pairs.

If only one model, then specify as { "0": 100 }, where "0" refers to this model being uploaded and 100 means 100% of the traffic.

If there are existing models on the endpoint, for which the traffic will be split, then use `model_id` to specify as { "0": percent, `model_id`: percent, . . . }, where `model_id` is the model ID of an existing model to the deployed endpoint. The percentages must add up to 100.

> Traffic splits help split traffic between two versions of a model. These versions can be used for A/B testing, which we will cover in the next section.

`machine_type`: The type of machine to use for training.

`accelerator_type`: The hardware accelerator type.

`accelerator_count`: The number of accelerators to attach to a worker replica.

`starting_replica_count`: The number of compute instances to initially provision.

`max_replica_count`: The maximum number of compute instances to scale to. In this tutorial, only one instance is provisioned.

You can deploy the model using the previous API or using the Google Cloud console.

Deploying a Model Using the Google Cloud Console

If you are using the GCP console, you can deploy the model by going to the Model Registry. The Model Registry is a centralized place to track versions of both AutoML and custom models. You can also choose the version you want to deploy. Vertex AI – trained AutoML and custom models appear in the Model Registry automatically. You can select the model and version, click the three dots, and select Deploy To Endpoint to deploy your model.

When you click Deploy To Endpoint in the Model Registry, you are redirected to the page to define the endpoint, as shown in Figure 10.5. In the Model settings section, you can define traffic split, compute resources, and autoscaling options, and in the Model monitoring section, you can enable the option to monitor the model in production for any drift.

FIGURE 10.5 Deploying to an endpoint

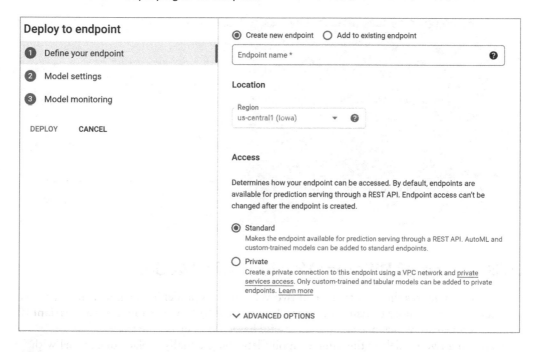

Your Model Registry has an IMPORT option to upload models from anywhere. If you have models trained in BigQuery ML, you can register them with the Vertex AI Model Registry.

Make Predictions

Before you can run the data through the endpoint, you need to preprocess it to match the format that your custom model defined in `task.py` expects. Use the `Endpoint` object's `predict` function, which takes the following parameters:

- You will see in the output for each prediction the confidence level for the prediction.

  ```
  predictions = endpoint.predict(instances=x_test)
  ```

  You get a REST endpoint ID that you can embed in a website or API gateway or App Engine to create an ML gateway for real-time prediction.

- If you're using one of the prebuilt containers to serve predictions using TensorFlow, scikit-learn, or XGBoost, your prediction input instances need to be formatted as JSON.

- If your model uses a custom container, your input must be formatted as JSON, and there is an additional parameters field that can be used for your container.

Go to the Endpoints page in the Vertex AI GCP console, select the endpoint, and click the sample request. You will then get instructions on how to preprocess your data to get predictions using the endpoint in REST and Python, as shown in Figure 10.6.

FIGURE 10.6   Sample prediction request

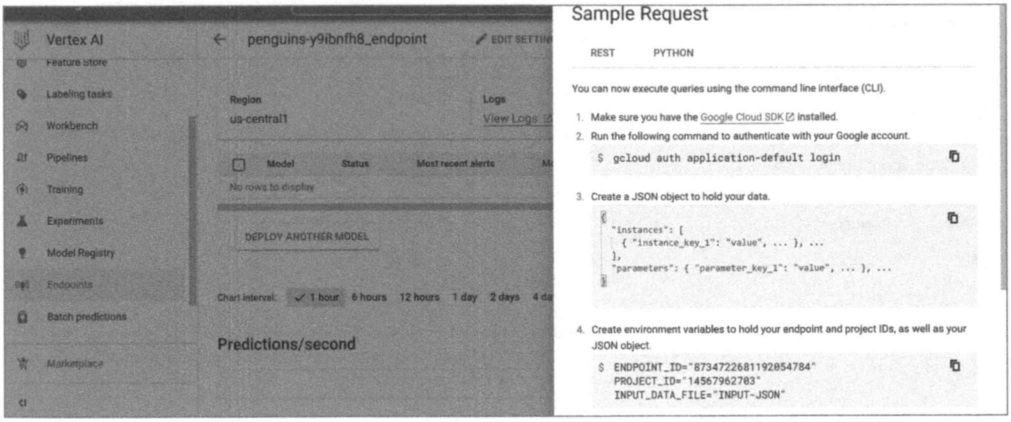

A/B Testing of Different Versions of a Model

A/B testing compares the performance of two versions of a model in machine learning to see which one appeals more to visitors/viewers. It tests a control (A) version against a variant (B) version to measure which one is most successful based on your key metrics.

Deploying two models to the same endpoint lets you gradually replace one model with the other. In scenarios for A/B testing where you don't want to create sudden changes in your application, you can add the new model to the same endpoint, serving a small percentage of traffic, and gradually increase the traffic split for the new model until it is serving 100 percent of the traffic.

For A/B testing in Vertex AI, we covered the traffic-split parameter while deploying a model. You can provide the model_id and the split value to split the traffic to this traffic-split parameter while hosting two models to the same endpoint. Here's an example using the gcloud command in the Cloud Shell:

```
gcloud ai endpoints update <Endpoint > --region=us-central1
 --traffic-split=[DEPLOYED_MODEL_ID=Value] --service-account= <Service account >
--project= <Project>
--traffic-split=[DEPLOYED_MODEL_ID=VALUE,...]
```

In the above code, traffic-split parameters take a list of deployed model id and their value set as traffic-split. Check out this link to learn more about the parameters to deploy models:

https://cloud.google.com/sdk/gcloud/reference/ai/endpoints/update

Since the resources are associated with the model rather than the endpoint, you could deploy models of different types to the same endpoint. However, the best practice is to deploy models of a specific type (for example, AutoML text, AutoML tabular, custom-trained) to an endpoint. This configuration is easier to manage.

Out of the box, other than using traffic-split, Vertex AI does not have all the capabilities that you typically have for A/B testing like controlling the model traffic, experimentation, tracking results, comparison, and so on.

However, you can use the Vertex AI model evaluations feature with Vertex AI Model Monitoring to create a setup for A/B testing. This feature is in experimental release right now.

The Vertex AI model evaluation feature allows you to run model evaluation jobs (measure model performance on a test dataset) regardless of which Vertex service is used to train the model (AutoML, managed pipelines, custom training, etc.), and store and visualize the evaluation results across multiple models in the Vertex AI Model Registry. With these capabilities, Vertex AI model evaluation enables users to decide which model(s) can progress to online testing or be put into production and, once they're in production, when models need to be retrained.

Undeploy Endpoints

If you do not have a critical business and you need to get endpoints up and running for a few hours in a day or during weekdays, you would need to undeploy the endpoints. You incur charges for a running endpoint. So, it's better to undeploy them when they're not in use. You can use the undeploy function to undeploy, as shown in the following Python code snippet:

```
deployed_model_id = endpoint.list_models()[0].id
endpoint.undeploy(deployed_model_id=deployed_model_id)
```

Send an Online Explanation Request

If you have configured your model for the Vertex Explainable AI, then you can get online explanations. Online explanation requests have the same format as online prediction requests, and they return similar responses; the only difference is that online explanation responses include feature attributions as well as predictions. The following sample Python code sends an online explanation request using the Vertex AI Python SDK:

```
aiplatform.init(project=project, location=location)

endpoint = aiplatform.Endpoint(endpoint_id)

response = endpoint.explain(instances=[instance_dict], parameters={})
```

Batch Predictions

In batch prediction, you point to the model and the input data (production data) in Google Cloud Storage and run a batch prediction job. The job runs the prediction using the model on the input data and saves the predictions output in Cloud Storage.

You need to make sure your input data is formatted as per the requirements for either an AutoML model (vision, video, image, text, tabular) or a custom model (prebuilt or custom container). To get batch predictions from a custom-trained model, prepare your input data in one of the ways described in Table 10.2.

TABLE 10.2   Input data options for batch training in Vertex AI

Input	Description
JSON Lines	Use a JSON Lines file to specify a list of input instances to make predictions about. Store the JSON Lines file in a Cloud Storage bucket.
TFRecord	You can optionally compress the TFRecord files with gzip. Store the TFRecord files in a Cloud Storage bucket. Vertex AI reads each instance in your TFRecord files as binary, then base64-encodes the instance as a JSON object with a single key named b64.
CSV files	Specify one input instance per row in a CSV file. The first row must be a header row. You must enclose all strings in double quotation marks (").
File list	Create a text file where each row is the Cloud Storage URI to a file. Example: gs://path/to/image/image1.jpg.
BigQuery	Specify a BigQuery table as projectId.datasetId.tableId. Vertex AI transforms each row from the table to a JSON instance.

Similar to online prediction, you can use either Vertex AI APIs or the Google Cloud console to create a batch prediction job (see Figure 10.7).

FIGURE 10.7   Batch prediction job in Console

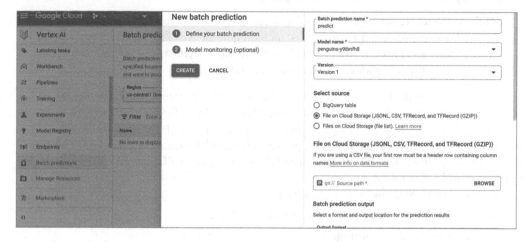

You can select for output either a BigQuery table or a Google Cloud Storage bucket. You can also enable model monitoring (in Preview) to detect skew.

For the exam, it's important to understand when to apply batch predictions and when to recommend online predictions in a use case. If the data is to be predicted in near real time, suggest online predictions; otherwise, suggest batch prediction.

Hosting Third-Party Pipelines (MLflow) on Google Cloud

In this section, we will cover various ways you can host third-party pipelines on Google Cloud that are specific to MLflow. MLflow (https://mlflow.org/docs/latest/concepts.html) is an open source platform for managing the end-to-end machine learning life cycle. It is library agnostic, and you can use it with any machine learning library and in any programming language. It tackles four primary functions:

MLflow Tracking   For experiment tracking and to record and compare parameters and results. You can think of this similar to Vertex AI Experiments used to track experiments in Vertex AI. We will cover experiments in upcoming Chapter 14.

MLflow Projects   For packaging ML code in a reusable, reproducible form in order to share with other data scientists or transfer to production.

MLflow Models   For managing and deploying models from a variety of ML libraries to a variety of model serving and inference platforms.

MLflow Model Registry   For providing a central model store to collaboratively manage the full life cycle of an MLFlow Model, including model versioning, stage transitions, and annotations. This is similar to the Vertex AI Model Registry, which is a centralized place to store models with versioning and annotations.

You can use each of these components on their own. For example, maybe you want to track experiments using MLflow without using MLflow Model Registry or Projects.

You would use MLflow on Google Cloud to leverage the scalability and availability provided by the Google Cloud Vertex AI platform for model training and hosting. You have access to high-performance compute such as GPUs, TPUs, and CPUs to run MLflow training and host workloads on Google Cloud.

To run or install MLflow on Google Cloud:

- Create a PostgreSQL DB for storing model metadata.

- Create a Google Cloud Storage bucket for storing artifacts.

- Create a Compute Engine instance to install MLFlow and run the MLFlow server, or you can run MLFlow Projects with Docker environments on Kubernetes.

You can also run MLFlow using a Google Cloud plug-in without needing to install the Docker image provided by MLFlow. Refer to this link for plug-in details:

```
https://pypi.org/project/google-cloud-mlflow
```

Testing for Target Performance

Some of the things you need to consider while testing your model for performance in production are as follows:

- You need to check for training-serving skew in the model and test the quality of the model in production with the real-time data.

- You can monitor the model age and performance throughout an ML pipeline.

- You can test that model weights and outputs are numerically stable. For example, during model training, your weights and layer outputs should not be NaN or null. You need to write tests to check for NaN and null values of model weights and layer outputs. Moreover, you need to test that more than half of the outputs of a layer are not zero.

Vertex AI has services such as Vertex AI Model Monitoring and Vertex AI Feature Store that can help solve some of the testing issues for your deployed model in production, such as detecting skew and monitoring model performance over time.

For more information, see `https://developers.google.com/machine-learning/testing-debugging/pipeline/production`.

Configuring Triggers and Pipeline Schedules

For this section, you need to know how to trigger a training or prediction job on the Vertex AI platform based on the use case.

For example, to trigger a real-time prediction job, you can set up the prediction endpoint on the Google Cloud App Engine to create a serverless ML gateway. We covered the architecture pattern in the section "Serving (Online, Batch, and Caching)" earlier in this chapter.

The following are some of the services that will help create a trigger and schedule the training or prediction jobs on Vertex AI:

- Cloud Scheduler can help you set up a cron job schedule to schedule your Vertex AI training or prediction jobs.

- With Vertex AI managed notebooks, you can execute and schedule a Vertex training and prediction job using the Jupyter Notebook. Refer to this link to learn more: `https://cloud.google.com/vertex-ai/docs/workbench/managed/schedule-managed-notebooks-run-quickstart`.

- Cloud Build is the CI/CD offering on GCP. If you want to retrain a model or build a Dockerfile and push it for custom training, use Cloud Build to kick it off. Cloud Run is a managed offering to deploy containers. Imagine that the container you're deploying is a Flask or FastAPI app that has your model. You can use Cloud Build to deploy your application to Cloud Run.

- You can also use event-driven serverless Cloud Functions and Cloud Pub/Sub. Cloud Functions are serverless and stateless functions as a service (FaaS), and Pub/Sub implements the publisher-subscriber pattern. You can use an event-based Cloud Storage trigger for a Cloud Function so that if a new version of a model is added to a bucket, you can activate a Cloud Function to start the deployment.

It's a challenge to use Cloud Function and Pub/Sub when there are multiple Cloud Functions doing multiple things. For example, Cloud Function A triggers data transform, then cloud function B triggers model training, and finally, Cloud Function C deploys the model. In this case, you would need an orchestrator to orchestrate these events in a pipeline. To orchestrate data cleaning, data transformation, model deployment, and model training using Cloud Functions, you can use Cloud *Workflows*.

Cloud Workflows orchestrate multiple HTTP-based services into a durable and stateful workflow. Workflows are great for chaining microservices together, automating infrastructure tasks like starting or stopping a VM, and integrating with external systems. Workflow connectors also support simple sequences of operations in Google Cloud services such as Cloud Storage and BigQuery.

If you do not want to orchestrate using a Cloud Function, use Cloud Scheduler and Workflows.

Vertex AI provides the orchestration choices such as Vertex AI pipelines listed in Table 10.3, which we will cover in detail in the next chapter (Chapter 11, "Designing ML Training Pipelines").

TABLE 10.3   ML orchestration options

Option	Description
Vertex AI Pipelines	Vertex AI Pipelines helps you to automate, monitor, and govern your ML systems by orchestrating your ML workflow in a serverless manner and storing your workflow's artifacts using Vertex ML Metadata. By storing the artifacts of your ML workflow in Vertex ML Metadata, you can analyze the lineage of your workflow's artifact.
Cloud Composer	Cloud Composer is designed to orchestrate data-driven workflows (particularly ETL/ELT). It's built on the Apache Airflow project, but Cloud Composer is fully managed. Cloud Composer supports your pipelines wherever they are, including on-premises or across multiple cloud platforms. All logic in Cloud Composer, including tasks and scheduling, is expressed in Python as directed acyclic graph (DAG) definition files.

 We also covered the TFX pipelines and Kubeflow pipelines to orchestrate Kubeflow and TensorFlow workloads in Chapter 5.

Read this blog for more information: `https://cloud.google.com/blog/topics/developers-practitioners/choosing-right-orchestrator-google-cloud`.

Summary

In this chapter, we covered the details of TF Serving in scaling prediction service.

We discussed the `predict` function in TF Serving and how to know the output based on the SignatureDef of the saved TF model.

Then we discussed architecture for online serving. We dove deep into static and dynamic reference architectures. Then we discussed the architecture to use pre-computing and caching while serving predictions.

We also covered how to deploy models using online and batch mode with Vertex AI Prediction and Google Cloud serving options. We covered the reasons for performance degradation in production when testing for target performance such as training-serving skew, change in data quality, and so on. You learned about tools such as Vertex AI Model Monitoring that can help in testing for models in production.

Last, you learned about ways to configure triggers and schedules to automate a model pipeline, such as Cloud Run, Cloud Build, Cloud Scheduler, Vertex AI managed notebooks, and Cloud Composer.

Exam Essentials

Understand TensorFlow Serving.   Understand what TensorFlow Serving is and how to deploy a trained TensorFlow model using TF Serving. Know the different ways to set up TF Serving with Docker. Understand the TF Serving prediction response based on a saved model's SignatureDef tensors.

Understand the scaling prediction services (online, batch, and caching).   Understand the difference between online batch and caching. For online serving, understand the differences in architecture and use cases with respect to input features that are fetched in real time to invoke the model for prediction (static reference features and dynamic reference features). Also, understand the caching strategies to improve serving latency.

Understand the Google Cloud serving options.   Understand how to set up real-time endpoints using Google Cloud Vertex AI Prediction for custom models or models trained outside Vertex AI; understand how to set up predictions using both APIs and the GCP console setup. Also, understand how to set up a batch job for any model using Vertex AI batch prediction.

Test for target performance.   Understand why model performance in production degrades. Also understand at a high level how Vertex AI services such as Vertex AI Model Monitoring can help with performance degradation issues.

Configure triggers and pipeline schedules.   Understand ways to set up a trigger to invoke a trained model or deploy a model for prediction on Google Cloud. Know how to schedule the triggers, such as using Cloud Scheduler and the Vertex AI managed notebooks scheduler. Also, learn how to automate the pipeline with Workflows, Vertex AI Pipelines, and Cloud Composer.

Review Questions

1. You are a data scientist working for an online travel agency. You have been asked to predict the most relevant web banner that a user should see next in near real time. The model latency requirements are 300ms@p99, and the inventory is thousands of web banners. You want to implement the simplest solution on Google Cloud. How should you configure the prediction pipeline?

    A. Embed the client on the website, and cache the predictions in a data store by creating a batch prediction job pointing to the data warehouse. Deploy the gateway on App Engine, and then deploy the model using Vertex AI Prediction.

    B. Deploy the model using TF Serving.

    C. Deploy the model using the Google Kubernetes engine.

    D. Embed the client on the website, deploy the gateway on App Engine, deploy the database on Cloud Bigtable for writing and for reading the user's navigation context, and then deploy the model on Vertex AI.

2. You are a data scientist training a text classification model in TensorFlow using the Vertex AI platform. You want to use the trained model for batch predictions on text data stored in Big-Query while minimizing computational overhead. What should you do?

    A. Submit a batch prediction job on Vertex AI that points to input data as a BigQuery table where text data is stored.

    B. Deploy and version the model on the Vertex AI platform.

    C. Use Dataflow with the SavedModel to read the data from BigQuery.

    D. Export the model to BigQuery ML.

3. You are a CTO of a global bank and you appointed an ML engineer to build an application for the bank that will be used by millions of customers. Your team has built a forecasting model that predicts customers' account balances three days in the future. Your team will use the results in a new feature that will notify users when their account balance is likely to drop below a certain amount. How should you serve your predictions?

    A. Create a Pub/Sub topic for each user. Deploy a Cloud Function that sends a notification when your model predicts that a user's account balance will drop below the threshold.

    B. Create a Pub/Sub topic for each user. Deploy an application on the App Engine environment that sends a notification when your model predicts that a user's account balance will drop below the threshold.

    C. Build a notification system on Firebase. Register each user with a user ID on the Firebase Cloud Messaging server, which sends a notification when the average of all account balance predictions drops below the threshold.

    D. Build a notification system on a Docker container. Set up cloud functions and Pub/Sub, which sends a notification when the average of all account balance predictions drops below the threshold.

4.   You are a data scientist and you trained a text classification model using TensorFlow. You have downloaded the saved model for TF Serving. The model has the following SignatureDefs:

```
input ['text'] tensor_info:
dtype: String
shape: (-1, 2)
name: dnn/head/predictions/textclassifier
SignatureDefs for output.
output ['text'] tensor_info:
dtype: String
shape: (-1, 2)
name: tfserving/predict
```

What is the correct way to write the predict request?

A.   json.dumps({'signature_name': 'serving_default'\ 'instances': [fab', 'be1, 'cd']]})

B.   json dumps({'signature_name': 'serving_default'! 'instances': [['a', 'b', 'c', 'd', 'e', 'f']]})

C.   json.dumps({'signature_name': 'serving_default, 'instances': [['a', 'b\ 'c'1, [d\ 'e\ T]]})

D.   json dumps({'signature_name': f,serving_default', 'instances': [['a', 'b'], [c\ 'd'], ['e\ T]]})

5.   You are an ML engineer who has trained a model on a dataset that required computationally expensive preprocessing operations. You need to execute the same preprocessing at prediction time. You deployed the model on the Vertex AI platform for high-throughput online prediction. Which architecture should you use?

A.   Send incoming prediction requests to a Pub/Sub topic. Set up a Cloud Function that is triggered when messages are published to the Pub/Sub topic. Implement your preprocessing logic in the Cloud Function. Submit a prediction request to the Vertex AI platform using the transformed data. Write the predictions to an outbound Pub/Sub queue.

B.   Stream incoming prediction request data into Cloud Spanner. Create a view to abstract your preprocessing logic. Query the view every second for new records. Submit a prediction request to the Vertex AI platform using the transformed data. Write the predictions to an outbound Pub/Sub queue.

C.   Send incoming prediction requests to a Pub/Sub topic. Transform the incoming data using a Dataflow job. Submit a prediction request to the Vertex AI platform using the transformed data. Write the predictions to an outbound Pub/Sub queue.

D.   Validate the accuracy of the model that you trained on preprocessed data. Create a new model that uses the raw data and is available in real time. Deploy the new model on to the Vertex AI platform for online prediction.

6. As the lead data scientist for your company, you are responsible for building ML models to digitize scanned customer forms. You have developed a TensorFlow model that converts the scanned images into text and stores them in Cloud Storage. You need to use your ML model on the aggregated data collected at the end of each day with minimal manual intervention. What should you do?

   A. Use the batch prediction functionality of the Vertex AI platform.

   B. Create a serving pipeline in Compute Engine for prediction.

   C. Use Cloud Functions for prediction each time a new data point is ingested.

   D. Deploy the model on the Vertex AI platform and create a version of it for online inference.

7. As the lead data scientist for your company, you need to create a schedule to run batch jobs using the Jupyter Notebook at the end of each day with minimal manual intervention. What should you do?

   A. Use the schedule function in Vertex AI managed notebooks.

   B. Create a serving pipeline in Compute Engine for prediction.

   C. Use Cloud Functions for prediction each time a new data point is ingested.

   D. Use Cloud Workflow to schedule the batch prediction Vertex AI job by cloud function.

8. You are a data scientist working for an online travel agency. Your management has asked you to predict the most relevant news article that a user should see next in near real time. The inventory is in a data warehouse, which has thousands of news articles. You want to implement the simplest solution on Google Cloud with the least latency while serving the model. How should you configure the prediction pipeline?

   A. Embed the client on the website, deploy the gateway on App Engine, and then deploy the model using Vertex AI Prediction.

   B. Deploy the model using TF Serving.

   C. Deploy the model using Google Kubernetes Engine.

   D. Embed the client on the website, deploy the gateway on App Engine, deploy the database on Cloud Bigtable for writing and for reading the user's navigation context, and then deploy the model on Vertex AI.

Chapter 11

Designing ML Training Pipelines

GOOGLE CLOUD PROFESSIONAL MACHINE LEARNING ENGINEER EXAM OBJECTIVES COVERED IN THIS CHAPTER:

✓ **5.1 Developing end-to-end ML pipelines. Considerations include:**

- Orchestration framework (e.g., Kubeflow Pipelines, Vertex AI Managed Pipelines, Cloud Composer)

- Hybrid or multicloud strategies

- System design with TFX components or Kubeflow DSL (e.g., Dataflow)

- Identifying components, parameters, triggers, and compute needs (e.g., Cloud Build, Cloud Run)

Delivering business value through machine learning (ML) is not only about building the best ML model for the use case at hand. Delivering this value is also about building an integrated ML system that operates continuously to adapt to changes in the dynamics of the business environment. Such an ML system involves collecting, processing, and managing ML datasets and features; training and evaluating models at scale; serving the model for predictions; monitoring the model performance in production; and tracking model metadata and artifacts.

The challenge with ML systems is that ML code is a small part of the overall ML component. You need to manage the relationship between models, data, and the ML code, as shown in Figure 11.1.

FIGURE 11.1 Relation between model data and ML code for MLOps

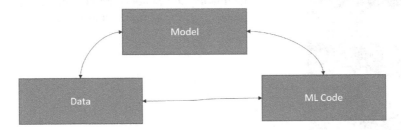

Machine learning operations (MLOps) supports ML development and deployment in the way that DevOps and DataOps support application engineering and data engineering. The difference is that when you deploy a web service, you care about resilience, queries per second, and load balancing. When you deploy an ML model, you also need to worry about changes in the data, changes in the model, and changes in the user behavior.

The MLOps process is an iterative process and expects inputs and has output that goes into the next steps, as shown in Figure 11.2. You can learn more at `https://services .google.com/fh/files/misc/practitioners_guide_to_mlops_whitepaper.pdf`.

The ML pipelines let you instrument, orchestrate, and automate the complex ML steps shown in Figure 11.2, from ML development to prediction serving.

Key functionalities in ML pipelines include triggering pipelines on demand, on a schedule, or in response to specified events. Pipelines also integrate with the ML metadata tracking capability to capture pipeline execution parameters and to produce artifacts.

FIGURE 11.2   End-to-end ML development workflow

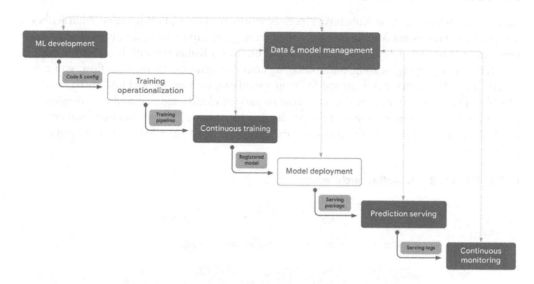

In this chapter, we will cover orchestration framework and tools to manage the ML pipeline such as Vertex AI Pipeline, Kubeflow Pipelines, and Cloud Composer.

Then we will cover how you can schedule workflows in these pipelines. We will go into the system design of Kubeflow and TFX (TensorFlow Extended) for setting up ML pipelines.

Last, we will cover some of the hybrid and multicloud strategies to set up ML workflows.

Orchestration Frameworks

You need an orchestrator to manage the various steps, such as cleaning data, transforming data, and training a model, in the ML pipeline. The orchestrator runs the pipeline in a sequence and automatically moves from one step to the next based on the defined conditions. For example, a defined condition might be executing the model-serving step after the model-evaluation step if the evaluation metrics meet the predefined thresholds. Orchestrating the ML pipeline is useful in both the development and production phases:

- During the development phase, orchestration helps the data scientists to run the ML experiment instead of having to manually execute each step.

- During the production phase, orchestration helps automate the execution of the ML pipeline based on a schedule or certain triggering conditions.

We will cover Kubeflow Pipelines, Vertex AI Pipelines, Apache Airflow, and Cloud Composer in the following sections as different ML pipeline orchestrators you can use.

Kubeflow Pipelines

Before understanding how Kubeflow Pipelines works, you should understand what Kubeflow is. Kubeflow is the ML toolkit for Kubernetes. (You can learn more about it at www.kubeflow.org/docs/started/architecture.) Kubeflow builds on Kubernetes as a system for deploying, scaling, and managing complex systems. Using Kubeflow, you can specify any ML framework required for your workflow, such as TensorFlow, PyTorch, or MXNet. Then you can deploy the workflow to various clouds or local and on-premises platforms for experimentation and for production use. Figure 11.3 shows how you can use Kubeflow as a platform for arranging the components of your ML system on top of Kubernetes.

FIGURE 11.3   Kubeflow architecture

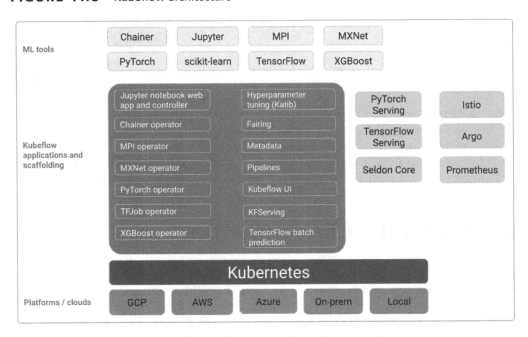

When you develop and deploy an ML system, the ML workflow typically consists of several stages. Developing an ML system is an iterative process. You need to evaluate the output at various stages of the ML workflow and apply changes to the model and parameters when necessary to ensure the model keeps producing the results you need.

Kubeflow Pipelines is a platform for building, deploying, and managing multistep ML workflows based on Docker containers.

A pipeline is a description of an ML workflow in the form of a graph, including all of the components in the workflow and how the components relate to each other. The pipeline configuration includes the definition of the inputs (parameters) required to run the pipeline and the inputs and outputs of each component.

When you run a pipeline, the system launches one or more Kubernetes pods corresponding to the steps (components) in your workflow (pipeline). The pods start Docker containers, and the containers in turn start your programs, as shown in Figure 11.4.

FIGURE 11.4 Kubeflow components and pods

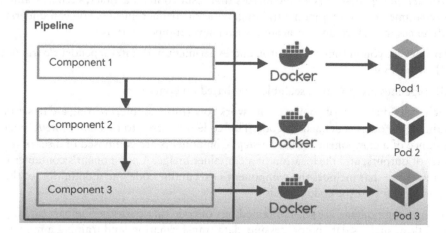

The Kubeflow Pipelines platform consists of the following:

- A user interface (UI) for managing and tracking experiments, jobs, and runs
- An engine for scheduling multistep ML workflows
- An SDK for defining and manipulating pipelines and components
- Notebooks for interacting with the system using the SDK
- Orchestration, experimentation, and reuse

You can install Kubeflow Pipelines on Google Cloud on GKE or use managed Vertex AI Pipelines to run Kubeflow Pipelines on Google Cloud.

 You can also install Kubeflow Pipelines on on-premises or local systems for testing purposes.

Vertex AI Pipelines

You can use Vertex AI Pipelines to run Kubeflow Pipelines or TensorFlow Extended pipelines without spinning any servers to set up the Kubeflow infrastructure or the TFX infrastructure. Vertex AI Pipelines automatically provisions the underlying infrastructure and manages it for you. You can bring your existing Kubeflow or TFX pipeline code and run it serverless on Vertex AI Pipelines.

Vertex AI Pipelines also provides data lineage. *Lineage* in machine learning means tracking the movement of data over time from the source system to transformations and to the data's consumption by a model. This includes all the transformations the data underwent along the way, starting from source system, how the data was transformed, what changed, and why. Each pipeline run produces *metadata* and ML *artifacts*, such as models or datasets. *Artifact lineage* describes all the factors that resulted in an artifact, such as training data or hyperparameters used for model training. By using artifact lineage, you can understand the differences in performance or accuracy over several pipeline runs:

- Pipelines let you automate, monitor, and experiment with interdependent parts of an ML workflow.

- ML pipelines are portable, scalable, and based on containers.

- Each individual part of your pipeline workflow (for example, creating a dataset or training a model) is defined by code. This code is referred to as a *component*. Each instance of a component is called a *step*. Components are composed of a set of inputs, a set of outputs, and the location of a container image. A component's container image is a package that includes the component's executable code and a definition of the environment that the code runs in.

- Pipeline components are self-contained sets of code that perform one part of a pipeline's workflow, such as data preprocessing, data transformation, and training a model.

- You can build custom components, or you can reuse pre-built components. To use features of Vertex AI like AutoML in your pipeline, use the Google Cloud pipeline components. You can learn more about using Google Cloud pipeline components in your pipeline at `https://cloud.google.com/vertex-ai/docs/pipelines/build-pipeline#google-cloud-components`.

Figure 11.5 shows Vertex AI Pipelines.

FIGURE 11.5   Vertex AI Pipelines

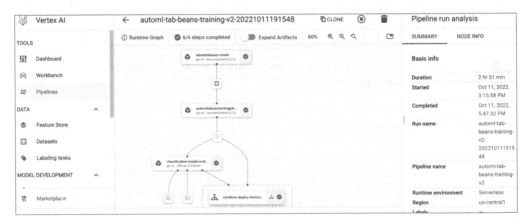

The pipeline in Figure 11.5 first created a dataset and then started an AutoML training job. The pipeline has set up a threshold to deploy a model only when the threshold for *area under the curve (AUC)* is more than 95 percent. You can add conditions and parameters to the pipeline before deploying the model in production, as shown in Figure 11.6.

FIGURE 11.6   Vertex AI Pipelines condition for deployment

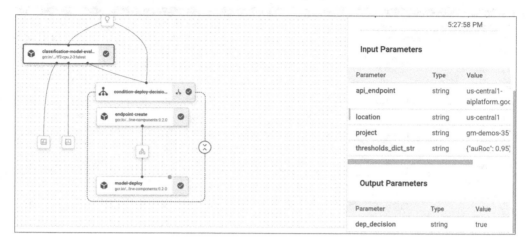

You can see the lineage of pipeline resources by clicking the resource and clicking Lineage. For example, click Endpoint, and then in the panel on the right you will see View Lineage, which will redirect you to the lineage graph, as shown in Figure 11.7.

FIGURE 11.7   Lineage tracking with Vertex AI Pipelines

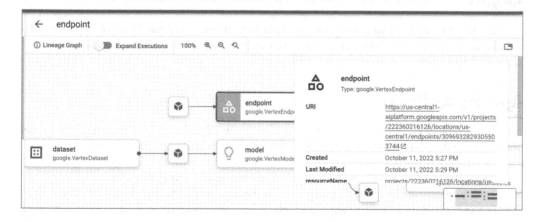

You can also track lineage by using Vertex ML Metadata, a feature of Vertex AI that stores artifacts and metadata for pipelines run using Vertex AI Pipelines, as shown in Figure 11.8.

FIGURE 11.8   Lineage tracking in Vertex AI Metadata store

By building a pipeline with the Kubeflow Pipelines SDK, you can implement your workflow by building custom components or reusing pre-built components, such as the Google Cloud Pipeline Components.

> **NOTE**   Vertex AI Pipelines can run pipelines built using the Kubeflow Pipelines SDK v1.8.9 or higher or TensorFlow Extended v0.30.0 or higher.

Refer to `https://cloud.google.com/vertex-ai/docs/pipelines/migrate-kfp` to learn more about how you can migrate your existing pipelines in Kubeflow Pipelines to Vertex AI Pipelines.

Apache Airflow

Apache Airflow is an open source workflow management platform for data engineering pipelines. It started at Airbnb in October 2014 as a solution to manage the company's increasingly complex workflows.

Airflow (`https://airflow.apache.org/docs/apache-airflow/stable/concepts/overview.html`) is a platform that lets you build and run workflows. A workflow is represented as a directed acyclic graph (DAG) and contains individual pieces of work called *tasks*, arranged with dependencies and data flows taken into account. It comes with a UI, a scheduler, and an executor.

Cloud Composer

Cloud Composer is a fully managed workflow orchestration service built on Apache Airflow.

By using Cloud Composer instead of a local instance of Apache Airflow, you can benefit from the best of Airflow with no installation or management overhead. Cloud Composer helps you create Airflow environments quickly and use Airflow-native tools, such as the powerful Airflow web interface and command-line tools, so you can focus on your workflows and not your infrastructure. Cloud Composer is designed to orchestrate data-driven workflows (particularly ETL/ELT).

Cloud Composer is best for batch workloads that can handle a few seconds of latency between task executions. You can use Cloud Composer to orchestrate services in your data pipelines, such as triggering a job in BigQuery or starting a Dataflow pipeline.

Comparison of Tools

Table 11.1 compares three orchestrators.

TABLE 11.1   Kubeflow Pipelines vs. Vertex AI Pipelines vs. Cloud Composer

	Kubeflow Pipelines	Vertex AI Pipelines	Cloud Composer
Management and support for frameworks	Kubeflow Pipelines is used to orchestrate ML workflows in any supported framework such as TensorFlow, PyTorch, or MXNet using Kubernetes. It can be set up on-premises or in any cloud.	Managed serverless pipeline to orchestrate either Kubeflow Pipelines or TFX Pipeline. No need to manage the infrastructure.	Managed way to orchestrate ETL/ELT pipelines using Apache Airflow. It's a Python-based implementation. You would use a workflow to solve complex data processing workflows in MLOps.
Failure handling	You would need to handle failures on metrics as this is not supported out of the box.	Since Vertex AI pipelines runs the Kubeflow Pipelines, you can use the Kubeflow failure management on metrics.	Failure management for built-in GCP metrics to take action on failure or success.

Identification of Components, Parameters, Triggers, and Compute Needs

We covered how to configure triggers and pipeline schedules in Chapter 10, "Scaling Models in Production," with respect to scheduling training jobs. In this part of the chapter, we will cover how to trigger an MLOps pipeline. You can automate the ML production pipelines to retrain your models with new data. You can trigger your pipeline on demand, on a schedule, on the availability of new data, on model performance degradation, on significant changes in the statistical properties of the data or based on other conditions.

The availability of new data is a trigger to retrain the ML model:

- To train a new ML model with new data, the previously deployed continuous training (CT) pipeline is executed. No new pipelines or components are deployed; only a new prediction service or newly trained model is served at the end of the pipeline.

- To train a new ML model with a new implementation, a new pipeline is deployed through a CI/CD pipeline.

Figure 11.9 shows the relationship between the CI/CD pipeline and the ML CT pipeline.

FIGURE 11.9   Continuous training and CI/CD

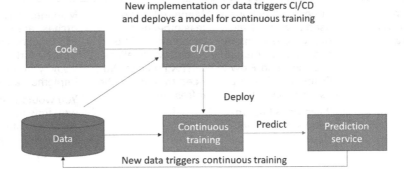

Schedule the Workflows with Kubeflow Pipelines

Let's look at how CI/CD works for Kubeflow Pipelines. See Figure 11.10.

FIGURE 11.10   CI/CD with Kubeflow Pipelines

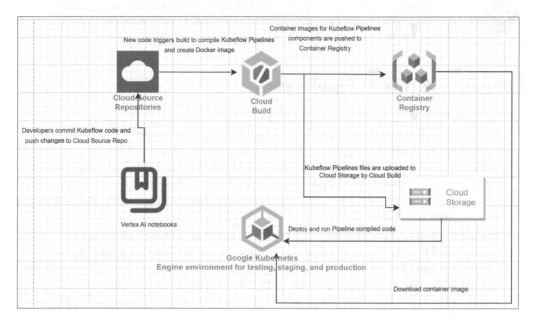

Kubeflow Pipelines provides a Python SDK to operate the pipeline programmatically using kfp.Client. By using the Kubeflow Pipelines SDK (`www.kubeflow.org/docs/components/pipelines/v1/sdk/sdk-overview`), you can invoke Kubeflow Pipelines using the following services:

- On a schedule, you can use Cloud Scheduler.

- Responding to an event, you can use Pub/Sub and Cloud Functions. For example, the event can be the availability of new data files in a Cloud Storage bucket.

- As part of a bigger data and process workflow, you can use Cloud Composer or Cloud Data Fusion.

- Kubeflow Pipelines also provides a built-in scheduler, Argo, for recurring pipelines in Kubeflow Pipelines.

- As an alternative to using Cloud Build, you can use other build systems such as Jenkins. A ready-to-go deployment of Jenkins is available on Google Cloud Marketplace.

- You can use Apache Airflow, a popular orchestration and scheduling framework, for general-purpose workflows, which you can run using the fully managed Cloud Composer service. For more information on how to orchestrate data pipelines with Cloud Composer and Cloud Build, refer to `https://cloud.google.com/architecture/cicd-pipeline-for-data-processing`.

You can configure the automated Cloud Build pipeline to skip triggers, for example, if only documentation files are edited or if the experimentation notebooks are modified.

Schedule Vertex AI Pipelines

There are two ways to schedule the Vertex AI pipeline:

- **Schedule pipeline execution with Cloud Scheduler:** You can schedule the execution of a precompiled pipeline using Cloud Scheduler with an event-driven Cloud Function with an HTTP trigger. To schedule a pipeline with Cloud Scheduler, build and compile a simple pipeline, upload the compiled pipeline JSON to a Cloud Storage bucket, create a Cloud Function with an HTTP trigger, and create a Cloud Scheduler job. You can manually run your job (optional).

- **Trigger a pipeline run with Cloud Pub/Sub:** You can schedule the execution of a precompiled pipeline using an event-driven Cloud Function with a Cloud Pub/Sub trigger. In Cloud Functions, a Pub/Sub trigger enables a function to be called in response to Pub/Sub messages. When you specify a Pub/Sub trigger for a function, you also specify a Pub/Sub topic. Your function will be called whenever a message is published to the specified topic.

System Design with Kubeflow/TFX

In the following sections, we will discuss system design with the Kubeflow DSL, and then we will cover system design with TFX.

System Design with Kubeflow DSL

Pipelines created in Kubeflow Pipelines are stored as YAML files executed by a program called Argo. Kubeflow Pipelines runs on Argo Workflows by default. Kubeflow exposes a Python domain-specific language (DSL) for authoring pipelines. The DSL is a Python representation of the operations performed in the ML workflow and built with ML workloads specifically in mind. The DSL also allows for some simple Python functions to be used as pipeline stages without you having to explicitly build a container.

For each container (with the Kubeflow Python SDK), you need to do the following:

1. Create the container either as a simple Python function or with any Docker container.

2. Create an operation that references that container as well as the command-line arguments, data mounts, and variables to pass the container.

3. Sequence the operations, defining which may happen in parallel and which must complete before moving on to a further step.

4. Compile this pipeline, defined in Python, into a YAML file that Kubeflow Pipelines can consume.

Kubeflow Pipelines Components

For a component to be invoked in the pipeline, you need to create a *component op*. You can create a component op using one of the following methods:

- **Implementing a lightweight Python component:** This component doesn't require that you build a new container image for every code change and is intended for fast iteration in a notebook environment. In a lightweight Python function, we define a Python function and then let Kubeflow take care of packaging that function into a container and creating an operation.

- **Creating a reusable component:** This functionality requires that your component includes a component specification in the component.yaml file. Component sops are automatically created from the component.yaml files using the ComponentStore.load_components function in the Kubeflow Pipelines SDK during pipeline compilation.

- **Using predefined Google Cloud components:** Kubeflow Pipelines provides predefined components that execute various managed services such as AutoML on Google Cloud by providing the required parameters. These components help you execute tasks using services such as BigQuery, Dataflow, Dataproc, and the AI platform. Similar to using reusable components, these component ops are automatically created from the predefined component specifications through ComponentStore.load_components. Other predefined components are available for executing jobs in Kubeflow and other platforms.

Figure 11.11 shows how in Kubeflow Pipelines, a containerized task can invoke other services such as BigQuery jobs, AI platform (distributed) training jobs, and Dataflow jobs. Cloud SQL is used as a metadata store.

FIGURE 11.11 Kubeflow Pipelines on GCP

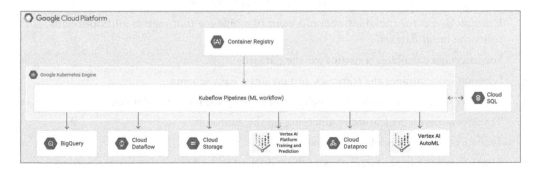

System Design with TFX

Before discussing TFX pipelines, let's understand what TFX is. TFX is a Google production-scale machine learning (ML) platform based on TensorFlow. It provides a configuration framework and shared libraries to make your ML code production-ready. TFX is a platform for building and managing ML workflows in a production environment. TFX provides the following:

- TFX pipelines let you orchestrate your ML workflow on several platforms, such as Apache Airflow, Apache Beam, and Kubeflow Pipelines.

- TFX provides components that you can use as a part of a pipeline or as a part of your ML training script.

- TFX provides libraries, which provide the base functionality for many of the standard components. TFX includes both libraries and pipeline components. We covered TFX libraries such as TFDV, etc., in Chapter 2, "Exploring Data and Building Data Pipelines." Figure 11.12 illustrates the relationships between TFX libraries and pipeline components.

FIGURE 11.12   TFX pipelines, libraries, and components

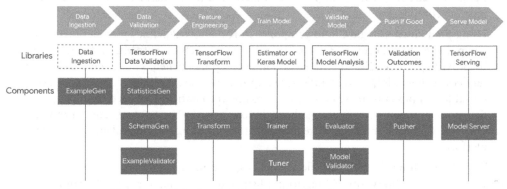

Source: www.tensorflow.org/tfx/guide#tfx_standard_components

A TFX pipeline typically includes the following components:

- ExampleGen is the initial input component of a pipeline that ingests and optionally splits the input dataset.
- StatisticsGen calculates statistics for the dataset.
- SchemaGen examines the statistics and creates a data schema.
- ExampleValidator looks for anomalies and missing values in the dataset.
- Transform performs feature engineering on the dataset.
- Trainer trains the model.
- Tuner tunes the hyperparameters of the model.

- Evaluator performs deep analysis of the training results and helps you validate your exported models, ensuring that they are "good enough" to be pushed to production.

- Model Validator checks that the model is actually servable from the infrastructure and prevents bad models from being pushed.

- Pusher deploys the model on a serving infrastructure.

- Model Server performs batch processing on a model with unlabeled inference requests.

It's important to have an understanding of the previous components for the exam.

The TFX ModelValidator component was used to check if a model was good enough to be used in production. Since the component Evaluator has already computed all the metrics you want to validate against, ModelValidator is deprecated and fused with Evaluator so you don't have to duplicate the computations.

A TFX pipeline is a sequence of components that implement an ML pipeline that is specifically designed for scalable, high-performance machine learning tasks. Components are built using TFX libraries, which can also be used individually. TFX uses a metadata store to maintain the state of the pipeline run.

You can orchestrate the TFX pipelines using an orchestration system such as Apache Airflow or Kubeflow.

You can orchestrate TFX pipelines on GCP by using one of the following methods:

- Use Kubeflow Pipelines running on GKE.

- Use Apache Airflow or Cloud Composer.

- Use Vertex AI Pipelines.

If you are using TFX and using Kubeflow Pipelines to orchestrate TFX stages such as data processing, training, and TFServing, then you can use the TFX Pipeline DSL and use TFX components with Kubeflow. TFX provides a command-line interface (CLI) that compiles the pipeline's Python code to a YAML file and describes the Argo workflow. Then you can submit the file to Kubeflow Pipelines.

Hybrid or Multicloud Strategies

Multicloud means there is an interconnection between two different cloud providers and describes setups that combine at least two public cloud providers. These are some of the ways you can operate as multicloud with GCP:

- GCP AI APIs can be integrated anywhere on-premises or in any application. You can call the pretrained APIs using an AWS Lambda function and take advantage of GCP ML.

- BigQuery Omni lets you run BigQuery analytics on data stored in Amazon S3 or Azure Blob Storage. If you want to join the data present in AWS or Azure with the data present in Google Cloud regions or if you want to utilize BigQuery ML capabilities, use the LOAD DATA SQL statement. This SQL statement lets you transfer data from Big-Query Omni–accessible S3 buckets into BigQuery native tables.

- To train custom ML models on Vertex AI, Vertex AI is integrated with BigQuery and you can access the data from BigQuery Omni (data in S3, Azure) to train an AutoML or custom ML model using Vertex AI Training. You can also use BigQuery ML on the data.

Hybrid cloud means combining a private computing environment, usually an existing on-premises data center and public cloud computing environment.

Anthos is the hybrid and multicloud cloud modernization platform. The following list includes some of the features of Anthos that support hybrid ML development:

- BigQuery Omni is powered by Anthos, and you will be able to query data without having to manage the underlying infrastructure.

- The hybrid AI offering is Speech-to-Text On-Prem, which is now generally available on Anthos through the Google Cloud Marketplace.

- You can run GKE on-premises, which means you can set up Kubeflow Pipelines for your ML workflow using Anthos.

- You can also run the service Cloud Run on-premises through Anthos, which gives you the ability to set up API-based pretrained AI services.

Summary

In this chapter, we covered orchestration for ML pipelines using tools such as Kubeflow, Vertex AI Pipelines, Apache Airflow, and Cloud Composer. We also covered the difference between all these tools and when to use each one for ML workflow automation. You saw that Vertex AI Pipelines is a managed serverless way to run Kubeflow and TFX workflows, while you can run Kubeflow on GCP on Google Kubernetes Engine.

Then we covered ways to schedule ML workflows using Kubeflow and Vertex AI Pipelines. For Kubeflow, you would use Cloud Build to trigger a deployment, while for Vertex AI Pipelines, you can use Cloud Function event triggers to schedule the pipeline. You can also run these pipelines manually.

We covered system design with Kubeflow and TensorFlow. In Kubeflow Pipelines, you create every task into a component and orchestrate the components. Kubeflow comes with a UI and TensorBoard to visualize these components. You can run TFX pipelines on Kubeflow. For TFX, we covered three TFX components and TFX libraries to define ML pipelines. To orchestrate an ML pipeline, TFX supports bringing your own orchestrator or runtime. You can use Cloud Composer, Kubeflow, or Vertex AI Pipelines to run TFX ML workflows.

Finally, we covered the high-level definition of *hybrid* and *multicloud*. You saw how to use BigQuery Omni and Anthos to set up hybrid and multicloud environments on GCP. You can use BigQuery Omni connectors to get data from AWS S3 and Azure storage. You can use Anthos to set up Kubeflow Pipelines on GKE on-premises.

Exam Essentials

Understand the different orchestration frameworks. Know what an orchestration framework is and why it's needed. You should know what Kubeflow Pipelines is and how you can run Kubeflow Pipelines on GCP. You should also know Vertex AI Pipelines and how you can run Kubeflow and TFX on Vertex AI Pipelines. Also learn about Apache Airflow and Cloud Composer. Finally, compare and contrast all four orchestration methods for automating ML workflows.

Identify the components, parameters, triggers, and compute needs on these frameworks. Know ways to schedule ML workflows using Kubeflow and Vertex AI Pipelines. For Kubeflow, understand how you would use Cloud Build to trigger a deployment. For Vertex AI Pipelines, understand how you can use Cloud Function event triggers to schedule the pipeline.

Understand the system design of TFX/Kubeflow. Know system design with Kubeflow and TensorFlow. Understand that in Kubeflow Pipelines, you create every task into a component and orchestrate the components. Understand how you can run TFX pipelines on Kubeflow and how to use TFX components and TFX libraries to define ML pipelines. Understand that to orchestrate ML pipelines using TFX, you can use any runtime or orchestrator such as Kubeflow or Apache Airflow. You can also run TFX on GCP using Vertex AI Pipelines.

Review Questions

1. You are a data scientist building a TensorFlow model with more than 100 input features, all with values between −1 and 1. You want to serve models that are trained on all available data but track your performance on specific subsets of data before pushing to production. What is the most streamlined and reliable way to perform this validation?

   A. Use the TFX ModelValidator component to specify performance metrics for production readiness.

   B. Use the entire dataset and treat the area under the curve receiver operating characteristic (AUC ROC) as the main metric.

   C. Use L1 regularization to reduce the coefficients of uninformative features to 0.

   D. Use k-fold cross-validation as a validation strategy to ensure that your model is ready for production.

2. Your team has developed an ML pipeline using Kubeflow to clean your dataset and save it in a Google Cloud Storage bucket. You created an ML model and want to use the data to refresh your model as soon as new data is available. As part of your CI/CD workflow, you want to automatically run a Kubeflow Pipelines job on GCP. How should you design this workflow with the least effort and in the most managed way?

   A. Configure a Cloud Storage trigger to send a message to a Pub/Sub topic when a new file is available in a storage bucket. Use a Pub/Sub–triggered Cloud Function to start the Vertex AI Pipelines.

   B. Use Cloud Scheduler to schedule jobs at a regular interval. For the first step of the job, check the time stamp of objects in your Cloud Storage bucket. If there are no new files since the last run, abort the job.

   C. Use App Engine to create a lightweight Python client that continuously polls Cloud Storage for new files. As soon as a file arrives, initiate the Kubeflow Pipelines job on GKE.

   D. Configure your pipeline with Dataflow, which saves the files in Cloud Storage. After the file is saved, you start the job on GKE.

3. You created an ML model and want to use the data to refresh your model as soon as new data is available in a Google Cloud Storage bucket. As part of your CI/CD workflow, you want to automatically run a Kubeflow Pipelines training job on GKE. How should you design this workflow with the least effort and in the most managed way?

   A. Configure a Cloud Storage trigger to send a message to a Pub/Sub topic when a new file is available in a storage bucket. Use a Pub/Sub–triggered Cloud Function to start the training job on GKE.

   B. Use Cloud Scheduler to schedule jobs at a regular interval. For the first step of the job, check the time stamp of objects in your Cloud Storage bucket to see if there are no new files since the last run.

   C. Use App Engine to create a lightweight Python client that continuously polls Cloud Storage for new files. As soon as a file arrives, initiate the Kubeflow Pipelines job on GKE.

   D. Configure your pipeline with Dataflow, which saves the files in Cloud Storage. After the file is saved, you can start the job on GKE.

4. You are an ML engineer for a global retail company. You are developing a Kubeflow pipeline on Google Kubernetes Engine for a recommendation system. The first step in the pipeline is to issue a query against BigQuery. You plan to use the results of that query as the input to the next step in your pipeline. Choose two ways you can create this pipeline.

A. Use the Google Cloud BigQuery component for Kubeflow Pipelines. Copy that component's URL, and use it to load the component into your pipeline. Use the component to execute queries against a BigQuery table.

B. Use the Kubeflow Pipelines domain-specific language to create a custom component that uses the Python BigQuery client library to execute queries.

C. Use the BigQuery console to execute your query and then save the query results into a new BigQuery table.

D. Write a Python script that uses the BigQuery API to execute queries against BigQuery. Execute this script as the first step in your pipeline in Kubeflow Pipelines.

5. You are a data scientist training a TensorFlow model with graph operations as operations that perform decoding and rounding tasks. You are using TensorFlow data transform to create data transformations and TFServing to serve your data. Your ML architect has asked you to set up MLOps and orchestrate the model serving only if data transformation is complete. Which of the following orchestrators can you choose to orchestrate your ML workflow? (Choose two.)

A. Apache Airflow

B. Kubeflow

C. TFX

D. Dataflow

6. You are a data scientist working on creating an image classification model on Vertex AI. You are using Kubeflow to automate the current ML workflow. Which of the following options will help you set up the pipeline on Google Cloud with the least amount of effort?

A. Set up Kubeflow Pipelines on GKE.

B. Use Vertex AI Pipelines to set up Kubeflow ML pipelines.

C. Set up Kubeflow Pipelines on an EC2 instance with autoscaling.

D. Set up Kubeflow Pipelines using Cloud Run.

7. As an ML engineer, you have written unit tests for a Kubeflow pipeline that require custom libraries. You want to automate the execution of unit tests with each new push to your development branch in Cloud Source Repositories. What is the recommended way?

A. Write a script that sequentially performs the push to your development branch and executes the unit tests on Cloud Run.

B. Create an event-based Cloud Function when new code is pushed to Cloud Source Repositories to trigger a build.

C. Using Cloud Build, set an automated trigger to execute the unit tests when changes are pushed to your development branch.

D. Set up a Cloud Logging sink to a Pub/Sub topic that captures interactions with Cloud Source Repositories. Execute the unit tests using a Cloud Function that is triggered when messages are sent to the Pub/Sub topic.

8. Your team is building a training pipeline on-premises. Due to security limitations, they cannot move the data and model to the cloud. What is the recommended way to scale the pipeline?

   A. Use Anthos to set up Kubeflow Pipelines on GKE on-premises.

   B. Use Anthos to set up Cloud Run to trigger training jobs on GKE on-premises. Orchestrate all of the runs manually.

   C. Use Anthos to set up Cloud Run on-premises to create a Vertex AI Pipelines job.

   D. Use Anthos to set up Cloud Run on-premises to create a Vertex AI Training job.

Chapter
12

Model Monitoring, Tracking, and Auditing Metadata

GOOGLE CLOUD PROFESSIONAL MACHINE LEARNING ENGINEER EXAM OBJECTIVES COVERED IN THIS CHAPTER:

✓ **2.3 Tracking and running ML experiments. Considerations include:**

- Choosing the appropriate Google Cloud environment for development and experimentation (e.g., Vertex AI Experiments, Kubeflow Pipelines, Vertex AI TensorBoard with TensorFlow and PyTorch) given the framework

✓ **5.3 Tracking and auditing metadata. Considerations include:**

- Tracking and comparing model artifacts and versions (e.g., Vertex AI Experiments, Vertex ML Metadata)

- Hooking into model and dataset versioning

- Model and data lineage

✓ **6.2 Monitoring, testing, and troubleshooting ML solutions. Considerations include:**

- Establishing continuous evaluation metrics (e.g., Vertex AI Model Monitoring, Explainable AI)

- Monitoring for training-serving skew

- Monitoring for feature attribution drift

- Monitoring model performance against baselines, simpler models, and across the time dimension

In the previous chapters you saw how to collect the data, train the model, find the best hyperparameter, and deploy the model. In this chapter, you will see how to monitor the model that was already deployed, the different logging strategies, and finally, how to track lineage using a metadata store.

Model Monitoring

You went through a great journey, from experimentation in a Jupyter Notebook to deploying a model in production, and you are now serving predictions using serverless architecture. Deployment is not the end of this workflow; rather, it is the first iteration of the machine learning model's life cycle.

While your model might have scored high in your evaluation metrics, how do you know if it will perform well on real-time data? What if there are massive changes in the world after you deploy, like a worldwide pandemic that changes human behavior? What if there are subtle changes to the input that are not obvious? In short, how do you know that your model works after deployment? Post-deployment, the model may not be fit for the original purpose after some time.

The world is a dynamic place and things keep changing. However, machine learning models are trained on historical data and, ideally, recently collected data. Imagine that a model is deployed and the environment slowly but surely starts to change; your model will become more and more irrelevant as time passes. This concept is called *drift*. There are two kinds of drift: concept drift and data drift.

There are two types of drift: concept drift and data drift. Know how to detect the different types of drift and methods to recover.

Concept Drift

In general, there is a relationship between the input variables and predicted variables that we try to approximate using a machine learning model. When this relationship is not static and changes, it is called *concept drift*. This often happens because the underlying assumptions of your model have changed.

A good example of this is email spam, which makes up the majority of all emails sent. As spam gets detected and filtered, spammers modify the emails to bypass the detection filter. In these cases, adversarial agents try to outdo one another and change their behavior.

Data Drift

Data drift refers to the change in the input data that is fed to the machine learning model compared to the data that was used to train the model. One example would be the changes in the statistical distribution, such as a model trained to predict the food preference of a customer failing if the age of the customer demography changes.

Another reason for data drift could be the change in the input schema at the source of your data. An example of this is the presence of new product labels (SKUs) not present in training data. A more subtle case is when the meaning of the columns change. For example, the meaning of the term *diabetic* might change over time based on the medical diagnostic levels of blood sugar.

The only way to act on model deterioration such as through drift is to keep an eye on the data, called *model monitoring*. The most direct way is to monitor the input data and continuously evaluate the model with the same metrics that were used during the training phase.

Model Monitoring on Vertex AI

Vertex AI offers model monitoring features as part of the model deployments. From the practical perspective, a model can be monitored for skew and drift:

- **Training-serving skew:** When there is a difference in the input feature distribution in production when compared to training data, it can impact the performance of the model. You can enable this feature if and only if you have access to the original data.

- **Prediction drift:** When the input's statistical distribution changes in production over time, it can also impact the performance. If the original training data is not available during prediction, you can use prediction drift detection to monitor your inputs.

These two features are not exclusive; you can enable both skew and drift detection in Vertex AI. In fact, you will realize that skew and drift need to be examined for each data type, and Vertex AI provides this for categorical and numerical features. Let's look at the data types for which these are available:

- **Categorical features:** These are features that have a limited number of possible values, typically grouped by qualitative properties. Examples are color, country, and zip code. See Figure 12.1 for an example distribution.

- **Numerical values:** These are features that can take any value. Examples are price ($), speed, and distance. See Figure 12.2 for an example distribution.

FIGURE 12.1 Categorical features

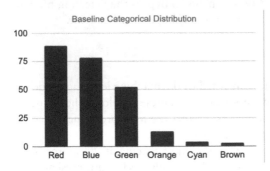
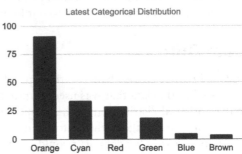

FIGURE 12.2 Numerical values

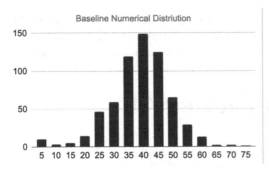
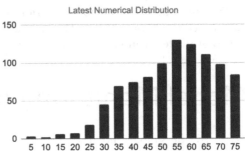

Drift and Skew Calculation

We will show you how to calculate a baseline distribution and then use the same method to calculate the distribution at prediction time and use a comparison method. These methods will differ by the data type.

1. Calculate a baseline.

   - **Baseline for skew detection:** The statistical distribution of the feature's values in the training data is the baseline.

   - **Baseline for drift detection:** The statistical distribution of the features values seen in the production in the recent past is the baseline.

   How these are applied depends on whether the data type is categorical or numerical. The distributions used for baseline are calculated as follows:

   - **Distribution calculations for categorical features:** The count or percentage of instances of each possible value.

   - **Distribution calculation for numerical features:** The count or percentage of the values that fall into buckets. (Full range is divided into equal-sized buckets.)

2. Calculate the statistical distribution using the previous method for the latest values seen in production.

3. Vertex AI then compares the baseline with the latest distribution calculated in step 2. A distance measure is calculated as follows:

   ▪ **Categorical features:** The distance score between the baseline distribution and latest production distribution is calculated using L-infinity distance. This is measured as the largest distance of the two vectors along any coordinate dimension.

   ▪ **Numerical features:** The distance score is calculated using Jensen-Shannon divergence. (The mathematical definition of this is beyond the scope of the exam.)

4. When the distance score hits a configured threshold value, Vertex AI identifies it as an anomaly (skew or drift).

Practical Considerations of Enabling Monitoring

There are a few things to keep in mind to effectively monitor the data and at the same time make it cost-effective:

▪ **Sampling rate:** Configure a *prediction request sampling rate* to only get a sample of the production inputs.

▪ **Monitoring frequency:** Configure a *frequency* to set the rate at which the model's logged inputs are monitored for skew or drift. This sets the monitoring window size of logged data that is analyzed in each run.

▪ **Alerting thresholds:** Configure the threshold for each feature you are interested in. When the statistical distance between the baseline and the production input feature distribution exceeds this threshold, an alert is generated. The default value is 0.3.

▪ **Multiple models in an endpoint:** When you enable and configure skew or drift detection on an endpoint, the configuration will be applied to all the models deployed behind that endpoint, including the following:

   ▪ Type of detection

   ▪ Sampling rate

   ▪ Monitoring frequency

Input Schemas

The input values are part of the payload of the prediction requests. Vertex AI should be able to parse the input values to monitor. You can specify a schema when you configure model monitoring to help parse this input.

The input schema is automatically parsed for AutoML models, so you don't have to provide one. You must provide one for custom-trained models that don't use a key/value input format.

Input values are automatically parsed for AutoML models.

Automatic Schema Parsing

Model monitoring can usually automatically parse the input schema when enabled for skew or drift. Vertex AI model monitoring will analyze the first 1,000 requests to detect the schema. The efficacy of this automatic detection is best if the input values are in the form of key/value pairs. Here *key* is the name of the feature and the actual value follows the colon. See the following for an example of an input (of a car) presented as key/value pairs:

```
{"make":"Ford", "model":"focus": year: "2011", "color":"black"}
```

Custom Schema

To make sure that Vertex AI correctly parses the input values, you can specify the schema in what is called an *analysis instance*. The analysis instance is expected to be in Open API schema format.

Here are the details of the schema expected:

- The "type" could be one of the following:
  - *object*: key/value pairs
  - *array*: array-like format
  - *string*: csv-string
- *Properties*: the type of each feature.
- For *array or csv*-string format, specify the order of the features.

 There are three types of schema formats: object, array, or string.

Here is an example of an input to a model that predicts the resale value of a car:

```
type: object
properties:
  make:
    type:string
  model:
    type:string
  year:
    type:number
  color:
    type:string
  known_defects:
    type: array
```

```
    items:
        type: string
required:
-make
-model
-year
-color
```

The previous schema is specified in `object` format. The features `make`, `model`, and `color` are string features, and `year` is a number. The feature `known_defects` is an array of strings. The last section tells you that all features are required except for `known_defects`.

In CSV format you can skip optional input features by providing empty fields. For example, say you are expecting five features: `["a","b",  ,"d","e"]`. Notice that the third feature was skipped. The third missing feature would be understood as a "null" value.

Logging Strategy

When you deploy a model for prediction, in addition to monitoring the inputs (which is to keep track of the trends in the input features), it may be useful to log the requests. In some domains (such as regulated financial verticals), logging is mandatory for all models for future audits. In other cases, it may be useful to collect monitoring data to update your training data.

In Vertex AI, you can enable prediction logs for AutoML tabular models, AutoML image models, and custom-trained models. This can be done during either model deployment or endpoint creation.

Types of Prediction Logs

You can enable three kinds of logs to get information from the prediction nodes. These three types of logs are independent of each other and so can be enabled or disabled independently.

Container Logging

This logs the *stdout* and *stderr* from your prediction nodes to Cloud Logging. This is highly useful and relevant for debugging your container or the model. It may be helpful to understand the larger logging platform on GCP.

Access Logging

This logs information such as a time stamp and latency for each request to Cloud Logging. This is enabled by default on v1 service endpoints; in addition, you can enable access logging when you deploy your model to the endpoint.

Request-Response Logging

This logs a sample of the online prediction requests and responses to a BigQuery table. This is the primary mechanism. With this you can create more data to augment your training or test data. Either you can enable this during creation of the prediction endpoint or you can update it later.

Log Settings

Log settings can be updated when you create the endpoint or when you deploy a model to the endpoint. It is important to be aware of the default settings for logging. If you have already deployed your model with default log settings but want to change the log settings, you must undeploy your model and redeploy it with new settings.

If you expect to see a huge number of requests for your model, in addition to scaling your deployment, you should consider the costs of logging. A high rate of "Queries per second," or QPS, will produce a significant number of logs.

Here is an example of the `gcloud` command to configure logging for an image classification model. Notice the last two lines where the logging configuration is specified.

```
gcloud ai endpoints deploy-model 1234567890\
  --region=us-central1 \
  --model=model_id_12345 \
  --display-name=image_classification \
  --machine-type=a2-highgpu-2g \
  --accelerator=count=2,type=nvidia-tesla-t4 \
  --disable-container-logging \
  --enable-access-logging
```

Model Monitoring and Logging

Both model monitoring and request-response logging use the same infrastructure in the backend (BigQuery table). Therefore, there are some restrictions when these two services are involved:

- If model monitoring is already enabled on an endpoint, you cannot enable request-response logging.

- If request-response logging is enabled first, and then model monitoring is enabled, the request-response logging cannot be modified.

Model and Dataset Lineage

When you are experimenting with different types of models, you will need a methodical approach to recording the parameters of the experiments and the corresponding observations. The parameters, artifacts, and metrics of an ML experiment are called *metadata* of the experiment. The metadata helps you to do the following:

- Detect degradation of the model after deployment.

- Compare the effectiveness of different sets of hyperparameters.

- Track the lineage of the ML artifacts, both datasets and models. Lineage helps find the source of all the artifacts and also find the descendant artifacts from a given model/dataset.

- Rerun an ML workflow with the same parameters.

- Track downstream usage of artifacts for audit purposes. This could also be used to understand what was affected by a given artifact.

Vertex ML Metadata

Using Vertex ML Metadata, you can record the metadata of the artifacts and query the metadata for analyzing, debugging, or auditing purposes. Vertex ML Metadata is based on the open source ML Metadata (MLMD) library that was developed by Google's TensorFlow Extended team.

The Vertex ML Metadata uses the following data model and the associated terminology:

- **Metadata store:** This is the top-level container for all the metadata resources. It is regional and within the scope of a Google Cloud project. Usually, one metadata store is shared by the entire organization.

- **Metadata resources:** Vertex ML Metadata uses a graph-like data model for representing the relationship between the resources. These resources are as follows:

  - **Artifacts:** An artifact is an entity or a piece of data that was created by or can be consumed by an ML workflow. Datasets, models, input files, training logs, and metrics are examples.

  - **Context:** A context is a group of artifacts and executions that can be queried. Say you are optimizing hyperparameters; each experiment would be a different execution with its own set of parameters and metrics. You can group these experiments into a context and then compare the metrics in this context to identify the best model.

  - **Execution:** This represents a step in a machine learning workflow and can be annotated with runtime parameters. An example could be a "training" operation, with annotation about time and number of GPUs used.

- **Events:** An event connects artifacts and executions. Details like an artifact being the output of an execution and the input of the next execution can be captured using events. It helps you determine origin of artifact when trying to trace lineage. Figure 12.3 shows a simple graph containing events, artifacts, execution, and context.

- **Metadataschema:** The metadataschema specifies the schema to be used by the particular types of data like artifact or execution. Type schemas are represented using OpenAPI schema objects in YAML format.

FIGURE 12.3   Vertex Metadata data model

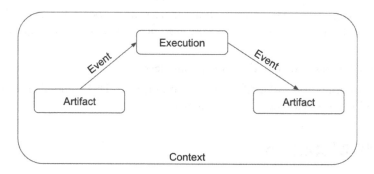

Manage ML Metadataschemas

Every metadata resource that is stored in Vertex ML Metadata follows a schema called `MetaDataSchema`. There are predefined schemas called *system schemas* for the most common types of resources stored. The system schemas come under the namespace `system`. Here is an example of a predefined model system type in YAML format:

```
title: system.Model
type: object
properties:
  framework:
    type: string
    description: "The ML framework used, eg: 'TensorFlow' or 'PyTorch'."
  framework_version:
    type: string
    description: "The version used, eg: '1.16' or '2.5'"
  payload_format:
    type: string
    description: "The format of the model stored: eg: 'SavedModel' or 'pkl'"
```

Let's look at two of the important operations: create artifacts and lookup artifacts. The other operations (not shown here) are delete artifacts, create executions, and context management. You can use REST, the command line, or Python to do these operations, and we show the examples in Python. Here is how to create an artifact in Python:

```python
def create_artifact_sample(
    project: str,
    location: str,
    uri: Optional[str] = None,
    artifact_id: Optional[str] = None,
    display_name: Optional[str] = None,
    schema_version: Optional[str] = None,
    description: Optional[str] = None,
    metadata: Optional[Dict] = None,
):
    system_artifact_schema = artifact_schema.Artifact(
        uri=uri,
        artifact_id=artifact_id,
        display_name=display_name,
        schema_version=schema_version,
        description=description,
        metadata=metadata,
    )
    return system_artifact_schema.create(project=project, location=location,)
```

In this example, we are defining a new function that takes in the details like URI, artifact ID, location, display name, schema version, description, and the metadata (properties that define the metadata itself). Inside the function we are calling the `artifact_schema` `.Artifact` function to create a system artifact instance and in the second step calling the `create()` function to create it in the metadata store.

In the next example, we see how to query or look up an artifact like dataset or model:

```python
def list_artifact_sample(
    project: str,
    location: str,
    display_name_fitler: Optional[str] = "display_name=\"my_model_*\"",
    create_date_filter:  Optional[str] = "create_time>\"2022-06-11\"",
):
    aiplatform.init(
        project=project,
        location=location)

    combined_filters = f"{display_name_fitler} AND {create_date_filter}"
    return aiplatform.Artifact.list(filter=combined_filters)
```

We use a similar method here, where we define a function called `list_artifact_sample`, which does the job for us. This also has only three lines of code, where the first line is the `init()` function, and the second line creates a `combined_filters` query. In the third line we call the `aiplatform.Artifact.list()` function with the `combined_filters` string as an argument. These code blocks and more information can be found in the documentation at `https://cloud.google.com/vertex-ai/docs/ml-metadata/managing-metadata`.

Vertex AI Pipelines

When you use Vertex AI Pipelines, the model metadata and artifacts are automatically stored in the metadata store for *lineage tracking*. Whenever you run a pipeline, it generates a series of artifacts. These could include dataset summaries, model evaluation metrics, metadata on the specific pipeline execution, and so on. Vertex AI Pipelines also provides a visual representation of the lineage, as shown in Figure 12.4. You can use this to understand which data the model was built on and which model version was deployed and also sort it by data schema and date.

FIGURE 12.4   Vertex AI Pipelines showing lineage

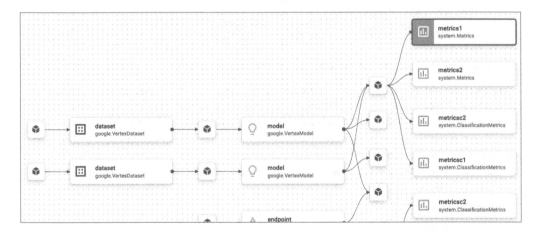

Vertex AI Experiments

When you are developing a ML model, the goal is to find the best model for the use case. You could experiment with various different libraries, algorithms, model architectures, hyperparameters, etc. Vertex AI Experiments helps you to keep track of these trials, and analyze the different variations.

In particular, Vertex AI Experiments helps you to:

- Track the steps of an experiment run (like preprocessing, embedding, training, etc.)
- Track input like algorithms, hyperparameters, datasets, etc.
- Track output of these steps like models, metrics, checkpoints, etc.

Based on the above you can understand what works and choose your direction of exploration. The Google Cloud console provides a single pane of glass to view your experiments, where you can slice and dice the results of the experiment runs, and zoom into the results of a single run. Using the Vertex AI SDK for Python you can access experiments, experiment runs, experiment run parameters, metrics, and artifacts. When used with Vertex ML Metadata you can track artifacts and view the lineage.

Vertex AI Debugging

Sometimes when training a model, you run into issues and suspect that the GPU is not being used efficiently or a permission issue restricts access to data. To debug these kinds of issues, Vertex AI allows you to directly connect to the container where your training is running. To do this, follow these steps:

1. Install the interactive Bash shell in the training container. The Bash shell comes installed in pre-built containers.

2. Run the custom training where interactive shells are supported.

3. Make sure that the user has the right permissions. If you are using a service account, make sure the service account has the right permissions.

4. Set the `enableWebAccess` API field to true to enable interactive shells.

5. Navigate to the URI provided by Vertex AI when you initiate the custom training job.

6. Use the interactive shell to do the following:

   a. Check permissions for the service account that Vertex AI uses for training code.

   b. Visualize Python execution with profiling tools like py-spy, which you can install using pip3.

   c. Analyze performance of your training node using perf.

   d. Check CPU and GPU usage.

Summary

In this chapter we looked at the steps beyond building a model and deploying it. This includes monitoring a deployed model to detect if there is a performance degradation. Later we also looked at the various different logging strategies available in Vertex AI. Finally, when building several models, we looked at how to track lineage of models using Vertex ML Metadata and track using Vertex AI Experiments.

Exam Essentials

Understand model monitoring. Understand the need to monitor the performance of the model after deployment. There are two main types of degradation: data drift and concept drift. Learn how to monitor continuously for these kinds of changes to input.

Learn logging strategies. Logging after deployment is crucial to be able to keep track of the deployment, including the performance, as well as create new training data. Learn how to use logging in addition to monitoring the models in Vertex AI.

Understand Vertex ML Metadata. ML metadata helps you to track lineage of the models and other artifacts. Vertex ML Metadata is a managed solution for storing and accessing metadata on GCP. Learn the data model as well as the basic operations of creating and querying metadata.

Review Questions

1. You spend several months fine-tuning your model and the model is performing very well in your evaluations based on test data. You have deployed your model, and over time you notice that the model accuracy is low. What happened and what should you do? (Choose two.)

    A. Nothing happened. There is only a temporary glitch.

    B. You need to enable monitoring to establish if the input data has drifted from the train/ test data.

    C. Throw away the model and retrain with a higher threshold of accuracy.

    D. Collect more data from your input stream and use that to create training data, then retrain the model.

2. You spend several months fine-tuning your model and the model is performing very well in your evaluations based on test data. You have deployed your model and it is performing well on real-time data as well based on an initial assessment. Do you still need to monitor the deployment?

    A. It is not necessary because it performed very well with test data.

    B. It is not necessary because it performed well with test data and also on real-time data on initial assessment.

    C. Yes. Monitoring the model is necessary no matter how well it might have performed on test data.

    D. It is not necessary because of cost constraints.

3. Which of the following are two types of drift?

    A. Data drift

    B. Technical drift

    C. Slow drift

    D. Concept drift

4. You trained a regression model to predict the longevity of a tree, and one of the input features was the height of the tree. When the model is deployed, you find that the average height of trees you are seeing is two standard deviations away from your input. What type of drift is this?

    A. Data drift

    B. Technical drift

    C. Slow drift

    D. Concept drift

5. You trained a classification model to predict fraudulent transactions and got a high F1 score. When the model was deployed initially, you had good results, but after a year, your model is not catching fraud. What type of drift is this?

    A. Data drift

    B. Technical drift

    C. Slow drift

    D. Concept drift

6. When there is a difference in the input feature distribution between the training data and the data in production, what is this called?

    A. Distribution drift

    B. Feature drift

    C. Training-serving skew

    D. Concept drift

7. When statistical distribution of the input feature in production data changes over time, what is this called in Vertex AI?

    A. Distribution drift

    B. Prediction drift

    C. Training-serving skew

    D. Concept drift

8. You trained a classification model to predict the number of plankton in an image of ocean water taken using a microscope to measure the amount of plankton in the ocean. When the model is deployed, you find that the average number of plankton is an order of magnitude away from your training data. Later, you investigate this and find out it is because the magnification of the microscope was different in the training data. What type of drift is this?

    A. Data drift

    B. Technical drift

    C. Slow drift

    D. Concept drift

9. What is needed to detect training-serving skew? (Choose two.)

    A. Baseline statistical distribution of input features in training data

    B. Baseline statistical distribution of input features in production data

    C. Continuous statistical distribution of features in training data

    D. Continuous statistical distribution of features in production data

10. What is needed to detect prediction drift? (Choose two.)

    A. Baseline statistical distribution of input features in training data

    B. Baseline statistical distribution of input features in production data

    C. Continuous statistical distribution of features in training data

    D. Continuous statistical distribution of features in production data

11. What is the distance score used for categorical features in Vertex AI?

   A. L-infinity distance

   B. Count of the number of times the categorical value occurs over time

   C. Jensen-Shannon divergence

   D. Normalized percentage of the time the categorical values differ

12. You deployed a model on an endpoint and enabled monitoring. You want to reduce cost. Which of the following is a valid approach?

   A. Periodically switch off monitoring to save money.

   B. Reduce the sampling rate to an appropriate level.

   C. Reduce the inputs to the model to reduce the monitoring footprint.

   D. Choose a high threshold so that alerts are not sent too often.

13. Which of the following are features of Vertex AI model monitoring? (Choose three.)

   A. Sampling rate: Configure a prediction request sampling rate.

   B. Monitoring frequency: Rate at which model's inputs are monitored.

   C. Choose different distance metrics: Choose one of the many distance scores for each feature.

   D. Alerting thresholds: Set the threshold at which alerts will be sent.

14. Which of the following is *not* a correct combination of model building and schema parsing in Vertex AI model monitoring?

   A. AutoML model with automatic schema parsing

   B. Custom model with automatic schema parsing with values in key/value pairs

   C. Custom model with automatic schema parsing with values not in key/value pairs

   D. Custom model with custom schema specified with values not in key/value pairs

15. Which of the following is *not* a valid data type in the model monitoring schema?

   A. String

   B. Number

   C. Array

   D. Category

16. Which of the following is *not* a valid logging type in Vertex AI?

   A. Container logging

   B. Input logging

   C. Access logging

   D. Request-response logging

17. How can you get a log of a sample of the prediction requests and responses?

    A. Container logging

    B. Input logging

    C. Access logging

    D. Request-response logging

18. Which of the following is a *not* a valid reason for using a metadata store?

    A. To compare the effectiveness of different sets of hyperparameters

    B. To track lineage

    C. To find the right proportion of train and test data

    D. To track downstream usage of artifacts for audit purposes

19. What is an artifact in a metadata store?

    A. Any piece of information in the metadata store

    B. The train and test dataset

    C. Any entity or a piece of data that was created by or can be consumed by an ML workflow

    D. A step in the ML workflow that can be annotated with runtime parameters

20. Which of the following is *not* part of the data model in a Vertex ML metadata store?

    A. Artifact

    B. Workflow step

    C. Context

    D. Execution

Chapter

13

Maintaining ML Solutions

GOOGLE CLOUD PROFESSIONAL MACHINE LEARNING ENGINEER EXAM OBJECTIVES COVERED IN THIS CHAPTER:

✓ **2.1 Exploring and preprocessing organization-wide data (e.g., Cloud Storage, BigQuery, Cloud Spanner, Cloud SQL, Apache Spark, Apache Hadoop). Considerations include:**

- Creating and consolidating features in Vertex AI Feature Store

✓ **4.2 Scaling online model serving. Considerations include:**

- Vertex AI Feature Store

✓ **5.2 Automating model retraining. Considerations include:**

- Determining an appropriate retraining policy

- Continuous integration and continuous delivery (CI/CD) model deployment (e.g., Cloud Build, Jenkins)

✓ **6.2 Monitoring, testing, and troubleshooting ML solutions. Considerations include:**

- Establishing continuous evaluation metrics (e.g., Vertex AI Model Monitoring, Explainable AI)

- Common training and serving errors

Maintaining ML
Solutions

In the previous chapters, you learned about training a model, deploying strategies, and monitoring deployed models. In this chapter, we will discuss some of the concepts that were not covered before but are important for creating a mature machine learning solution and maintaining it.

This includes retraining policy, MLOps maturity (Level 0, 1, 2), and a common design pattern that solves a problem that occurs frequently as MLOps matures.

MLOps is the application of DevOps principles to machine learning operations. This provides architectural and policy guidance to the ML engineers managing the operations. In this chapter, you will learn that it is not a one-size-fits-all approach to MLOps but rather a graded approach based on the maturity of the organization in adopting machine learning.

Later we will also discuss two important problems that are faced by ML engineers in the implementation of MLOps. First, determining the retraining policy for ML models and to match it with the organizational objectives, followed by a useful convention for versioning models. Second, complexity of scaling out machine learning to multiple teams within the organization that invests heavily in feature engineering. These two problems are solved using solutions we describe as design patterns.

MLOps Maturity

Organizations go through a journey starting with experimenting with machine learning technology and then progressively bringing the concepts of continuous integration/continuous deployment (CI/CD) into machine learning. This application of DevOps principles to machine learning is called MLOps.

While there are similarities between MLOps and DevOps, there are some key differences.

We have found that organizations first start experimenting with machine learning by manually training models and then bring automation to the process using pipelines; they later enter into a transformational phase as they fully automate. These three phases that they journey through use different technologies and reflect their "AI readiness."

Before we look at each of these phases in detail, let's first look at the steps in ML:

1. Data

   a. **Extraction:** Collect data from different sources, aggregate the data, and make it available for the ML process downstream.

   b. **Analysis:** Perform exploratory data analysis (EDA) on the data collected to understand the schema, statistical distributions, and relationships. Identify the feature engineering and data preparation requirements that will have to be performed.

   c. **Preparation:** Apply transformations and feature engineering on the data. Split the data into train, test, and validation for the ML task.

2. Model

   a. **Training:** Set up ML training using the input data, and predict the output. Experiment with different algorithms and hyperparameters to identify the best-performing model.

   b. **Evaluation:** Evaluate the model using a holdout set and assess the quality of the model based on predefined metrics.

   c. **Validation:** Validate if the model is qualified for deployment, that is, if the metrics meet a certain baseline performance criterion.

3. Deployment

   a. **Serving:** Deploy the model to serve online or batch predictions. For online predictions, create and maintain a RESTful endpoint for the model, and provision to scale based on demand. This could also include making batch predictions.

   b. **Monitor:** Continuously monitor the model after deployment to detect anomalies, drift, and skew.

We looked at all of these steps in the previous chapters, and so you should be familiar with them. The level of automation of these steps defines the maturity of the MLOps. Google characterizes MLOps as having three levels: MLOps level 0 (manual phase), MLOps level 1(strategic automation phase), and MLOps level 2 (CI/CD automation, transformational phase).

MLOps Level 0: Manual/Tactical Phase

Organizations that start to experiment with ML are in this phase. In this phase, the focus is to build proof of concepts and test out some AI/ML use cases. The idea is to validate some ideas of how a business can be improved by using ML.

In this phase, there is usually an individual or a team that is experimenting and training models. The output of their effort is the model, which is handed off to the release or deployment team using a model registry as shown in Figure 13.1. The model is then picked up by the deployment team and will be deployed to serve predictions.

FIGURE 13.1 Steps in MLOps level 0

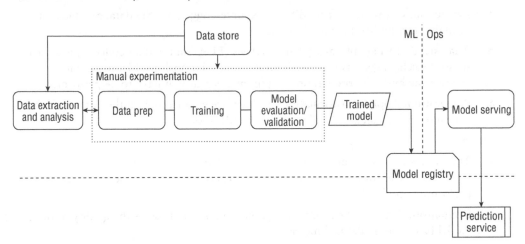

Key Features of Level 0

Let's look at the key points of the process in this tactical phase:

1. **Manual:** There is no automation in any of the steps. Each of the tasks is manually performed, including data analysis, preparation, training, and validation. It is not surprising to see most of these steps done in a Jupyter Notebook of a data scientist.

2. **Division between ML and MLOps:** The data scientists and engineers that serve the model are completely separated, and the only point of contact is the model handoff. Even the handoff could be storing the model file in a storage location to be picked up by the deployment team, or a slightly more mature team could use a model registry for the handoff. This division negatively affects the ability to detect training-serving skew.

3. **Manual iterations:** Since training is manual in this phase, there is no regularity in retraining, and so the process doesn't scale to more than a few models.

4. **Continuous integration:** Testing usually happens only as part of the Jupyter Notebooks, but otherwise CI is not even a consideration here.

5. **Continuous deployment:** These models are not frequently updated, so CD is not given much thought.

6. **Deployment for prediction service:** Typically, the deployment here is a microservice of a model, which is consumed through a REST API, as opposed to deploying an entire ML system.

7. **Monitoring:** Typically, this process does not consider monitoring or model degradation.

Challenges

The most important challenge in this phase is the model degradation. Well-trained models frequently underperform in real life due to differences between training data and real data. The only way to mitigate these problems is to actively monitor the quality of predictions, to frequently retrain the models, and to frequently experiment with new algorithms or implementations of the model to leverage improvements in technology.

MLOps Level 1: Strategic Automation Phase

Organizations in this phase usually have identified business objectives and have prioritized ML to solve some problems. This phase involves the use of pipelines to automate continuous training of the model, and continuous delivery of the model prediction service. There are new services required to achieve this, including automated data and model validation steps, pipeline triggers, the Feature Store, and metadata management, as shown in Figure 13.2.

FIGURE 13.2   MLOps Level 1 or strategic phase

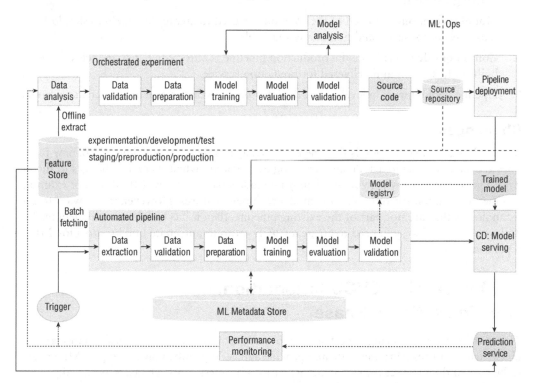

In this phase, there is infrastructure to share artifacts between teams, and there is a clear distinction between development and production environments. The development of ML models happens in an orchestrated environment. The source code for the data pipelines is stored in a central repository and model training is automated.

Key Features of MLOps Level 1

This phase has some distinct features that make it more mature than level 0, and we will list them here:

1. **Experimentation:** Each step in the experimentation phase is orchestrated. Since the transition between the steps is automated, it increases the speed of iterating through experiments.

2. **Continuous training:** The model is trained automatically in production, triggered by new data.

3. **Experiment-operational symmetry:** The code used to create the experimentation pipeline is also used in the production environment, which aligns well with the best practices of unifying MLOps.

4. **Modular components:** Each of the components used to create the pipelines should be reusable, composable, and potentially shareable.

5. **Continuous delivery:** Since the production pipeline is automated, new models can be built on fresh data and delivered for prediction service.

6. **Pipeline deployment:** In level 1, you deploy a pipeline that is executed to create a model.

Challenges

In this phase, the expectation is that the team manages only a few pipelines. Also, new pipelines are manually deployed. Pipelines are triggered mainly when there are changes to the data. This is not ideal when you are deploying models based on new ML ideas. For example, this method is good for retraining the model with new features. However, if you want to use technologies that are not part of the existing pipeline, then it has to be manually deployed. To be able to do that, you need to create a CI/CD setup to automate build/test/deploy ML pipelines.

MLOps Level 2: CI/CD Automation, Transformational Phase

This is the level of maturing expected of an organization that is in the transformational phase, where it uses AI to innovate and provide agility. Typically, you can expect ML experts to be part of the product teams and across various business units. Datasets are usually accessible across the silos, and ML projects shared between product groups. As shown in Figure 13.3, the entire pipeline goes through the CI/CD automation (not just the model).

So, if you want to update your library from TensorFlow 2.1 to TensorFlow 2.5, it will go through the CI/CD automation steps naturally and the process doesn't have to be done manually.

FIGURE 13.3   MLOps level 2, the transformational phase

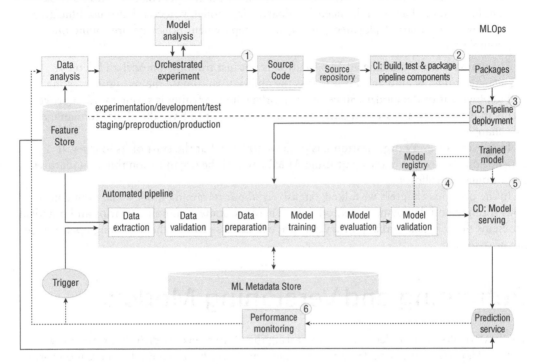

Key Features of Level 2

The striking feature of moving to level 2 is the complete adoption of the CI/CD model. Let's look at some of the features in detail:

1. **Pipeline:** The first stage is the development and experimentation of new ML algorithms, possibly using new libraries. The output is the source code for the pipeline that is shared using a code repository. From that point on, automation takes over, from building pipeline code, running various tests on the pipeline code, creating artifacts for the pipeline code (like packages, executables, etc.), later deploying this pipeline, and producing the model artifacts. The trained model is automatically deployed for continuous delivery. After deployment monitoring is enabled, the monitored data is collected to create more training data and training is automatically triggered.

2. **Testing:** Testing is a must for continuous integration of the pipeline, starting from testing the feature engineering logic, model training convergence checks, checking errors

in model output (like NaN values), validating the artifacts created at each stage, and integration between each of the pipeline components.

3. Delivery: To be able to provide continuous delivery, you need to verify the compatibility of the model with the software and hardware infrastructure in the serving environment. Test the prediction service for conforming to the API schema, load test, and so on. In addition, based on the need for a particular model, you could also use blue/green deployment, canary deployment, or a shadow deployment policy before rolling out completely.

To summarize, maintaining an ML solution is not just training a model and deploying a single model behind an API. It means the ability to automate the retraining, testing, and deployment of the models. Since the field of machine learning is seeing rapid improvements in technology almost on a daily basis, it is important to have the ability to manage this change.

However, not every organization has to move to level 2 at the start of its journey. It depends on the level of maturity of using AI/ML, and as the organization thinking matures, the automation follows.

In the previous chapters we talked extensively about retraining models and even continuous training and deployment methodology. There are some common scenarios and practical problems that happen in that journey, and we will address two of them as design patterns in the next section.

Retraining and Versioning Models

You have deployed a model and are monitoring the predictions for drift. Now, we know that model performance can degrade over time, which can be measured from the monitoring data. However, at what point do you retrain the model? This is not just a question out of curiosity, but one that has to be answered to configure the continuous training pipeline.

Vertex AI Model Monitoring offers you the ability to monitor for drift detection and training-serving skew. As you monitor the performance, it is also important to collect this real data. This will be used for evaluation of the model as well as for creation of new training datasets. Now, when do we use this training dataset to train a new model? Or what is our retraining frequency?

   When you enable monitoring, have measures to collect the data for the creation of fresh, new training and test data.

Triggers for Retraining

Model performance usually degrades over time. To fix this we need to retrain the model. The idea is to trigger a retrain pipeline based on a policy. Here are a couple of available policies:

- **Absolute threshold:** You can set an absolute threshold for retraining. For example, whenever accuracy falls below 90 percent, you can trigger. Determining what this absolute threshold is would depend on your use case.

- **Rate of degradation:** You can trigger retraining whenever there is a sudden dip in performance. For example, if you see a drop of more than 2 percent in accuracy in a day, you can trigger a retraining.

Now considering the preceding policies, there are a few main points to think about:

- **Training costs:** There is a cost to training models. Frequently training models could be expensive. So it is important to make sure the policy does not frequently trigger retraining.

- **Training time:** Some models train in a few minutes, but others take weeks to train. The deployed model could degrade further when waiting for the newly trained model.

- **Delayed training:** If the threshold is too low, the model could degrade too much before the new model is deployed. This not only affects the performance of the ML service, it also shows inconsistency in the ML performance, which may not be tolerated by the end user.

- **Scheduled training:** A much simpler policy could be a retraining on a fixed schedule. This would incorporate new data on a regular basis and the costs are predictable.

Retraining policy should take into account the cost of retraining, the time to retrain, and also the degradation in performance.

Versioning Models

When you are building multiple models and sharing them with other teams, it is important to have some way to find them. One method is to use metadata to identify artifacts; however, users external to the organization access a deployed model using an API, and to them the metadata store might not be accessible. This is where versioning can be used.

The problem with having multiple models is that, when users are accessing through an API, they expect a certain performance and behavior from the model. If there is a sudden change in behavior from the same API, it causes unexpected disruption. However, there is a need for the model to update or change. For example, say there is a model to identify objects and humans in an image and it accurately detects all the human faces. Later, say you have updated the model and it now has the ability to also detect dogs and other pets; this could cause a disruption. In this case, the user needs the ability to choose the older model.

The solution is to use model versioning. Model versioning allows you to deploy an additional model to the existing model, with the ability to select it using a version ID. In this case, both the models can be accessed by the end user by specifying the version. This solves the problem of backward compatibility; that is, this works well for models that have the same inputs and outputs.

For models that behave in a different way (say a model has the ability to provide model explanations), they can be deployed as a new model (and not a new version of an existing model).

In both cases, there should be the ability to access these models using REST endpoints, separately and conveniently for the users. Enabling monitoring on all the deployed model versions allows you the ability to compare the different versions.

Feature Store

Feature engineering is an important factor in the ability to build good ML models. However, it has been observed that, practically, feature engineering is more time-consuming than experimenting with ML models. For this reason, a valuable feature that has been engineered provides a huge value for the entire ML solution.

So, feature engineering is a huge investment for any organization. In order to optimize their models, many teams work on creating new features. At times these features would have been valuable to other teams as well. Unfortunately, sharing these features is tricky and so the same feature engineering tasks are done over and over again. This creates several problems:

- **Non-reusable:** Features are created ad hoc and not intended to be used by others. Each team creates a feature with the purpose of only using it themselves. These ad hoc features are not automated in pipelines and are sometimes derived from other expensive data preprocessing pipelines.

- **Governance:** Diversity of sources of the methods of creating these features creates a very complex situation for data governance.

- **Cross-collaboration:** Due to the ad hoc nature of these features not being shared, more divisions between teams are created and they continue to go separate ways.

- **Training and serving differences:** When features are built ad hoc and not automated, this creates differences between training data and serving data and reduces the effectiveness of the ML solution.

- **Productizing features:** While these ad hoc features are useful during experimentation, they cannot be productized because of the lack of automation and the need for low-latency retrieval of the features.

Solution

The solution is to have a central location to store the features as well as the metadata about the features that can be shared between the data engineers and ML engineers. This also allows the application of the software engineering principles of versioning, documentation, and access control of these features.

Feature stores also has two key features: the ability to process large feature sets quickly and the ability to access the features with low latency for real-time prediction and batch access for training time and batch predictions.

Feast is an open-source Feature Store created by Google and Gojek that is available as a software download. Feast was designed with Redis and Google Cloud services BigQuery and Apache Beam. Google Cloud also offers a managed service called Vertex AI Feature Store that allows you to scale dynamically based on your needs.

Data Model

We will now discuss the data model used by the Vertex AI Feature Store service. It uses a time-series model to store all the data, which enables you to manage the data as it changes over time. All the data in Vertex AI Feature Store is arranged in a hierarchy with the top level called a featurestore. This featurestore is a container that can have one or more entity types, which represents a certain type of feature. In your entity type you can store similar or related features.

Featurestore → EntityType → Feature

As an example, Table 13.1 has data of baseball batters. The first step is to create a featurestore called baseballfs.

TABLE 13.1   Table of baseball batters

Row	player_id	Team	Batting_avg	Age
1	player_1	RedSox	0.289	29
2	player_2	Giants	0.301	32
3	player_3	Yankees	0.241	35

You can then create an EntityType called batters and map the column header player_id to that entity. You can then add team, batting_avg, and age as features to this EntityType.

Here player_1 and player_2 are entities in this EntityType. Entities must always be unique and must always be of type String.

RedSox, Giants, and Yankees are featurevalues in the featurestore.

Ingestion and Serving

Vertex AI Feature Store supports both batch and streaming ingestion. A typical method to do this is to have the feature stored in BigQuery and then ingested into the Feature Store.

For retrieving features from the Feature Store, there are two methods: batch and online. The batch method is used for the model training phase and the online method is used for online inference. When you request data from time t, the Vertex AI Feature Store returns values at or before time t.

Vertex AI Permissions Model

It is essential to manage access to various different resources like datasets, models, and so on and also to provide permission to perform various operations like training, deploying, and monitoring. Identity and Access Management (IAM) is the mechanism to enforce that. Refer to Chapter 6, "Building Secure ML Pipelines," for a discussion of IAM.

 Revisit GCP's IAM fundamentals before diving into the Vertex AI permissions model.

You may already have experience with GCP's IAM model—for example, in Compute Engine or Google Cloud Storage—which will come in handy.

It is important to emphasize following best practices to use IAM security. The following are some of the high-level points:

- **Least privilege:** Restrict the users and applications to do only what is necessary.

- **Manage service accounts and service account keys:** Actively manage these security assets and periodically check them.

- **Auditing:** Enable audit logs and use cloud logging roles.

- **Policy management:** Use a higher-level check to make sure the policies are being implemented at every level.

For more details on IAM best practices, refer to this URL:

```
https://cloud.google.com/blog/products/identity-security/
iam-best-practice-guides-available-now
```

We looked at general IAM best practices, and now we will look at some special cases for Vertex AI.

Custom Service Account

When you run a Vertex AI training job, it uses one of several *service accounts* that Google automatically creates for your Google Cloud Project. However, these service accounts might have more permissions than required, like access to BigQuery and GCS. It is better to use custom service accounts with just the right set of permissions.

Access Transparency in Vertex AI

To verify who is accessing your content, and what is being accessed, you need logs. In many domains, there are legal and compliance requirements for such logging. Importantly, it also provides you with access logs that capture the actions of Google personnel in your project. There are two types of access logs. *Cloud Audit logs* are logs of users from your organization. *Access Transparency logs* are logs of Google personnel. Most services are supported in this, but there are some features that are not covered.

For a full list of services supported, refer to this URL:

```
https://cloud.google.com/vertex-ai/docs/general/access-transparency
```

Common Training and Serving Errors

In the following sections, we will look at some of the errors you frequently see during training and serving. Knowledge of the types of errors will help you debug problems effectively. While the errors are dependent on the framework used, we will use TensorFlow as the framework in this discussion.

Training Time Errors

During the training phase, the most relevant errors are seen when you run `Model.fit()`.Errors happen when the following scenarios occur:

1. Input data is not transformed or not encoded.
2. Tensor shape is mismatched.
3. Out of memory errors occur because of instance size (CPU and GPU).

Serving Time Errors

The serving time errors are seen only during deployment and the nature of the errors is also different. The typical errors are as follows:

1. Input data is not transformed or not encoded.
2. Signature mismatch has occurred.

Refer to this URL for a full list of TensorFlow errors:

```
www.tensorflow.org/api_docs/python/tf/errors
```

TensorFlow Data Validation

To prevent and reduce these errors, you can use TensorFlow Data Validation (TFDV). TFDV can analyze training and serving data as follows:

1. To compute statistics

2. To infer schema

3. To detect anomalies

    Refer here for full documentation:

    ```
    https://cloud.google.com/vertex-ai/docs/training/monitor-debug-
    interactive-shell
    ```

Vertex AI Debugging Shell

Vertex AI provides an interactive shell to debug training for both pre-built containers and custom containers. You can use an interactive shell to inspect the training container to debug problems in your training code or the Vertex AI configuration. Using that you can do the following:

1. Run tracing and profiling tools.

2. Analyze GPU utilization.

3. Validate IAM permissions for the container.

    Refer to this URL for full documentation:

    ```
    https://cloud.google.com/vertex-ai/docs/training/monitor-debug-
    interactive-shell
    ```

Summary

In this chapter we looked at the long-term maintenance of a ML application. ML operations or MLOps is based on CI/CD principles of maintaining software applications. During this process we look at how to automate training, deployment, and monitoring. Retraining policy of models is an important concept that has to be balanced between model quality and cost of training. Another important problem that arises in large enterprises is the inability to share features between departments, which causes lots of inefficiencies. To solve this problem the idea of feature store was invented, which can be implemented either using open source software or Vertex AI Feature Store.

Exam Essentials

Understand MLOps maturity.   Learn different levels of maturity of MLOps and how it matches with the organizational goals. Know the MLOps architecture at the experimental phase, then a strategic phase where there is some automation, and finally a fully mature CI/CD-inspired MLOps architecture.

Understand model versioning and retraining triggers.   A common problem faced in MLOps is knowing when to trigger new training. It could be based on model degradation as observed in model monitoring, or it could be time-based. When retraining a model, learn how to add it as a new version or a new model.

Understand the use of feature store.   Feature engineering is an expensive operation, so the features generated using those methods are more useful if shared between teams. Vertex AI Feature Store is a managed service, and Feast is an open source feature store by Google.

Review Questions

1. Which of the following is *not* one of the major steps in the MLOps workflow?

   A. Data processing, including extraction, analysis, and preparation

   B. Integration with third-party software and identifying further use cases for similar models

   C. Model training, testing, and validation

   D. Deployment of the model, monitoring, and triggering retraining

2. You are on a small ML team in a very old retail organization, and the organization is looking to start exploring machine learning for predicting daily sales of products. What level of MLOps would you implement in this situation?

   A. No MLOps, will build ML models ad hoc

   B. MLOps level 0

   C. MLOps level 1

   D. MLOps level 2

3. You are a data scientist working as part of an ML team that has experimented with ML for its online fashion retail store. The models you build match customers to the right size/fit of clothes. Organization has decided to build this out, and you are leading this effort. What is the level of MLOps you would implement here?

   A. No MLOps, will build ML models ad hoc

   B. MLOps level 0

   C. MLOps level 1

   D. MLOps level 2

4. You have been hired as an ML engineer to work in a large organization that works on processing photos and images. The team creates models to identify objects in photos, faces in photos, and the orientation of photos (to automatically turn) and also models to adjust the colors of photos. The organization is also experimenting with new algorithms that can automatically create images from text. What is the level of MLOps you would recommend?

   A. No MLOps, ad hoc because they are using new algorithms

   B. MLOps level 0

   C. MLOps level 1

   D. MLOps level 2

5. What problems does MLOps level 0 solve?

   A. It is ad hoc building of models so it does not solve any problems.

   B. It automates training so building models is a repeatable process.

   C. Model training is manual but deployment is automated once there is model handoff.

   D. It is complete automation from data to deployment.

6. Which of these statements is **false** regarding MLOps level 1 (strategic phase)?

    A. Building models becomes a repeatable process due to training automation.

    B. Model training is triggered automatically by new data.

    C. Trained models are automatically packaged and deployed.

    D. The pipeline is automated to handle new libraries and algorithms.

7. You are part of an ML engineering team of a large organization that has started using ML extensively across multiple products. It is experimenting with different algorithms and even creating its own new ML algorithms. What should be its MLOps maturity level to be able to scale?

    A. Ad hoc is the only level that works for the organization because it is using custom algorithms.

    B. MLOps level 0.

    C. MLOps level 1.

    D. MLOps level 2.

8. In MLOps level 1 of maturity (strategic phase), what is handed off to deployment?

    A. The model file

    B. The container containing the model

    C. The pipeline to train a model

    D. The TensorFlow or ML framework libraries

9. In MLOps level 0 of maturity (tactical phase) what is handed off to the deployment?

    A. The model file

    B. The container containing the model

    C. The pipeline to train a model

    D. The TensorFlow or ML framework libraries

10. What triggers building a new model in MLOps level 2?

    A. Feature store

    B. Random trigger

    C. Performance degradation from monitoring

    D. ML Metadata Store

11. What should you consider when you are setting the trigger for retraining a model? (Choose two.)

    A. The algorithm

    B. The frequency of triggering retrains

    C. Cost of retraining

    D. Time to access data

12. What are reasonable policies to apply for triggering retraining from a model monitoring data? (Choose two.)

    A. The amount of prediction requests to a model

    B. Model performance degradation below a threshold

    C. Security breach

    D. Sudden drop in performance of the model

13. When you train or retrain a model, when do you deploy a new version (as opposed to deploy as a new model)?

    A. Every time you train a model, it is deployed as a new version.

    B. Only models that have been uptrained from pretrained models get a new version.

    C. Never create a new version, always a new model.

    D. Whenever the model has similar inputs and outputs and is used for the same purpose.

14. Which of the following are good reasons to use a feature store? (Choose two.)

    A. There are many features for a model.

    B. There are many engineered features that have not been shared between teams.

    C. The features created by the data teams are not available during serving time, and this is creating training/serving differences.

    D. The models are built on a variety of features, including categorical variables and continuous variables.

15. Which service does Feast *not* use?

    A. BigQuery

    B. Redis

    C. Gojek

    D. Apache Beam

16. What is the hierarchy of the Vertex AI Feature Store data model?

    A. Featurestore - > EntityType -> Feature

    B. Featurestore - > Entity -> Feature

    C. Featurestore - > Feature -> FeatureValue

    D. Featurestore -> Entity - > FeatureValue

17. What is the highest level in the hierarchy of the data model of a Vertex AI Feature Store called?

    A. Featurestore

    B. Entity

    C. Feature

    D. EntityType

18. You are working in a small organization and dealing with structured data, and you have worked on creating multiple high-value features. Now you want to use these features for machine learning training and make these features available for real-time serving as well. You are given only a day to implement a good solution for this and then move on to a different project. Which options work best for you?

    A. Store the features in BigQuery and retrieve using the BigQuery Python client.

    B. Create a Feature Store from scratch using BigQuery, Redis, and Apache Beam.

    C. Download and install open-source Feast.

    D. Use Vertex AI Feature Store.

19. Which of these statements is false?

    A. Vertex AI Feature Store can ingest from BigQuery.

    B. Vertex AI Feature Store can ingest from Google Cloud Storage.

    C. Vertex AI Feature Store can even store images.

    D. Vertex AI Feature Store serves features with low latency.

20. Which of these statements is true?

    A. Vertex AI Feature Store uses a time-series model to store all data.

    B. Vertex AI Feature Store cannot ingest from Google Cloud Storage.

    C. Vertex AI Feature Store can even store images.

    D. Vertex AI Feature Store cannot serve features with low latency.

Chapter

14

BigQuery ML

BigQuery is the flagship data warehouse product in Google Cloud. It is a fully managed serverless service that can work with petabytes of data. BigQuery was released (generally available) in November 2011. Over 10 years, the popular service has grown significantly in user base as well as number of features.

You might have noticed that BigQuery ML was mentioned in many of the previous chapters. Although the current exam guide (as of writing this book) does not have a separate section for it, this is one of the most important topics for the ML certification.

In BigQuery, data is analyzed using SQL, including creating and training models. We will explain usage of BigQuery using an example. Suppose we have a dataset that has data about credit card customers and the objective is to find if a customer defaulted on their credit card payment.

BigQuery ML revolutionized the industry because it was a radical change to the status quo. Traditionally, machine learning was only accessible to expert machine learning engineers who wrote code (say Python). BigQuery ML made it possible for data analysts that are familiar with SQL to be able to leverage the ML tools.

Data analysts and others who are familiar with SQL prefer to use Big-Query ML instead of other methods.

In a big way, BigQuery ML democratized machine learning and made it available to many more people. This created a rapid change in the usage of machine learning, especially for structured data.

BigQuery – Data Access

There are three ways of accessing the data. The most common method is using the web console to write a SQL query (shown in Figure 14.1). The results of the query are displayed below the query editor.

The second method is to run the same query in a Jupyter Notebook, by using the magic command %%bigquery, as shown in Figure 14.2. The figure shows the execution and the query result from BigQuery being run on a Jupyter Notebook running Vertex AI Workbench.

FIGURE 14.1   Running a SQL query in the web console

FIGURE 14.2   Running the same SQL query through a Jupyter Notebook on Vertex AI Workbench

```
[3]: %%bigquery

SELECT

* FROM

    `projectname.dataset1.table1`

LIMIT 10
```

```
Query complete after 0.00s: 100%|██████████| 1/1 [00:00<00:00, 452.85query/s]
Downloading: 100%|██████████| 10/10 [00:00<00:00, 12.03rows/s]
```

	ID	LIMITBAL	SEX	EDUCATION	MARRIAGE	AGE	PAY0	PAY2	PAY3	PAY4	...	BILLAMT4	BILLAMT5
0	3	90000	2	2	2	34	0	0	0	0	...	14331	14948
1	4	50000	2	2	1	37	0	0	0	0	...	28314	28959
2	6	50000	1	1	2	37	0	0	0	0	...	19394	19619
3	7	500000	1	1	2	29	0	0	0	0	...	542653	483003

The third method is to use a Python API to run the same query in Jupyter Notebook using the Python API. See the following code for reference. The first part is importing the BigQuery library and then creating a client. Pass the query as a string and the results are captured in a Pandas DataFrame.

```
from google.cloud import bigquery
import pandas
client = bigquery.Client(location="us-central1",project="projectname")
query = """
    SELECT * FROM `projectname.dataset1.table1` LIMIT 10
"""
```

continues

(continued)
```
query_job = client.query(
    query,
    location="us-central1",
)
df = query_job.to_dataframe()
```

BigQuery ML Algorithms

BigQuery ML (previously called BQML) allows you to create machine learning models using standard SQL queries. You can create models and train, test, validate, and predict using models with only SQL queries. You don't have to write any Python code to use machine learning in BigQuery. Moreover, it is completely serverless.

 BigQuery ML is a completely serverless method to train and predict.

Model Training

To create a model, the keyword to use is `CREATE MODEL`. This statement is similar to the `CREATE TABLE` DDL statement. When you run a query with the `CREATE MODEL` statement, a query job is generated and processes the query. Similar to `CREATE MODEL`, you also have `CREATE MODEL IF NOT EXISTS` and `CREATE OR REPLACE MODEL`, commands with names that are intuitive to help us reuse model names for our convenience.

```
CREATE MODEL modelname1
    OPTIONS(model_type='linear_reg', input_label_cols=['label_col'])
AS SELECT * FROM table1
```

In the preceding SQL command, after the keyword, you must provide two options, model_type and input_label_cols. The model type specifies what kind of model you are trying to build. There are regression, classification, and time-series models available for you to choose from. See Table 14.1 for the full list of models available today. The second option is input_label_cols, which identifies the target column in the data provided below.

Finally, the last part of the SQL command ("SELECT * FROM table1) identifies the tables you are going to use for training. Notice that it appears as a simple selection query, which means the query result is being passed to the training job. In this line, you can select some columns, select some rows, join multiple tables to generate a result, and so on to create your training dataset. The only restriction is to make sure that the target column exists and there are enough rows to train a model.

TABLE 14.1   Models available on BigQuery ML

Model Category	Model Type	Description
Regression	LINEAR_REG, BOOSTED_ TREE_REGRESSOR, DNN_REGRESSOR, AUTOML_REGRESSION	To predict a real value
Classification	LOGISTIC_REG, BOOSTED_ TREE_CLASSIFIER, DNN_CLASSIFIER, DNN_ LINEAR_COMBINED_CLASSI- FIER, AUTOML_CLASSIFIER	To predict either a binary label or multiple labels
Deep and wide models	DNN_LINEAR_COMBINED_ REGRESSOR, DNN_LINEAR_COMBINED_ CLASSIFIER	Deep and wide models used for recommendation systems and personalization
Clustering	KMEANS	Unsupervised clustering models
Collaborative filtering	MATRIX_FACTORIZATION	For recommendations
Dimensionality reduction	PCA, AUTOENCODER	Unsupervised preprocessing step
Time-series forecasting	ARIMA_PLUS	Forecasting
General	TENSORFLOW	Generic TensorFlow model

If you take a look at the list in Table 14.1, there are several kinds of available models. The expected ones are in linear regression, classification, and clustering and are easy to define using SQL. However, as you go down the list, you may see DNN, which stands for *deep neural network*. In BigQuery ML, you have the complete flexibility to define and train DNN models by passing the right parameters in the options section. See Figure 14.3 for the full list of options for DNN_CLASSIFIER and DNN_REGRESSOR. These models are built using TensorFlow estimators. Notice that you have all the flexibility you need to build the model of your choice.

We created a model for our small dataset, and it was complete in a few minutes:

```
CREATE OR REPLACE MODEL
    `test.creditcard_model1`
```

continues

(continued)

```
OPTIONS(model_type='logistic_reg',
       input_label_cols=['defaultpaymentnextmonth'])
AS
SELECT * FROM `test.creditcardtable`
```

FIGURE 14.3 SQL options for DNN_CLASSIFIER and DNN_REGRESSOR

```
{CREATE MODEL | CREATE MODEL IF NOT EXISTS | CREATE OR REPLACE MODEL} model_name
[OPTIONS(MODEL_TYPE = { 'DNN_CLASSIFIER' | 'DNN_REGRESSOR' },
        ACTIVATION_FN = { 'RELU' | 'RELU6' | 'CRELU' | 'ELU' | 'SELU' | 'SIGMOID' | 'TANH' },
        AUTO_CLASS_WEIGHTS = { TRUE | FALSE },
        BATCH_SIZE = int64_value,
        CLASS_WEIGHTS = struct_array,
        DROPOUT = float64_value,
        EARLY_STOP = { TRUE | FALSE },
        HIDDEN_UNITS = int_array,
        L1_REG = float64_value,
        L2_REG = float64_value,
        LEARN_RATE = float64_value,
        INPUT_LABEL_COLS = string_array,
        MAX_ITERATIONS = int64_value,
        MIN_REL_PROGRESS = float64_value,
        OPTIMIZER = { 'ADAGRAD' | 'ADAM' | 'FTRL' | 'RMSPROP' | 'SGD' },
        WARM_START = { TRUE | FALSE },
        DATA_SPLIT_METHOD = { 'AUTO_SPLIT' | 'RANDOM' | 'CUSTOM' | 'SEQ' | 'NO_SPLIT' },
        DATA_SPLIT_EVAL_FRACTION = float64_value,
        DATA_SPLIT_COL = string_value,
        ENABLE_GLOBAL_EXPLAIN = { TRUE | FALSE },
        INTEGRATED_GRADIENTS_NUM_STEPS = int64_value,
)];
```

When we train a classification model, we can view the results of the training, the iterations, and also the evaluations, including aggregate metrics, score threshold, ROC curve, PR curves, and the confusion matrix. These are calculated automatically.

Model Evaluation

However, it is recommended to use a separate dataset not seen by the model for evaluating the model using the keyword ML.EVALUATE.

```
SELECT * FROM
ML.EVALUATE(MODEL `projectid.test.creditcard_model1`,
  ( SELECT * FROM `test.creditcardtable`))
```

This gave us the result shown in Figure 14.4 in a few seconds, which shows the query and the results below it in the web interface.

 Supervised and unsupervised learning model evaluations work differently.

FIGURE 14.4   Query showing results of model evaluation

Prediction

The `ML.PREDICT` function is used for prediction in BigQuery ML. You can pass an entire table to predict and the output will be a table with all the input columns and the same number of rows, along with two new columns, *predicted_<label_column_name>* and *predicted_<label_column_name>_probs*. Here the <label_column_name> is the name of the label column in the training data. There are some differences.

Here is the example SQL for making predictions from the model we created:

```
select * from
 ML.PREDICT (MODEL `dataset1.creditcard_model1` ,
        (select * FROM `dataset1.creditcardpredict` limit 1))
```

Here we are specifying the model `creditcard_model1` that was created earlier and selecting one row from a table called `creditcardpredict` and passing it to the `ML.PREDICT` function. The `select` in the first line allows me to select only certain columns from the output.

Here is the same example with only the predictions selected:

```
select
      predicted_defaultpaymentnextmonth,
      predicted_defaultpaymentnextmonth_probs
 from
 ML.PREDICT (MODEL `dataset1.creditcard_model1` ,
     (select  * FROM `dataset1.creditcardtable` limit 1))
```

The result of the preceding query is shown in Figure 14.5. Notice that the predictions probability is shown for each label.

FIGURE 14.5   Query results showing only the predictions

Query results			
JOB INFORMATION	RESULTS	JSON	EXECUTION DETAILS
Row	predicted_defaultpaymentnextmonth	predic...label	predic...prob
1	0	1	0.22607946403...
		0	0.77392053596...

Explainability in BigQuery ML

Explainability is important to debug models and improve transparency, and in some domains it is even a regulatory requirement. In BigQuery, you can get global feature importance values at the model level or you can get explanations for each prediction. These are also accessed using SQL functions.

To have explanations at the global level, you must set `enable_global_explain=TRUE` during training. Here is the sample SQL for our previous example:

```
CREATE OR REPLACE MODEL
      `model1`

OPTIONS(model_type='logistic_reg',
      enable_global_explain=TRUE,
      input_label_cols=['defaultpaymentnextmonth']) AS SELECT
  *
FROM ` dataset1.creditcardtable`
```

And after the model has trained, you can query the model's global explanations, which are returned as a table (Figure 14.6); each row contains the input features with the floating-point number representing the importance.

```
SELECT  *
FROM
ML.GLOBAL_EXPLAIN(MODEL ` model1`)
```

The numbers next to the features represent the impact of a feature on making the predictions. The higher the attribution, the higher the relevance to model and vice versa. However, note that the attributions are not normalized (they do not add up to 1). See Table 14.2.

FIGURE 14.6 Global feature importance returned for our model

Row	feature	attribution
1	PAY0	0.34025237617099363
2	PAY2	0.11768674830782758
3	LIMITBAL	0.07408092345060201
4	MARRIAGE	0.07286064114290507
5	PAY3	0.06566790235259186
6	AGE	0.05685299936790562
7	EDUCATION	0.051288064334038874
8	SEX	0.04843962733428721
9	BILLAMT1	0.04125181574956304
10	PAYAMT2	0.039422534029275515
11	PAYAMT1	0.03912628720654249
12	PAY4	0.03487845016572051
13	PAY5	0.03305366012064719
14	BILLAMT3	0.025391484056269387
15	PAY6	0.025171480923831053

TABLE 14.2 Model types

Model Type	Explainability Method	Description
Linear and logistic regression	Shapley values and standard errors, p-values	This is the average of all the marginal contributions to all possible coalitions.
Boosted Trees	Tree SHAP, Gini-based feature importance	Shapley values optimized for decision tree–based models.
Deep Neural Network and Wide-and-Deep	Integrated gradients	A gradients-based method to efficiently compute feature attributions with same axiomatic properties as Shapley.
Arima_PLUS	Time-series decomposition	Decompose into multiple components if present in the time series.

There is a computational cost to adding explainability to predictions. This is especially true for methods like Shapley where the complexity increases exponentially with the number of features.

In the following SQL code, we are using EXPLAIN_PREDICT instead of the PREDICT function. We are selecting all columns from a table called dataset1.credit_card_test and only one row. The result is shown in Figure 14.7.

FIGURE 14.7   Prediction result

baseline_prediction_value	prediction_value
-1.412493199732077	-1.2813410910646574

```
SELECT  *
FROM  ML.EXPLAIN_PREDICT(
MODEL `creditcard_model1`,
    (
      SELECT * FROM
        `dataset1.credit_card_test` limit 1
    ),
STRUCT(5 AS top_k_features))
```

In our case, predicted value is −1.281. Now let us look at the top five features that were reported as part of the query result (Figure 14.8). One thing to notice is that these individual feature contributions are two orders of magnitude lower than the baseline.

FIGURE 14.8   Top feature attributions for the prediction

top_feature_attributions.feature	top_feature_attributions.attribution
MARRIAGE	-0.06667881581378379
LIMITBAL	0.061773120858242034
SEX	-0.03908922859885329
PAYAMT1	0.026788378166783776
BILLAMT2	0.019992252732497153

After you have analyzed the explanations, you may also want to record the global explanations as part of your metadata. At a model level, you may always set aside a dataset just to run explanations on. Store the feature attributions for every prediction along with the predictions.

BigQuery ML vs. Vertex AI Tables

BigQuery ML deals with tables and so does Vertex AI. These two products have similarities, but there are key differences because they cater to different kinds of users. BigQuery is a serverless data warehouse, where users are SQL experts and think in terms of tables, joins, GROUP-BY statements, and so on. Some of the BigQuery customers have written thousands of queries, and some of them are very complex queries, are automated using BigQuery_ scheduled queries, and use visualization tools like Looker and Looker Studio.

The Vertex AI customer is very familiar with Kubeflow and most proficient in Java or Python. This data scientist uses Jupyter Notebooks on a daily basis and mainly uses Pandas DataFrames to manipulate the data. This machine learning engineer is building interesting new neural networks, and sometimes custom TensorFlow operations, and thinking about using TPUs. This user wants fine-grained control over the flow of the data and the training process.

In summary, although the two products have largely similar features, the interface and the method to train and predict are very different and are aimed at different audiences.

 If you have a question where the user is an analyst or business user, you want to consider BigQuery. On the other hand, if you have machine learning engineers, consider Vertex AI.

Interoperability with Vertex AI

Although Vertex AI and BigQuery ML are very distinct products, they have been designed to interoperate at every point in the machine learning pipeline. There are at least six integration points that make it easy to use both products together seamlessly.

Access BigQuery Public Dataset

BigQuery has more than 200 public datasets that are made available to the general public through the Google Cloud Public Datasets Program. Google pays for the storage of the datasets and you can access them through your GCP project. You pay only for the queries that you run on these datasets.

You can also access these datasets from Vertex AI to train your ML models or to augment your existing data. For example, say you are predicting the traffic conditions in a location; you can combine your dataset with BigQuery's public weather dataset to improve your model.

Import BigQuery Data into Vertex AI

When you create a dataset in Vertex AI, you provide the source URL to start with. You can directly provide a BigQuery URL that points to a BigQuery dataset to create a Vertex AI dataset. You can do this in just a few steps in the console or like this in Python:

```
from google.cloud import aiplatform
dataset = aiplatform.TabularDataset.create(
    display_name="my-tabular-dataset",
    bq_source="bq://project.dataset.table_name",
)
```

Notice that we are not exporting the data from BigQuery and then importing into Vertex AI. Thanks to this integration, you can now seamlessly connect to data in BigQuery.

Access BigQuery Data from Vertex AI Workbench Notebooks

When you use a Jupyter Notebook from a managed notebook instance in Vertex AI Workbench, you can directly browse your BigQuery dataset, run SQL queries, or download into a Pandas DataFrame.

This is highly useful for data scientists who use Jupyter Notebooks for exploratory analysis, create visualizations, experiment with machine learning models, or perform feature engineering with different datasets.

Analyze Test Prediction Data in BigQuery

This feature is similar to the dataset creation integration but works in the other direction. When you train a model, you provide a train and test dataset, and as part of the process you get the predictions for the test dataset. You have the ability to export this directly to BigQuery. This is useful when you want to further analyze the test predictions using various SQL methods.

Export Vertex AI Batch Prediction Results

When you are making batch predictions in Vertex AI, you can directly point to a BigQuery table as the input data and, in addition, send the predictions back to BigQuery to be stored as a table. This is very useful if you have standardized your MLOps using Vertex AI, but the data is in BigQuery.

Export BigQuery Models into Vertex AI

When you build a model in BigQuery, you can export the model from BigQuery into GCS and then import it into Vertex AI. This gives you complete freedom to train it and use it anywhere. Going forward, if you use the Vertex AI Model Registry, you can register your BigQuery ML models directly into it. This step saves you the additional work of exporting the model files into GCS and makes it seamless. Both BigQuery inbuilt models and TensorFlow models are supported. Currently there is a limitation on exporting ARIMA_PLUS models, XGBoost models, and models that use a transform.

BigQuery Design Patterns

There are several situations in data science and machine learning that recur frequently enough to be considered a pattern, and there are some clever well-thought-out solutions to address them, called design patterns. Because BigQuery ML is a revolutionary technology that approaches machine learning from a novel perspective, there have been some elegant new solutions to some of the old problems.

Hashed Feature

This solution addresses three problems faced by categorical variables:

- Incomplete vocabulary: The input data might not have the full set of the values that a categorical variable could take. This creates a problem if the data is fed directly into a ML model.

- High cardinality: Zip code is an example of a categorical variable with high cardinality, which creates some scaling issues in ML.

- Cold start problem: There could be new values added to the categorical variable that might not have existed in the training dataset—for example, the creation of a new employee ID when a person joins.

One method to deal with this problem is to transform this high cardinal variable into a low cardinal domain by hashing. This can be done very easily in BigQuery like this:

```
ABS(MOD(FARM_FINGERPRINT(zipcode), numbuckets))
```

This uses a hashing function called FarmHash, a family of hashing algorithms that are deterministic, well-distributed, and available in a number of programming languages.

Transforms

Sometimes inputs to models are modified or enhanced or engineered before feeding into the model like the hashing example. There is valuable information in the transformations applied to the inputs. The transformations applied to the inputs to the training dataset must also be applied to the inputs if the model is deployed in production. So the code to transform is part of the pipeline when you are making the predictions. BigQuery has an elegant solution to this called the TRANSFORM clause that is part of the CREATE_MODEL function:

```
CREATE OR REPLACE MODEL m
  TRANSFORM(ML.FEATURE_CROSS(STRUCT(f1, f2)) as cross_f,
            ML.QUANTILE_BUCKETIZE(f3) OVER() as buckets,
            label_col)
  OPTIONS(model_type='linear_reg', input_label_cols=['label_col'])
AS SELECT * FROM t
```

In the preceding example SQL, we are creating a "feature cross" transform over f1 and f2, and the second transform is a quantile bucketizing the feature f3. These transformations will be applied to the input fields f1, f2, and f3 to create new features called "cross_f" and "buckets". BigQuery ML will then automatically add this transform code to the model that is built. Therefore, during prediction, when you pass inputs f1, f2, and f3, it will automatically perform these transformations before sending the inputs to the model.

BigQuery offers many such useful transforms like POLYNOMIAL_EXPAND, FEATURE_CROSS, NGRAMS, QUANTILE_BUCKET, HASH_BUCKETIZE, MIN_MAX_SCALER and STANDARD_SCALER.

For more details on the TRANSFORM clause, refer to the documentation:

```
https://cloud.google.com/bigquery-ml/docs/reference/standard-sql/
bigqueryml-preprocessing-functions
```

The caveat for this design pattern is that these models with transforms will not work outside BigQuery ML, say, if you export the model to Vertex AI.

Summary

BigQuery is an important service that revolutionized the use of ML in the SQL community. BigQuery ML democratized machine learning and made it available to many more people.

In this chapter we saw how to use SQL to perform all actions of a ML pipeline. We also learned how to apply transformations to input values directly using SQL, which reduces the time to create models. Although BigQueryML is a separate service, it is highly interoperable with Vertex AI. Lastly we also saw some interesting design patterns which are unique to BigQuery ML.

Exam Essentials

Understand BigQuery and ML.   Learn the history of BigQuery and the innovation of bringing machine learning into a data warehouse and to data analysis and anyone familiar with SQL. Learn how to train, predict, and provide model explanations using SQL.

Be able to explain the differences between BigQuery ML and Vertex AI and how they work together.   These services offer similar features but are designed for different users. BigQuery ML is designed for analysts and anyone familiar with SQL, and Vertex AI is designed for ML engineers. Learn the various different integration points that make it seamless to work between the two services.

Understand BigQuery design patterns.   BigQuery has elegant solutions to recurring problems in machine learning. Hashing, transforms, and serverless predictions are easy to apply to your ML pipeline.

Review Questions

1. You work as part of a large data analyst team in a company that owns a global footwear brand. The company manufactures in South Asia and distributes all over the globe. Its sales were affected during the COVID-19 pandemic and so was distribution. Your team has been asked to forecast sales per country with new data about the spread of the illness and a plan for recovery. Currently your data is on-prem and sales data comes from all over the world weekly. What will you use to forecast?

    A. Use Vertex AI AutoML Tables to forecast sales as this is a distributed case.

    B. User Vertex AI AutoML Tables with custom models (TensorFlow) because this is a special case due to COVID-19.

    C. Use BigQuery ML, experiment with a TensorFlow model and DNN models to find the best results.

    D. Use BigQuery ML with ARIMA_PLUS, and use the BigQuery COVID-19 public dataset for trends.

2. You are part of a startup that rents bicycles, and you want to predict the amount of time a bicycle will be used and the distance it will be taken based on current location and userid. You are part of a small team of data analysts, and currently all the data is sitting in a data warehouse. Your manager asks you to quickly create a machine learning model so that they can evaluate this idea. Your manager wants to show this prototype to the CEO to improve sales. What will you choose?

    A. Use a TensorFlow model on Vertex AI tables to predict time and distance.

    B. Use the advanced path prediction algorithm in Google Maps.

    C. Use BigQuery ML.

    D. Use a Vertex AI custom model to get better results because the inputs include map coordinates.

3. You are a data analyst for a large video sharing website. The website has thousands of users that provide 5-star ratings for videos. You have been asked to provide recommendations per user. What would you use?

    A. Use BigQuery classification `model_type`.

    B. Use a Vertex AI custom model to build a collaborative filtering model and serve it online.

    C. Use the matrix factorization model in BigQuery ML to create recommendations using explicit feedback.

    D. Use Vertex AI AutoML for matrix factorization.

4. You are a data analyst and your manager gave you a TensorFlow SavedModel to use for a classification. You need to get some predictions quickly but don't want to set up any instances or create pipelines. What would be your approach?

A. Use BigQuery ML and choose TensorFlow as the model type to run predictions.

B. Use Vertex AI custom models, and create a custom container with the TensorFlow SavedModel.

C. TensorFlow SavedModel can only be used locally, so download the data onto a Jupyter Notebook and predict locally.

D. Use Kubeflow to create predictions.

5. You are working as a data scientist in the finance industry and there are regulations about collecting and storing explanations for every machine learning prediction. You have been tasked to provide an initial machine learning model to classify good loans and loans that have defaulted. The model that you provide will be used initially and is expected to be improved further by a data analyst team. What is your solution?

A. Use Kubeflow Pipelines to create a Vertex AI AutoML Table with explanations.

B. Use Vertex AI Pipelines to create a Vertex AI AutoML Table with explanations and store them in BigQuery for analysts to work on.

C. Use BigQuery ML, and select "classification" as the model type and enable explanations.

D. Use Vertex AI AutoML Tables with explanations and store the results in BigQuery ML for analysts.

6. You are a data scientist and have built extensive Vertex AI Pipelines which use Vertex AI AutoML Tables. Your manager is asking you to build a new model with data in BigQuery. How do you want to proceed?

A. Create a Vertex AI pipeline component to download the BigQuery dataset to a GCS bucket and then run Vertex AI AutoML Tables.

B. Create a new Vertex AI pipeline component to train BigQuery ML models on the Big-Query data.

C. Create a Vertex AI pipeline component to execute Vertex AI AutoML by directly importing a BigQuery dataset.

D. Create a schedule query to train a model in BigQuery.

7. You are a data scientist and have built extensive Vertex AI Pipelines which use Vertex AI AutoML Tables. Your manager is asking you to build a new model with a BigQuery public dataset. How do you want to proceed?

A. Create a Vertex AI pipeline component to download the BigQuery dataset to a GCS bucket and then run Vertex AI AutoML Tables.

B. Create a new Vertex AI pipeline component to train BigQuery ML models on the Big-Query data.

C. Create a Vertex AI pipeline component to execute Vertex AI AutoML by directly importing the BigQuery public dataset.

D. Train a model in BigQuery ML because it is not possible to access BigQuery public datasets from Vertex AI.

8. You are a data scientist, and your team extensively uses Jupyter Notebooks. You are merging with the data analytics team, which uses only BigQuery. You have been asked to build models with new data that the analyst team created in BigQuery. How do you want to access it?

    A. Export the BigQuery data to GCS and then download it to the Vertex AI notebook.

    B. Create an automated Vertex AI pipeline job to download the BigQuery data to a GCS bucket and then download it to the Vertex AI notebook.

    C. Use Vertex AI managed notebooks, which can directly access BigQuery tables.

    D. Start using BigQuery console to accommodate the analysts.

9. You are a data scientist, and your team extensively uses Vertex AI AutoML Tables and pipelines. Your manager wants you to send the predictions of new test data to test for bias and fairness. The fairness test will be done by the analytics team that is comfortable with SQL. How do you want to access it?

    A. Export the test prediction data from GCS and create an automation job to transfer it to BigQuery for analysis.

    B. Move your model to BigQuery ML and create predictions there.

    C. Deploy the model and run a batch prediction on the new dataset to save in GCS and then transfer to BigQuery.

    D. Add the new data to your AutoML Tables test set, and configure the Vertex AI tables to export test results to BigQuery.

10. You are a data scientist, and your team extensively uses Vertex AI AutoML Tables and pipelines. Your manager wants you to send predictions to test for bias and fairness. The fairness test will be done by the analytics team that is comfortable with SQL. How do you want to access it?

    A. Export the test prediction data from GCS and create an automation job to transfer it to BigQuery for analysis.

    B. Move your model to BigQuery ML and create predictions there.

    C. Deploy the model and run a batch prediction on the new dataset to save in GCS and then transfer to BigQuery.

    D. Deploy the model and run a batch prediction on the new dataset to export directly to BigQuery.

11. You are a data scientist, and your team extensively uses Vertex AI AutoML Tables and pipelines. Another team of analysts has built some highly accurate models on BigQuery ML. You want to use those models also as part of your pipeline. What is your solution?

    A. Run predictions in BigQuery and export the prediction data from BigQuery into GCS and then load it into your pipeline.

    B. Retrain the models on Vertex AI tables with the same data and hyperparameters.

    C. Load the models in the Vertex AI model repository and run batch predictions in Vertex AI.

    D. Download the model and create a container for Vertex AI custom models and run batch predictions.

12. You are a data analyst and working with structured data. You are exploring different machine learning options, including Vertex AI and BigQuery ML. You have found that your model accuracy is suffering because of a categorical feature (zipcode) that has high cardinality. You do not know if this feature is causing it. How can you fix this?

   A. Use the hashing function (`ABS(MOD(FARM_FINGERPRINT(zipcode),buckets))`) in BigQuery to bucketize.

   B. Remove the input feature and train without it.

   C. Don't change the input as it affects accuracy.

   D. Vertex AI tables will automatically take care of this.

13. You are a data analyst working with structured data in BigQuery and you want to perform some simple feature engineering (hashing, bucketizing) to improve your model accuracy. What are your options?

   A. Use the BigQuery TRANSFORM clause during CREATE_MODEL for your feature engineering.

   B. Have a sequence of queries to transform your data and then use this data for BigQuery ML training.

   C. Use Data Fusion to perform feature engineering and then load it into BigQuery.

   D. Build Vertex AI AutoML Tables which can automatically take care of this problem.

14. You are part of a data analyst team working with structured data in BigQuery but also considering using Vertex AI AutoML. Which of the following statements is wrong?

   A. You can run BigQuery ML models in Vertex AI AutoML Tables.

   B. You can use BigQuery public datasets in AutoML Tables.

   C. You can import data from BigQuery into AutoML.

   D. You can use SQL queries on Vertex AI AutoML Tables.

15. Which of the following statements is wrong?

   A. You can run SQL in BigQuery through Python.

   B. You can run SQL in BigQuery through the CLI.

   C. You can run SQL in BigQuery through R.

   D. You can run SQL in BigQuery through Vertex AI.

16. You are training models on BigQuery but also use Vertex AI AutoML Tables and custom models. You want flexibility in using data and models and want portability. Which of the following is a bad idea?

   A. Bring TensorFlow models into BigQuery ML.

   B. Use TRANSFORM functionality in BigQuery ML.

   C. Use BigQuery public datasets for training.

   D. Use Vertex AI Pipelines for automation.

17. You want to standardize your MLOps using Vertex AI, especially AutoML Tables and Vertex AI Pipelines, etc., but some of your team is using BigQuery ML. Which of the following is incorrect?

    A. Vertex AI Pipelines will work with BigQuery.

    B. BigQuery ML models that include TRANSFORM can also be run on AutoML.

    C. BigQuery public datasets can be used in Vertex AI AutoML Tables.

    D. You can use BigQuery and BigQuery ML through Python from Vertex AI managed notebooks.

18. Which of these statements about BigQuery ML is incorrect?

    A. BigQuery ML supports both supervised and unsupervised models.

    B. BigQuery ML supports models for recommendation engines.

    C. You can control the various hyperparameters of a deep learning model like dropouts in BigQuery ML.

    D. BigQuery ML models with TRANSFORM clause can be ported to Vertex AI.

19. Which of these statements about comparing BigQuery ML explanations is incorrect?

    A. All BigQuery ML models provide explanations with each prediction.

    B. Feature attributions are provided both at the global level and for each prediction.

    C. The explanations vary by the type of model used.

    D. Not all models have global explanations.

20. You work as part of a large data analyst team in a company that owns hundreds of retail stores across the country. Their sales were affected due to bad weather. Currently your data is on-prem and sales data comes from all across the country. What will you use to forecast sales using weather data?

    A. Use Vertex AI AutoML Tables to forecast with previous sales data.

    B. User Vertex AI AutoML Tables with a custom model (TensorFlow) and augment the data with weather data.

    C. Use BigQeury ML, and use the Wide-and-Deep model to forecast sales for a wide number of stores as well as deep into the future.

    D. Use BigQuery ML with ARIMA_PLUS, and use the BigQuery public weather dataset for trends.

Appendix

Answers to Review Questions

Chapter 1: Framing ML Problems

1. A, B, D. First understand the use case, and then look for the details such as impact, success criteria, and budget and time frames. Finding the algorithm comes later.

2. B. Hyperparameters are variables that cannot be learned. You will use a hyperparameter optimization (HPO) algorithm to automatically find the best hyperparameters. This is not considered when you are trying to match a business case to an ML problem.

3. B. The input data is time-series data and predicting for next 7 days is typical of a forecasting problem.

4. B. A prediction has only two outputs: either valid or not valid. This is binary classification. If there are more than two classes, it is multiclass classification. Linear regression is predicting a number. Option C is popular with support tickets to identify clusters of topics but cannot be used in this case.

5. C. When you are trying to identify an object across several frames, this is video object tracking. Option A is factually incorrect. Option B is for images, not video. Scene detection or action detection classifies whether an "action" has taken place in video, a different type of problem, so option D is also wrong.

6. D. Topic modeling is an unsupervised ML problem. Given a set of documents, it would cluster them into groups and also provide the keywords that define each cluster.

7. C. Precision is a metric for unbalanced classification problems.

8. A. The root-mean-squared error (RMSE) is the best option if you are trying to reduce extreme errors.

9. A. RMSE, MAPE, and R^2 are regression metrics. Accuracy is the only classification metric here.

10. C. We can eliminate RMSE because it is a regression metric. Accuracy is also wrong because it is a poor metric for imbalanced (1:100) datasets. So, the correct answer is either precision or recall. In this case, a false negative could cause severe problems later on, so we want to choose a metric that minimizes false negatives. So, the answer is recall.

11. B. "No labeled data" means you cannot have supervised learning or semi-supervised learning. Reinforcement learning is when an agent actively explores an environment (like a robot), which is not relevant here. Only unsupervised learning can be applied to purely unlabeled data.

12. C. The Like button here is the explicit feedback that users provide on content and can be used for training. Collaborative filtering is the class of algorithm that can be used for recommendations such as in this case.

13. B. Option B is the bad idea because you need to update the data related to the new products. The idea of a "golden dataset" exists, but in this case, the dataset needs to be updated.

14. D. Use supervised learning when you have labeled data. Use unsupervised learning when you have unlabeled data. Use semi-supervised learning when you have a mix. There is no such thing as hyper-supervised learning.

15. A, D. Option A is absolutely true and is done throughout the industry. Option B is incorrect because it is done frequently in practice. Option C is partially true because it may amplify errors, but that does not mean you never feed one. Option D is correct because there is an entire class of models that help in transforming data for downstream prediction.

16. D. Whenever dealing with customer data and sensitive data, it is important to test your model for biases and apply responsible AI practices.

17. C. More testing data is not going to achieve much here. But that does not mean we cannot do anything. You can't always remove all the fields that may cause bias because some details might be hidden in other fields. The correct answer is to use model interpretability and explanations.

18. C. The model was deployed properly. Most Android phones can handle deep learning models very well. We cannot say much about the metric because it is unknown. This fun Android app could be used by a wide variety of people and was possibly not tested on a representative sample dataset.

19. B, D. There are many kinds of private data, not just photographs. Scans are also private data. There should always be concerns when using sensitive data.

20. B. While you can use the data creatively, there is always a privacy concern when dealing with customer data. Option A is true because you usually recommend other products at checkout. Option C is true because changes in user behavior and in the product catalog require retraining. Option D is true because you can use important information about products, like similar products or complementary products, to sell more.

Chapter 2: Exploring Data and Building Data Pipelines

1. D. Oversampling is the way to improve the imbalanced data class.

2. A. The model performed poorly on new patient data due to label leakage because you are training the model on hospital name.

3. A. Monitoring the model for skew and retraining will help with data distribution.

4. B. Model retraining will help with data distribution and minimizing data skew.

5. B. Downsample the majority data with unweighting to create 10 percent samples.

6. D. Transforming data before splitting for testing and training will avoid data leakage and will lead to better performance during model training.

7. C. Removing features with missing values will help because the dataset has columns with missing values.

8. A, B, and D. All of the options describe reasons for data leakage except option C, removing features with missing values.

Chapter 3: Feature Engineering

1. C. With one hot encoding you can convert categorical features to numeric features. Moreover, not all algorithms works well on categorical features.

2. B. Normalizing the data will help convert the range into a normalized format and will help converge the model.

3. C. For imbalanced datasets, AUC PR is a way to minimize false positives compared to AUC ROC.

4. B. Since the model is performing well with training data, it is a case of data leakage. Cross-validation is one of the strategies to overcome data leakage. We covered this in Chapter 2.

5. A, B. With TensorFlow data, prefectching and interleaving are techniques to improve processing time.

6. A. Use a tf.data.Dataset.prefetch transformation.

7. C. We will get one feature cross of binned latitude, binned longitude, and binned roomsPerPerson.

8. A. Cloud Data Fusion is the UI-based tool for ETL.

9. A. TensorFlow Transform is the most scalable way to transform your training and testing data for production workloads.

10. D. Since the model is underperforming with production data, there is a training-serving skew. Using a tf.Transform pipeline helps prevent this skew by creating transformations separately for training and testing.

Chapter 4: Choosing the Right ML Infrastructure

1. C. Always start with a pretrained model and see how well it solves your problem. If that does not work, you can move to AutoML. Custom models should always be the last resort.

2. C. "Glossary" is a feature that is intended to solve this exact problem. If you have some terms that need to be translated in a certain way, you can create a list of these in a XML document and pass it to Google Translate. Choose the Advanced option and not Basic. Whenever these specific words/phrases appear, it will replace them with your translation from the glossary.

3. D. It is true that there is no "translated subtitle" service; however, you can combine two services to suit your needs. Option A is wrong because there is no AutoML in Vertex AI today. Options B and C are possible but should not be the first step.

4. A. This is a classification problem. Using the AutoML Edge model type is the right approach because the model will be deployed on the edge device. While both Coral.ai and Android app deployment are right, if you want to go to market quickly, it is better to go with Android application using ML Kit.

5. A. You get the error "not found" when a GPU is not available in the selected region. Not all regions have all GPUs. If you have insufficient quota, you will get the error "Quota 'NVIDIA_V100_GPUS' exceeded."

6. D. Option A is wrong because n1-standard-2 is too small for GPUs, and option B is wrong because it is still using CPUs. Option D is better because it is better to go with 1 TPU than 8 GPUs, especially when you don't have any manual placements.

7. D. "Recommended for you" is intended for home pages, which brings attention to the most likely products based on current trends and user behavior. "Similar items" is based on product information only, which helps customers choose between similar products. "Others you may like" is the right choice for content based on the user's browsing history. "Frequently bought together" is intended to be shown at checkout when they can quickly add more into their cart.

8. B. "Frequently bought together" is intended to be shown at checkout when customers can quickly add more into their cart. "Recommended for you" is intended for home pages, which brings attention to the most likely product. "Similar items" is based on product information only, which helps customers choose between similar products. "Others you may like" is the right choice for showing content based on the user's browsing history.

9. A. When you want the customer to "engage more," it means you want them to spend more time in the website/app browsing through the products. "Frequently bought together" is intended to be shown at checkout when customers can quickly add more into their cart. "Recommended for you" is intended for home pages and brings attention to the most likely product, and "Similar items" is based on product information only, which helps customers to choose between similar products. "Others you may like" is the right choice for showing content based on the user's browsing history.

10. C. When you do not have browsing data, or "user events," you have to create recommendations based on project catalog information only. The only model that does not require "user information" in this list is "Similar items," which shows the products that are similar to the one the user is currently viewing.

11. B. The objective of "click-through rate" is based on the number of times the user clicks and follows a link, whereas the "revenue per order" captures the effectiveness for a recommendation being made at checkout.

12. D. Option A is wrong because there is no AutoML for this today. Currently there is no pre-trained API available for this on GCP. A Vertex AI custom job is the most appropriate.

13. B. Option A is wrong because the Natural Language API does not accept voice. While options C and D are also correct, these are custom models that will take time.

14. C. TPUs do not support custom TensorFlow operations. GPUs are the best options here.

15. A. Only A2 and N1 machine series support GPUs. Option C is wrong because you cannot have 3 GPUs in an instance.

16. A. Pushing a large model to an Android device without hardware support might slow the device significantly. Using devices with Edge TPU installed is the best answer here.

17. A, C. You cannot have TPU and GPU in a single instance. You would not usually go for a cluster of TPU VMs.

18. C. If you have a sparse matrix, TPUs will not provide the necessary efficiency.

19. C. TPUs are not used for high-precision predictions.

20. C, D. Options A and B increase the size of the instance without identifying the root cause. The question mentions that model has been already deployed on a big instance (32-core). The next step should be to identify the root cause of the latency, so Option C is a correct choice. Also, checking the code to see if it is single-threaded is correct, because it is not always a hardware problem; it could be a configuration issue or a software issue of being single threaded code.

Chapter 5: Architecting ML Solutions

1. B. The question is asking for the simplest solution, so we do not need Memorystore and Bigtable as the latency requirement is 300ms@p99. The best and simplest way to handle this is using App Engine to deploy the applications and call the model endpoint on the Vertex AI Prediction.

2. B. Bigtable is designed for very low latency reads of very large datasets.

3. A. To preprocess data you will use Dataflow, and then you can use the Vertex AI platform for training and serving. Since it's a recommendation use case, Cloud BigQuery is the recommended NoSQL store to manage this use case storage at scale and reduce latency.

4. A. Since you want to minimize the infrastructure overhead, you can use the Vertex AI platform for distributed training.

5. A, C. With Document AI, you can get started quickly because it's a solution offering built on the top layer of your AI stack with the least infrastructure heavy lifting needed by you to set up. Cloud Storage is the recommended data storage solution to create a document data lake.

6. A. When the question asks for retraining, look for a pipeline that can automate and orchestrate the task. Kubeflow Pipelines is the only option here that can help automate the retraining workflow.

7. D. Kubeflow Pipelines is the only choice that comes with an experiment tracking feature. See `www.kubeflow.org/docs/components/pipelines/concepts/experiment`.

8. C. You can use a Cloud Storage trigger to send a message to a Pub/Sub topic and create a Cloud Function that can trigger the GKE training jobs. See `https://cloud.google .com/architecture/architecture-for-mlops-using-tfx-kubeflow- pipelines-and-cloud-build#triggering-and-scheduling-kubeflow- pipelines`.

9. A. Use Kubeflow experiments for training and executing experiments.

10. A. You can use the batch prediction functionality because the data is aggregated at the end of the day and you do not need prediction in near real time.

11. B. TensorFlow's BigQueryClient uses the Storage API to efficiently read data directly out of BigQuery storage. The tf.data.datasetreader is used to create a input data pipeline and not to load data efficiently into tensorflow from BigQuery.

12. A, B, C. You can use all three connectors to connect to various framework datasets in BigQuery. Refer to Table 5.3 in this chapter.

13. A. A Vertex AI–managed dataset is the best way to organize and manage your data for training and prediction in the Vertex AI platform.

14. A, B. You should avoid storing data in block and file storage for ML use cases due to latency issues.

Chapter 6: Building Secure ML Pipelines

1. B. You would use the federated learning technique and deploy the ML model on the device where the data is stored.

2. B. Setting up different resources in separate projects can help separate the use of resources.

3. D. Masking replaces the value with surrogate characters such as # and the asterisk.

4. A, B, C. You need a service account key and authentication with GOOGLE_APPLICATION_ CREDENTIALS to use APIs. You also need to provide Vertex AI IAM access to the service account role created by the Vertex AI Workbench compute instance.

5. B, C. Cloud DLP can help redact and mask the PII, and VPC security control can manage data access.

6. A. You need to use a Vertex AI–managed notebook, which will take care of auto shutdown of idle instances automatically.

7. B. Cloud Healthcare API helps de-identify PHI data from an FHIR-type dataset.

8. A. Using architecture best practices, you can stream the files to Google Cloud and use Cloud Dataflow to write it to BigQuery. You can bulk-scan the tables using DLP API.

Chapter 7: Model Building

1. C. The question talks about a future change (6 months later) in data distribution causing the model to perform poorly. This sounds like training-serving skew or possibly prediction drift. The recommended best practice in either case is to monitor for it and retrain when necessary. `https://developers.google.com/machine-learning/guides/rules-of-ml#training-serving_skew`.

2. C. The model is already memorizing the training data, as seen from the good performance on training data but poor performance on validation data. Doubling the number of neurons will only make this worse, which rules out answer D. A 20% dropout would help the model generalize without drastically increasing training time. So, answer is C. Also L1 and L2 regularization will not help in this scenario.

3. B. The size of the images is too large to fit the GPUs. Changing batch size will help resolve the out of memory error.

4. D. In case of multiclass classification problems, we use sparse categorical cross-entropy.

5. D. Oscillating loss curves indicate that the model is repeatedly overcorrecting. This is usually due to the learning rate being too high. Increasing the learning rate will only make this worse. See `https://developers.google.com/machine-learning/testing-debugging/metrics/interpretic#1.-my-model-wont-train`.

6. B. The image classification model is a deep learning model. You minimize the loss of deep learning models to get the best model. So comparing loss performance for each model on validation data is the correct answer.

7. B. In order to minimize the training time without impacting the accuracy, you need to modify the batch size of the model because the model will train faster due to increase in batch size per epoch. This will lead to less time to train the same model.

8. B. Since the data is one-hot encoded, you will use categorical cross-entropy.

9. B, D. Since the model is converging in training and not while testing, it is an overfitting problem, which can be resolved by regularizing it with L2.

10. C. Since there is a bias and variance trade-off, you need to make sure that while training a model, both of the parameters are considered.

11. D, E. L1 is used for feature selection and k-means is a clustering algorithm.

12. B. When you have limited data, you can use the data augmentation techniques covered in this chapter.

13. B. Sigmoid is the activation function used for binary classification problems.

14. B. This is an example of tuning hyperparameters.

15. A. MirroredStrategy uses a single machine. Refer to Table 7.1.

Chapter 8: Model Training and Hyperparameter Tuning

1. A. In order to train TensorFlow code with less overhead from on-premises to cloud, you can use the custom training option on Vertex AI.

2. A. Since the question asks for the least manual intervention and less computation time, Big-Query SQL is the easiest way to do that compared to other options.

3. C. In order to evaluate the model metric while the job is running, you need to enable an interactive shell.

4. A, B, C. With Vertex AI hyperparameter tuning, you can configure the number of trials and the search algorithm as well as range of parameters.

5. B. You need a Cloud Dataproc connector to transform the data from PySpark to Spark SQL.

6. A. Using a Vertex AI training custom container is the most managed way to set up training for any framework.

7. B. For a large dataset, you can directly use Bigtable to train a TensorFlow model using a Big-table connector.

8. A. Pub/Sub with Cloud Dataflow is the most managed way of ingesting streaming data in Google Cloud.

9. A. From Pub/Sub, you can preprocess data in Dataflow and send it for ML training in Vertex AI, storing it in BigQuery. Store the results back into BigQuery after training and visualize in Data/Looker Studio.

10. C. You can directly access BigQuery tables using BigQuery magic in a Vertex AI notebook and then use the BigQuery client to convert it into a DataFrame.

11. B. From Pub/Sub you can preprocess data in Dataflow and send it for ML training in BigQuery ML. Store the results back into BigQuery after training and visualize in Data/ Looker Studio.

12. A. Using an established text classification model, and to have full control on the code, you will use custom Vertex AI training.

13. A, B. You can use both an interactive shell and TF Profiler to track metrics.

14. A. In order to monitor performance, you need TensorFlow Profiler.

15. A. The question is asking for a cost-effective approach. So the answer is option A.

16. B. The What-If Tool helps visualize TF models for regression and classification and LIT is for NLP models.

Chapter 9: Model Explainability on Vertex AI

1. B. Shapley values provide the informative, or important, features in a model.

2. B. For image data, integrated gradient is the preferred method.

3. A, B, and C. Vertex Explainable AI supports custom TensorFlow models and AutoML Tables and images.

4. A, B, E. Sampled Shapley, integrated gradients, and XRAI are three techniques for feature attribution.

5. A. Since this model is a nondifferentiable model, you can use sampled Shapley. Nondifferentiable models include nondifferentiable operations in the TensorFlow graph, such as operations that perform decoding and rounding tasks. To get feature attributions for nondifferentiable models, use the sampled Shapley method.

6. B, C. Both integrated gradients and XRAI are attribution techniques that are supported.

7. A. You can use local kernel explanations because the Explainable AI SDK is available in user-managed notebooks.

8. A. Vertex example–based explanations can help with detecting misclassifications in the predictions.

Chapter 10: Scaling Models in Production

1. D. Since the features are dynamic and it is a low-latency serving requirement, you would choose Bigtable for dynamic feature lookup. Moreover, you are also going to implement caching predictions in a datastore for a faster lookup.

2. A. You can use a BigQuery table for batch prediction with Vertex AI.

3. A. You can set up a notification with Pub/Sub and Cloud Function when your model predicts the user account balance drops below a certain threshold.

4. A. Pub/Sub to a Cloud Function for notification is the most suitable architecture.

5. A. Creating a daily batch prediction job will require minimal effort.

6. A. Creating a daily batch prediction job will require minimal effort using the schedule function in Vertex AI managed notebooks.

7. D. Since the question is asking about a solution with the least latency, you need to select a datastore, which will provide the least latency. Option D talks about using Cloud Bigtable for writing and reading the user navigation context. This is a classic architecture pattern discussed in topic online predictions.

8. A. The question is asking for a solution which requires the least effort to setup. Embed the client on the website, deploy the gateway on App Engine, and then deploy the model using Vertex AI Prediction.

Chapter 11: Designing ML Training Pipelines

1. A. You can use the TFX Evaluator or TFX ModelValidator component to create performance benchmarks for a model in production. Evaluator performs deep analysis of the training results and helps you validate your exported models, ensuring that they are "good enough" to be pushed to production.

2. A. For the setup that is the most managed and requires the least effort, you would use event-based Cloud Storage triggers to schedule Vertex AI Pipelines.

3. A. For the most managed setup that requires the least effort, you would use event-based Cloud Storage triggers to schedule a Kubeflow Pipelines job on GKE.

4. A, D. You can load the Kubeflow BigQuery component URL `https://github.com/kubeflow/pipelines/blob/master/components/gcp/bigquery/query/sample.ipynb` and query BigQuery in Kubeflow Pipelines.

5. A, B. With TFX, you can use either Apache Airflow or Kubeflow to orchestrate the Tensor-Flow pipeline.

6. B. Setting up Kubeflow Pipelines using Vertex AI is the most managed way as it will require the least effort to set up because it's serverless.

7. C. Using Cloud Build, you can automate the testing of Kubeflow Pipelines.

8. A. You can set up Kubeflow Pipelines using GKE on-premises with Anthos.

Chapter 12: Model Monitoring, Tracking, and Auditing Metadata

1. **B, D.** Option A is wrong because it is very clear that the data has drifted away from the training data. This may or may not be a temporary problem. Option C is wrong because retraining a model with higher accuracy is not going to solve this problem because you have not updated the training data. Option B and then followed by option D is the right approach.

2. **C.** Option A is wrong; the performance of the model on test data is irrelevant after deployment because the input data might change. Option B is wrong because the initial assessment is not sufficient. Option D is wrong because, although monitoring costs money, it is not a reason to not monitor the model.

3. **A, D.** Data drift is when the distribution of the input data changes. Concept drift is when the relationship between the input and predicted value changes.

4. **A.** Data drift is when the distribution of the input data changes. Here the distribution "height" feature of the training data and the real data are two standard deviations apart, which is significant.

5. **D.** Concept drift is when the relationship between the input and predicted value changes. In this case, most likely the fraudsters have changed their modus operandi and are using techniques to evade detection. You have to collect new data and retrain.

6. **C.** This is the definition of training-serving skew.

7. **B.** This is the definition of prediction drift.

8. **A.** Data drift is when the distribution of the input data changes. Here the number of plankton in training data and the real data are an order of magnitude different, which is significant.

9. **A, D.** For training-serving skew, you need a statistical distribution of input features of the training data for reference, and then you compare that with the continuous statistical distribution of the inputs in production.

10. **B, D.** For prediction drift, you need a baseline statistical distribution of input features of the production data for reference, and then you compare that with the continuous statistical distribution of the inputs in production over time.

11. **A.** L-infinity distance, or Chebyshev distance, is the greatest distance between two vectors.

12. **B.** Sampling rate is an option to tune to reduce the amount of data that is consumed by a service.

13. **A, B, D.** Option C is wrong because currently this is not a configuration; there is only one distance metric in Vertex AI.

14. **C.** If schema is not specified for custom models, the values may not be parsed properly. Option A is valid because AutoML models do not require schema. Option B is valid because custom models were the input is in key:value pairs are fine. Option D is valid because a schema is specified.

15. D. Options A and B are valid because string and number are supported. Option C is valid because you can define an array of strings or numbers. There is no data type called "category."

16. B. While the wording "input logging" may sound intuitive, that is not a type of logging on Vertex AI. Container logging, access logging, and request-response logging are valid.

17. D. Request-response logging gives you a sample saved in a BigQuery table.

18. C. Options A, B, and D valid as they are the primary usage for a metadata store. Option C does not make sense here.

19. C. Option C is the definition of an artifact. Option A is wrong because not all information on a metadata store is an artifact. Option B is only partially true, because an artifact is not limited to the train and test dataset. Option D is the definition of *execution*.

20. B. Artifact, context, and execution are valid elements in the data model.

Chapter 13: Maintaining ML Solutions

1. B. Option B is not part of MLOps. While it is a valid endeavor to look for other use cases to solve, it is not part of the MLOps workflow. Options A, C, and D are the major steps in MLOps.

2. B. This is an old organization that is just starting to explore and experiment with machine learning, so the best approach is to go with level 0. Option A is wrong because building ad hoc models is not a disciplined approach for any organization. Options C and D are for more mature situations.

3. C. Option A is wrong because ad hoc model building does not suit this level of maturity. Option B is wrong because MLOps level 0 is for organizations just experimenting and running proof of concepts. MLOps level 1 (strategic) is the right level for this organization. Also, since we are dealing with only one model, it fits this level. Option D is wrong because that is usually intended for organizations dealing with dozens or hundreds of models and experimenting with different algorithms and technologies.

4. D. Option A is wrong because ad hoc model building does not suit this level of maturity. Option B is wrong because MLOps level 0 is for organizations just experimenting and running proof of concepts. Option C is also wrong because MLOps level 1 (strategic) is usually for organizations that operate a few models. MLOps level 2 is the right level because they are dealing with many models in parallel and experimenting with different algorithms and technologies.

5. C. Option A is wrong because, although model training might be claimed as ad hoc, it does solve some problems. Option B is wrong because MLOps level 0 does not automate training. Option D is wrong because level 0 does not automate the whole process. Option C is factually correct.

6. D. Option D is not handled in MLOps level 1 but only in level 2. All other options, A, B and C are valid in level 1.

7. D. This organization is in an advanced stage of machine learning usage, and that level of maturity should also be reflected in the MLOps, so level 2 is the correct answer.

8. C. At this level, the data scientist experiments with the model and then creates a pipeline to generate the model. This pipeline code is submitted through a code repository, which will be orchestrated in the production environment.

9. A. At this level, the data scientist experiments with the model and then creates a model. This file is provided to the deployment team.

10. C. While they are important components, the Feature Store and Metadata Store do not trigger the training workflow. Also, a random trigger is not used. When a model degrades over time, as seen in monitoring data, it is triggered.

11. B, C. Retraining a model has infrastructure costs, and the more frequently a model is retrained, the more these costs will increase. So, options B and C are correct. The algorithm has no bearing on triggering retraining. Time to access data is not a factor in this at all.

12. B, D. When model monitoring is enabled, we evaluate the performance of the model at regular intervals. Retraining could be triggered if there is a sudden drop in performance or if performance degrades below a threshold. So, the correct answers are options B and D. The number of predictions or a security breach should not trigger retraining.

13. D. Generally, when you train/retrain a model that has the same inputs/outputs and is expected to be used in the same way as the previous version, to avoid disruption downstream, it is recommended to create a new version. Option A is wrong because if you a train a model that does completely different things, it shouldn't be deployed as a new version of an existing model. Option B is wrong because, while uptrained models are usually deployed as new versions, it is not the only case. Option C is wrong because versioning of new models is a common design pattern.

14. B, C. When teams are siloed, they tend to create the same or similar features repeatedly and that creates redundancies. It is better to create the features once and store them for future use or even for others to use. Option A is wrong because the number of features one model uses is not a good reason for creating a featurestore. Similarly, option D is wrong because the number of types of inputs to a model is not a reason to use a featurestore.

15. C. Feast uses BigQuery, Redis, and Apache Beam. It does not use Gojek, which is a contributor to the Feast open source project.

16. A. Featurestore is the high-level container and contains EntityType, which contains many Features.

17. A. Featurestore is the highest-level container and contains EntityType, which can contain many Features.

18. D. Option A is wrong because you cannot do real-time serving from BigQuery. Option B is not a good solution because it takes a long time to create a Feature Store. Option C would work, but since you have been given only a day and asked to move on to a different project, you should make it easy to maintain and hand off. So, a managed service is preferred here. Option D is the correct answer; Vertex AI Feature Store is a managed Feature Store that fits this use case best.

19. C. Vertex AI Feature Store cannot store images. All of the other statements are true.

20. A. Vertex AI Feature Store uses a time-series model to store data. This helps it to retrieve historical data to help with consistency of downstream ML workflows.

Chapter 14: BigQuery ML

1. D. Option A is wrong because this is not a distributed use case (sales might be distributed, but data and compute are not). Option B is wrong because you are part of a data analyst team and may not have TensorFlow expertise. Option C is correct but is missing ARIMA_ PLUS, the main algorithm for forecasting. Option D is better because you use ARIMA_PLUS and also leverage COVID-19 public datasets.

2. C. Options A and D are wrong because you are part of a small team of data analysts and may not have expertise for custom models or TensorFlow models. The key point is that your manager wants it quickly. Also, the inputs, including map coordinates, are not relevant. Option B is wrong because there is no such feature on Google Maps today. Option C is the correct answer because BigQuery lets you create models with SQL and that can be done quickly.

3. C. The BigQuery ML matrix factorization model type is intended for this use. There is even a tutorial in the Google documentation to do this. Option A is not suited because recommendations are a special type of classification. Option B is technically correct but not suited here because the question specifies that you are a data analyst. Option D is wrong because there is no AutoML for matrix factorization today.

4. A. Option A is the correct answer because analysts prefer BigQuery and it is quick. Option B is technically possible but not the best suited solution for data analysts. Option C is factually incorrect. Option D is wrong because the question states that you don't want to create pipelines.

5. C. Options A and B are also possible, but creating pipelines is overkill for an "initial model." Option A is also wrong because the next stage is usage by analysts who prefer BigQuery. Option D is also feasible but not the simplest and not elegant. Option C is a simple and elegant solution and works for analysts as well.

6. C. Option A is possible but downloading and then creating a Vertex AI dataset is unnecessary when you can directly import it from BigQuery. Options B and D are wrong because the question specifies that you have built extensive pipelines with AutoML Tables, so we don't have to disrupt that. Option C is the solution that fits this situation.

7. C. Option A is possible, but downloading and then creating a Vertex AI dataset is unnecessary when you can directly import it from BigQuery. Option B is wrong because the question specifies that you have built extensive pipelines with AutoML Tables, so you don't have to disrupt that. Option C is the solution that fits this situation. Option D is factually wrong. You *can* access BigQuery public datasets from Vertex AI.

8. C. Option A is possible but unnecessarily exports out of BigQuery. Option B is the same as option A but is only automated with a pipeline job. Option D is not convenient for your team. Option C is correct because it effectively uses a nice feature of Vertex AI managed notebooks.

9. D. Option D is the best answer because it effectively uses a Vertex AI and BigQuery integration that solves this exact problem. Option A is wrong because it is less efficient. Generally avoid data transfers. Option B is wrong because moving models is not necessary here. Option C is also possible but then again involves a data transfer.

10. D. Option D is the best answer because it effectively uses a Vertex AI and BigQuery integration that solves this exact problem. Option C is similar to option D but less effective so not correct here. It is better to avoid data transfers if possible. Option B is wrong because moving models is not necessary here. Option A is also possible but then again involves a data transfer.

11. C. Option A is possible, but it involves a data transfer from BigQuery to GCS, which is unnecessary. Option B is wrong because retraining the model is redundant. Option D is wrong because this is the long route to solving this problem. Option C is the correct answer because it elegantly uses one of the six integrations of BigQuery with Vertex AI.

12. A. This is a common problem seen in datasets, and the design pattern is to use a hashing function. BigQuery has an elegant solution provided in option A. Option B is wrong because removing a feature is counterproductive. Option C is wrong because we can transform this feature to improve accuracy. Option D is wrong because, although Vertex AI has some transformations, it doesn't have this level of advanced features engineering.

13. A. This is a common problem seen in datasets, and the design pattern is described in option A. Option B is wrong because these transformations are now separated from the model, which causes problems during prediction. Option C is wrong because we don't have to leave BigQuery for these simple transformations. Option D is wrong because although Vertex AI has some transformations, it does have this level of advanced feature engineering.

14. D. Option D is factually incorrect. Options A, B, and C are correct.

15. D. Option D is factually wrong. Options A, B, and C are factually correct.

16. B. Option B is the correct answer because you cannot port BigQuery models that have a TRANSFORM clause, which affects model portability. Regarding option D, Vertex AI pipelines has inbuilt components that support BigQuery operations.

17. B. The statement in option B is incorrect because you cannot port BigQuery models that have a TRANSFORM clause. The other statements are correct.

18. D. The statement in option D is incorrect. The other statements are true.

19. A. The statement in option A is incorrect because you have to enable explanations while training to get explanations. The other statements are true.

20. D. Options A and B are wrong because this is a data analyst team and BigQuery is better suited for them. Option C is wrong because Wide-and-Deep models are used for recommending engine type problems, not forecasting. Option D is the best fit.

Index

N

O

Q

R

S

Online Test Bank

To help you study for your Google Cloud Professional Machine Learning Engineer certification exams, register to gain one year of FREE access after activation to the online interactive test bank—included with your purchase of this book! All of the practice questions in this book are included in the online test bank so you can study in a timed and graded setting.

Register and Access the Online Test Bank

To register your book and get access to the online test bank, follow these steps:

1. Go to www.wiley.com/go/sybextestprep. You'll see the "**How to Register Your Book for Online Access**" instructions.
2. Click "here to register" and then select your book from the list.
3. Complete the required registration information, including answering the security verification to prove book ownership. You will be emailed a pin code.
4. Follow the directions in the email or go to www.wiley.com/go/sybextestprep.
5. Find your book on that page and click the "Register or Login" link with it. Then enter the pin code you received and click the "Activate PIN" button.
6. On the Create an Account or Login page, enter your username and password, and click Login or, if you don't have an account already, create a new account.
7. At this point, you should be in the test bank site with your new test bank listed at the top of the page. If you do not see it there, please refresh the page or log out and log back in.